Ulrike Davy, Antje Flüchter (eds.)
Imagining Unequals, Imagining Equals

**BiUP General**

**Ulrike Davy**, born in 1955, is a law professor at the Faculty of Law at Universität Bielefeld and member of the university council. Her fields of expertise include human rights law, anti-discrimination law, migration and refugee law, global and European social policy, German social security law, and welfare state theory.

**Antje Flüchter**, born in 1969, is a professor of early modern history at the Faculty of History, Philosophy and Theology at Universität Bielefeld. Her fields of expertise are early modern global history, history of religion and piety, cultural history of the political, gender and history of knowledge and theory.

SFB 1288 "Practices of Comparing. Ordering and Changing the World".

**SFB 1288**
PRACTICES OF
COMPARING

**Bibliographic information published by the Deutsche Nationalbibliothek**

The Deutsche Nationalbibliothek lists this publication in the Deutsche National-bibliografie; detailed bibliographic data are available in the Internet at http://dnb.d-nb.de

© 2022 Ulrike Davy, Antje Flüchter (eds.), chapters by respective authors.
Published by Bielefeld University Press, an Imprint of transcript Verlag.

http://www.bielefeld-university-press.de

Cover layout: Maria Arndt, Bielefeld

Print-ISBN 978-3-8376-5887-3
PDF-ISBN 978-3-8394-5887-7
https://doi.org/10.14361/9783839458877

Ulrike Davy, Antje Flüchter (eds.)

# Imagining Unequals, Imagining Equals

Concepts of Equality in History and Law

[transcript]

# Contents

# Acknowledgments

This book has been made possible through the help of many people. Our efforts started at a conference in late November 2019 at Bielefeld University, organised by two subprojects of the SFB 1288 "Practices of comparing. Ordering and Changing the World," one focusing on practices of comparing in intercultural jurisprudence from the seventeenth century through the nineteenth century, the other focusing on international legal norms outlawing racial discrimination.

At our November 2019 conference we asked: Why did "equality" become prominent in European societies based on hierarchy during the Enlightenment? What does "equality" imply for societies, politics, or legal systems? We explored and discussed concepts of equality from the perspectives of history and law, drawing on the idea that practices of comparing were essential when it came to imagining others as equals, fighting discrimination, or scandalising social inequalities. We owe our thanks to Cornelia Aust and Malika Mansouri, who were crucial for the organisation and realization of the conference. Moreover, the workshop was strongly supported by Sabrina Diab-Helmer, scientific manager of the SFB, and her team. Andreas Becker and Anna Dönecke wrote a conference report and thus made us reflect on equality once more in the aftermath of the conference. Yüsra Şimşek helped with the cite checking. Julia Bartneck joined the proofreading, equipped with an eagle's eye. Thank you all!

We owe particular thanks to the participants of the November 2019 conference, who revised their papers and contributed to the book. We also thank Demetrius Lynn Eudell (Weslian University, Middletown), Saul Dubow (University of Cambridge) and Gila Stopler (College of Law and Business, Tel Aviv) who enriched the discussions at our conference und inspired our thinking on equality concepts.

We are grateful to the BiUP team, most of all Vera Breitner, for her help in the various stages of preparing the book, to the anonymous peer reviewers for valuable comments, to Johannes Kroll for editing and polishing the English of the texts of the German speaking contributors so skilfully, and to the publishing house transcript for their support.

Last but not least, it is thanks to the generous support of the German Research Foundation (DFG) that we had the opportunity to explore the questions set out here in detail and great depth.

*Bielefeld, December 2021*

*Ulrike Davy and Antje Flüchter*

*For Fanny Lewald*

# Concepts of Equality: Why, Who, What for?[1]

*Ulrike Davy and Antje Flüchter*

## Roots

'Equality' is one of the key values of the European Enlightenment. When the revolutionaries in France demanded "liberté, égalité, fraternité," the notion of 'equality' must have seemed particularly ambitious and desirable. At the time, law and society in Europe were not unified and homogenous, but in many ways divided and sub-divided: Political entities encompassed a variety of social groups, and each had its own legal order, a structure that strengthened social hierarchies. Nonetheless, 'equality' rapidly made it into the texts of the nineteenth century constitutions in Europe and the Americas. After 1945, 'equality' became part of human rights law at both the global and the regional level (Universal Declaration of Human Rights 1948; American Declaration of the Rights and Duties of Man 1948; European Convention for the Protection of Human Rights and Fundamental Freedoms 1950). Today, almost all constitutions around the world guarantee a right to equality before the law, with rare exceptions. The constitution of China and the Basic Laws of Israel are current examples of such exceptions; the constitution of Apartheid-era South Africa is a former one. The concept of equality is at least as popular as the concept of individual freedoms catalogued at the level of national constitutions, and certainly more popular and less contentious than the concept of fraternity or solidarity. Also, equality clauses never ceased to appeal to popular hopes and aspirations. Once the idea of equality took root in the minds of the people and was embedded in law, more and more people—women, workers, indigenous peoples, people of color, homosexuals, or transgenders—demanded to be acknowledged and recognized as 'equals', with probably more claims to

1    This contribution draws on research conducted in the context of the Collaborative Research Center "Practices of Comparing. Ordering and Changing the World" (SFB 1288).

come. In other words, 'equality' was and is becoming part of the normative framework that guides us in our everyday lives.[2]

## Scholarly Interests

Concepts of equality were and are discussed in various academic circles, most notably in the fields of political or moral philosophy.[3] In philosophy, equality is often linked to justice. The egalitarian proposition is that a just or perfect society is a society that realizes equality. Sociologists have a strong focus on social or economic inequality; many sociological monographs or articles are based on empirical or statistical data. Sociologists measure social or economic inequalities (e.g., in terms of income; health; education; participation in the labor market), but they rarely elaborate on the premise underlying their investigations, namely, that equality (of wealth or life chances) is something societies ought to strive for.[4] Economic inequalities are also a major topic in economics, and have been so for a long time.[5] Recently, economic inequalities

2    Willibald Steinmetz, *Europa im 19. Jahrhundert*, Frankfurt 2019, 428–488.

3    See, e.g., John Rawls, *A Theory of Justice*, Cambridge, MA 1971; Ronald Dworkin, What is Equality? Part 1: Equality of Welfare, in: *Philosophy & Public Affairs* 10 (3/1981), 185–246; Ronald Dworkin, What is Equality? Part 2: Equality of Resources, in: *Philosophy & Public Affairs* 10 (4/1981), 283–345; Thomas Nagel, *Equality and Partiality*, New York 1991; Elizabeth S. Anderson, What is the Point of Equality?, in: *Ethics* 109 (2/1999), 287–337; Samuel Scheffler, What is Egalitarianism?, in: *Philosophy and Public Affairs* 30 (1/2003), 5–39.

4    There is an abundance of sociological literature concentrating on the various kinds of social inequalities, in particular in recent decades. For a more theoretical or global perspective, see, e.g., Aage B. Sørensen, The Structural Basis of Social Inequality, in: *American Journal of Sociology* 101 (5/1996), 1333–1365; Charles Tilly, *Durable Inequality*, Berkeley and Los Angeles 1998; Göran Therborn, *The Killing Fields of Inequality*, Cambridge 2013.

5    See, e.g., Friedrich Engels, *Die Lage der Arbeitenden Klasse in England. Nach eigner Anschauung und authentischen Quellen*, 2nd ed., Stuttgart 1892; Simon Kuznets, Economic Growth and Income Inequality, in: *The American Economic Review* 45 (1/1955), 1–28; James Tobin, On Limiting the Domain of Inequality, in: *Journal of Law and Economics* 13 (2/1970), 263–278; John E. Roemer, *Equality of Opportunity*, Cambridge, MA 1998; Wiemer Salverda/Brian Nolan/Timothy M. Smeeding (eds.), *The Oxford Handbook of Economic Inequality*, Oxford 2009.

became the subject of moral concerns, voiced by leading economists.[6] In law and history, however, 'equality' has not so far received as much attention.

The scholarly literature in the field of law tends to concentrate on gender equality and anti-discrimination measures, in particular in the context of European (labor) law.[7] Racial and social equality receive some—but considerably less—attention. The International Convention on the Elimination of All Forms of Racial Discrimination has prompted scholars closely involved with the international human rights machinery to engage with racial discrimination.[8] That circle of scholars, however, is rather small. Since 2016, the rise of

---

6    See, e.g., Amartya Sen, *Inequality Reexamined*, Oxford 1995; Amartya Sen, *On Economic Inequality*, Oxford 1997; Anthony B. Atkinson/Thomas Piketty (eds.), *Top Incomes: A Global Perspective*, Oxford 2010; Anthony B. Atkinson, *Inequality: What Can Be Done?*, Cambridge 2015; Branko Milanovic, *Global Inequality: A New Approach for the Age of Globalization*, Cambridge, MA 2016; Thomas Piketty, *Capital in the Twenty-First Century*, Cambridge, MA and London 2017. See also the contributions in: Kenneth Arrow/Samuel Bowles/Steven Durlauf (eds.), *Meritocracy and Economic Inequality*, Princeton 2000.

7    See, e.g., Mark Bell, *Anti-Discrimination Law and the European Union*, Oxford 2002; Christopher McCrudden/Sacha Prechel, *The Concepts of Equality and Non-Discrimination in Europe: A Practical Approach*, Brussels 2009; Alexander Somek, *Engineering Equality: An Essay on European Anti-Discrimination Law*, Oxford Scholarship online 2011; Dagmar Schiek/Anna Lawson (eds.), *European Union Non-Discrimination Law and Intersectionality: Investigating the Triangle of Racial, Gender and Disability Discrimination*, Surrey 2011; Evelyn Ellis/Philippa Watson, *EU Anti-Discrimination Law*, Oxford Scholarship online 2013; Eva Kocher, § 5 Arbeitsrechtlicher Diskriminierungsschutz, in: Monika Schlachter/Hans Michael Heinig (eds.), *Europäisches Arbeits- und Sozialrecht*, Baden-Baden 2016, 219–292; Valérie Verbist, *Reverse Discrimination in the European Union. A Recurring Balancing Act*, Cambridge, Antwerp, Portland 2017. For a global perspective, see Marsha A. Freeman/Christine Chinkin/Beate Rudolf (eds.), *The UN Convention on the Elimination of All Forms of Discrimination against Women. A Commentary*, Oxford 2012; Elisabeth Veronika Henn, *International Human Rights Law and Structural Discrimination: The Example of Violence against Women*, Berlin 2019.

8    Natan Lerner, *The U.N. Convention on the Elimination of All Forms of Racial Discrimination. A Commentary*, Leyden 1970, reprint 2015; Patrick Thornberry, Confronting Racial Discrimination: A CERD Perspective, in: *Human Rights Law Review* 5 (2/2005), 239–269; Patrick Thornberry, *The International Convention on the Elimination of All Forms of Racial Discrimination. A Commentary*, Oxford 2016; David Keane, *Caste-Based Discrimination in International Human Rights Law*, Aldershot 2007; David Keane, Mapping the International Convention on the Elimination of All Forms of Racial Discrimination as a Living Instrument, in: *Human Rights Law Review* 20 (2/2020), 236–268. But see also Michaela Fries, *Die Bedeutung von Artikel 5(f) der Rassendiskriminierungskonvention im deutschen Recht: Diskriminierung durch Private beim Zugang zu Gaststätten*, Berlin 2003.

authoritarian parties in Europe and other Western countries has put the issue of racism and the question of how to deal with it on the table.[9] Social
or economic equality and solidarity have become a major focus of EU politics, perhaps most prominently so in the context of migration.[10] Or, to turn
to one of the legal systems that institutionalized equality clauses during the
second half of the nineteenth century and thereafter, German-speaking scholars deal with 'equality' in commentaries to the constitutional clauses, but tend
to ignore the issue otherwise,[11] their monographs being primarily doctrinal
in outlook.[12]

Historians, particularly with the rise of social history as a key paradigm,
have understood social inequality as a pivotal axis of societies and history.[13]

---

9    Michael G. Hanchard, *The Spectre of Race. How Discrimination Haunts Western Democracy*,
     Princeton and Oxford 2018, 207–215.

10   Thorsten Kingreen, *Das Sozialstaatsprinzip im Europäischen Verfassungsverbund. Gemein-
     schaftsrechtliche Einflüsse auf das deutsche Recht der gesetzlichen Krankenversicherung*,
     Tübingen 2003; Constanze Janda, *Migranten im Sozialstaat*, Tübingen 2012; Anusceh
     Farahat, Rechtsunsicherheiten beim Zugang zur Gesundheitsversorgung von Mi-
     granten, in: *Zeitschrift für europäisches Arbeits- und Sozialrecht* 13 (2014), 269–278;
     Anusceh Farahat, Solidarität und Inklusion. Umstrittene Dimensionen der Unions-
     bürgerschaft, in: *Die Öffentliche Verwaltung* 69 (2/2016), 45–55; Ulrike Davy, Refugee Cri-
     sis in Germany and the Right to a Subsistence Minimum: Differences That Ought Not
     Be, in: *Georgia Journal of International and Comparative Law* 47 (2/2019), 367–450; Ulrike
     Davy, Asylum Seekers' Dignity—Elusive in Europe and Lost in Crisis. At the Threshold of
     Universality, in: Stephanie Arel/Levi Cooper/Vanessa Hellmann (eds.), *Probing Human
     Dignity. Exploring Thresholds from an Interdisciplinary Perspective*, Berlin 2022 (in print).

11   Ulrike Davy, Wenn Gleichheit in Gefahr ist. Staatliche Schutzpflichten und
     Schutzbedürftigkeit am Beispiel des Minderheitenschutzes und des Schutzes
     vor rassischer Diskriminierung, in: *Zeitschrift für öffentliches Recht* 74 (4/2019), 773–844,
     see 778.

12   Stefan Huster, *Rechte und Ziele. Zur Dogmatik des allgemeinen Gleichheitssatzes*, Berlin
     1993; Alexander Somek, *Rationalität und Diskriminierung*, Wien 2001; Magdalena
     Pöschl, *Gleichheit vor dem Gesetz*, Wien 2008. But see also Claudia Hofmann, *Jenseits
     von Gleichheit. Gleichheitsorientierte Maßnahmen im internationalen, europäischen und na-
     tionalen Recht*, Tübingen 2019.

13   Hans-Ulrich Wehler, *Deutsche Gesellschaftsgeschichte, Bd. 1: Vom Feudalismus des Alten Rei-
     ches bis zur Defensiven Modernisierung der Reformära 1700–1815*, 2nd ed., Munich 1989,
     11, 124–217; Hans-Ulrich Wehler, Vorüberlegung zur historischen Analyse sozialer Un-
     gleichheit, in: Hans-Ulrich Wehler (ed.), *Klassen in der europäischen Sozialgeschichte*, Göt-
     tingen 1979, 9–32; Cornelia Klinger/Gudrun-Axeli Knapp/Birgit Sauer, *Achsen der Un-
     gleichheit: Zum Verhältnis von Klasse, Geschlecht und Ethnizität*, Frankfurt 2007. The 2008
     Annual conference of the Germany history association was about inequality: Mar-

For many scholars concerned with modern history, equality was part of what they perceived as the progress of humankind that had been taking place since the nineteenth century.[14] Equality became an essential element of the traditional Western master narrative.[15] Some scholars, however, contrasted the rise of equality with opposing currents: The granting of legal equality, they argue, had given rise to fear and thus to even more social exclusion, for instance, in the growth of antisemitism during and after World War I as a response to Jewish emancipation and assimilation.[16] Moreover, with the rise of global history as a new scholarly perspective, ideas about equality in Europe, which arose with the Enlightenment, were contrasted with blatant inequalities and horrific crimes in the context of colonialism and imperialism.[17]

Historians who deal with the periods prior to the French Revolution are more interested in order or hierarchy than in equality. For centuries, at least in Christian Europe, social and political entities were conceptualized as being based on hierarchies of social status and rank.[18] Yet to some extent, precursors of modern concepts of equality were present either in the context of spiritual movements or in the context of social uprisings.[19]

Moreover, equality and inequality have become crucial topics for the growing sub-disciplines in history studies. For scholars promoting black, subaltern, or gender studies, for instance, equality was a normative concept that

---

tin Jehne/Winfried Müller/Peter E. Fässler, *Ungleichheiten: 47. Deutscher Historikertag in Dresden 2008: Berichtsband*, Göttingen 2009.

14    Otto Dann, *Gleichheit und Gleichberechtigung. Das Gleichheitspostulat in der alteuropäischen Tradition und in Deutschland bis zum ausgehenden 19. Jahrhundert*, Berlin 1980.

15    Jörg Fisch, *Europa zwischen Wachstum und Gleichheit 1850–1914*, Stuttgart 2002.

16    Martina Kessel, *Gewalt und Gelächter. "Deutschsein" 1914–1945*, Stuttgart 2019. More generally Steinmetz, *Europa im 19. Jahrhundert*, 428–488.

17    Roland Wenzlhuemer/Monica Juneja, *Die Neuzeit 1789–1914*, Konstanz 2013, 169–222; Gayatri Spivak, The Rani of Simur, in: Francis Barker/Peter Hulme/Margaret Iverson/ Diana Loxley (eds.), *Europe and Its Others*, vol. 1, Colchester 1985, 54–67.

18    For the German context, see Thomas Weller, Soziale Ungleichheit und ständische Gesellschaft. Stand und Perspektiven der Forschung, in: *Zeitsprünge. Forschungen zur Frühen Neuzeit* 15 (1/2011), 3–23; Claudia Ulbrich, Ständische Ungleichheit und Geschlechterforschung, in: Marian Füssel/Thomas Weller (eds.), *Soziale Ungleichheit und ständische Gesellschaft. Theorien und Debatten in der Frühneuzeitforschung (Zeitensprünge 15)*, 2011, 85–104.

19    Joachim Eibach, Versprochene Gleichheit—verhandelte Ungleichheit. Zum sozialen Aspekt in der Strafjustiz der Frühen Neuzeit, in: *Geschichte und Gesellschaft* 35 (4/2009), 488–533.

was and (still) is not matched by the realities on the ground.[20] Their focus is, consequently, on illegitimate inequalities, in other words, the lack of equality.

## Our Approach

Our edited volume draws on a workshop organized in Bielefeld late in November 2019 under the aegis of the Collaborative Research Center "Practices of Comparing. Ordering and Changing the World" (SFB 1288). The workshop focused on "Concepts of Equality and their Limits—Critical Junctures in History and Law." Amartya Sen inspired the philosophical discourse on the subject when he insisted on asking "Equality of What?"[21] The question drew academic attention to the respects, or the dimensions, of any proposition given as an answer to the question of as to how goods ought to be distributed in order to ensure equal treatment in a just society. Our take is different. Our focus is on a "why" question, a "who" question, and a question related to claims. From the point of view of history, the question we seek to answer is: Why did equality emerge at a time when European societies were seemingly firmly based on order and rank and had been based on order and rank for many centuries? With respect to right holders, we ask: Equality clauses promise some sort of equal treatment, but equal treatment among whom? And, from the perspective of specified right holders, we want to know: What does equality entail? What is it that right holders may claim based on the right to equality?

Equality is neither an analytical nor a clearly defined term. Equality has been differently understood and valued in the course of time and in various cultural contexts. The same is true for imagining others as one's equals. In any

---

20   Joseph P. Reidy, *Illusions of Emancipation: The Pursuit of Freedom and Equality in the Twilight of Slavery*, Chapel Hill 2019; Demetrius Lynn Eudell, *The Political Languages of Emancipation in the British Caribbean and the US South*, Chapel Hill 2002; Ute Gerhard (ed.), *Differenz und Gleichheit. Menschenrechte haben (k)ein Geschlecht*, Frankfurt 1990; Martin Duberman/Martha Vicinus/George Chauncey Jr. (eds.), *Hidden from History: Reclaiming the Gay and Lesbian Past*, London 1991.

21   Amartya Sen, *Equality of What? The Tanner Lecture on Human Values. Delivered at Stanford University*, May 22, 1979, <https://www.ophi.org.uk/wp-content/uploads/Sen-1979_Equality-of-What.pdf> [last accessed: October 30, 2021].

case, concepts of equality are closely connected to practices of comparing[22] or even produced by such practices.[23] Practices of comparing start from the assumption that the entities that are compared (*comparata*) have at least one characteristic in common. This assumption ensures comparability and serves as a prerequisite for acts of comparing. Where comparability is lacking (i.e., is not assumed), acts of comparing will not take place or fail. Where comparability is, however, assumed, various acts of comparing may then highlight differences or similarities between the *comparata*, according to the chosen *tertium comparationis*. If my starting point is 'mankind' and my *tertium comparationis* is skin color, I may end up generating many 'races.' If my starting point is 'mankind' and my *tertium comparationis* is having a soul, I may end up generating one group only. Consequently, difference and similarity are not a given, but obviously determined by the chosen *tertium*. Again, the choice of *tertium* is not free or arbitrary, but structured by a specific "regime of comparatism" which is "determined by the horizon of knowledge in which each individual comparison is formed, received and judged."[24]

---

22    Otto Dann, Gleichheit, in: Otto Brunner/Werner Conze/Reinhart Koselleck (eds.), *Geschichtliche Grundbegriffe. Historisches Lexikon zur politisch-sozialen Sprache in Deutschland (Studienausgabe)*, Bd. 2, E–G, Stuttgart 2004, 997–1046.

23    Ulrike Davy/Johannes Grave/Marcus Hartner/Ralf Schneider/Willibald Steinmetz, Grundbegriffe für eine Theorie des Vergleichens. Ein Zwischenbericht, in: *Praktiken des Vergleichens. Working Paper 3 des SFB 1288*, Bielefeld 2019, <https://pub.uni-bielefeld. de/record/2939563> [last accessed: October 30, 2021]; Angelika Epple, Inventing White Beauty and Fighting Black Slavery. How Blumenbach, Humboldt, and Arango y Parreño Contributed to Cuban Race Comparisons in the Long Nineteenth Century, in: Angelika Epple/Walter Erhart/Johannes Grave (eds.), *Practices of Comparing. Towards a New Understanding of a Fundamental Human Practice*, Bielefeld 2020, 295–328; Angelika Epple /Walter Erhart, Practices of Comparing. A New Research Agenda Between Typological and Historical Approaches, in: Angelika Epple/Walter Erhart/Johannes Grave (eds.), *Practices of Comparing. Towards a New Understanding of a Fundamental Human Practice*, Bielefeld 2020, 11–38; Angelika Epple/Antje Flüchter/Thomas Müller, Praktiken des Vergleichens: praxistheoretische Fundierung und heuristische Typologien. Ein Bericht von unterwegs, in: *Praktiken des Vergleichens. Working Paper 6 des SFB 1288*, Bielefeld, 2020, <https://pub.uni-bielefeld.de/record/2943010> [last accessed: October 30, 2021].

24    Renaud Gagné, Introduction: Regimes of Comparatism, in: Renaud Gagné/Simon Goldhill/Geoffrey E.R. Lloyd (eds.), *Regimes of Comparatism*, Leiden 2019, 1–17, see 2.

## Preview

The contributions to this edited volume overlap in many respects.

*Levels of Discourses and Practices*. The contributors to this edited volume follow up on our lead questions (why? who? what for?) at various levels, at the level of discourses as well as that of practices. Lynn Hunt explores practices of visualization and debates in revolutionary France that effectively undermined God-given hierarchies and opened up new spaces for thinking 'equality.' Helmut Walser Smith demonstrates how nineteenth-century German nationalism bridged existing stark differences and inequalities between rural and urban populations and, even more astonishingly, between the wealthy and the poor. The idea of an existing "deep horizontal comradeship," encompassing all who were deemed German, was crucial in the process. Gautam Bhatia presents the legal discourse on equality from the perspective of both constitutional law-making and decision-making by the courts in India. Lawmakers and courts confronted and still confront societal hierarchies that challenge any legal concept of equality: How can those hierarchies be overcome through the means of a constitutional equality clause? Antje Flüchter—describing early modern societies in Europe and in India—moves beyond national boundaries. She asks: Is there a concept of equality in India that predates the strong European move toward 'equality' during and after the Enlightenment? Ulrike Davy, Malika Mansouri, and David Keane deal with international discourses and practices. Ulrike Davy elaborates on the understanding of equality underlying the system of minority protection that was created by the Allied powers when World War I was formally brought to an end and the maps of Europe were redrawn in Paris in 1919: How were minority rights and equality linked in the 1919 treaty system, and what did equality mean for minorities and for majorities? Malika Mansouri turns to venues that emerged after World War II, namely, the United Nations and the human rights treaty bodies sponsored by the United Nations. Concentrating on the norms explicitly outlawing racial discrimination, Malika Mansouri gives an account on why the idea of prohibiting racial discrimination came into being, how the idea of racial discrimination relates to 'equality,' and how the idea then evolved in the hands of the Committee on the Elimination of Racial Discrimination since the 1980s. David Keane, finally, discusses a dispute between India and the Committee on the Elimination of All Forms of Racial Discrimination over the issue of caste: The committee holds that the caste system constitutes a form of racial discrimination and hence that the system must be considered internationally outlawed and stigmatized. India rejects that position quite firmly and has done so for many years. David Keane explains the background and the details of the dispute and offers legal paths to resolving the dispute.

*Imagining Being Equal.* As we have already remarked, differences and similarities are not a given, nor is equality. It is not self-evident that all human beings are to be deemed equals. Imagining other human beings as equal to oneself depends on assumptions on comparability and hence is contingent. Modern declarations of human rights proclaim that all human beings are equal and therefore have a right to be treated equally under the law. In the sixteenth century, however, Europeans discussed whether indigenous peoples were indeed human beings, for instance in the Valladolid debate of 1550/51 between Bartolomé de las Casas and Juan Ginés de Sepúlveda. In Asian and Latin American thinking, the boundaries between human beings and animals might be blurry—due to the idea of reincarnation, for example.[25] And for premodern Christian Europeans, it was normal to imagine a fundamental difference between peasants and nobles (as in France) or the members of different religions, such as Jews, Moslems, and Christians (as in Spain).[26] At the turn to the nineteenth century, the difference between men and women was deemed to be a biological one, and therefore an unchangeable difference.[27] We should thus be wary of reading the modern understanding of equality into earlier concepts that may seem at first glance to be all-encompassing ("all men are equal"). Otherwise, we run the risk of arguing in anachronistic terms.[28]

---

25   Descola analyzed relations between nature and culture like animism or totemism, which are fundamentally different from the Western naturalism and also encompass the relation between human beings and animals. See Philippe Descola, *Beyond Nature and Culture*, Chicago and London 2013. Descola refers to indigenous cultures in South America and in the Amazon region. His criticism of Eurocentric naturalism can be transferred to many other regions, for example India; see Axel Michaels, Notions of nature in traditional hinduism, in: E. Ehlers/C.F. Gethmann (eds.), *Environment across Cultures. Wissenschaftsethik und Technikfolgenbeurteilung*, Heidelberg 2003, 111–121.

26   André Devyver, *Le sang épuré, les préjugés de race chez les français de l'Ancien Régime (1560–1720)*, Brüssel 1973; María Elena Martínez/David Nirenberg/Max-Sebastián Hering Torres, *Race and Blood in the Iberian World*, Münster 2012.

27   Claudia Honegger, *Die Ordnung der Geschlechter. Die Wissenschaft vom Menschen und das Weib, 1750–1850*, Frankfurt 1991.

28   The Virginia Bill of Rights (1776) did not 'lie' when declaring that all men were created equal. The authors just did not imagine women, slaves, and other groups as being their equals—these groups were simply not deemed "men".

Early modern travelers to India imagined people as equal to themselves if the social status of the others was deemed similar to their own, as Antje Flüchter shows in her contribution: Travelers of higher rank imagined the elite at the Mughal court as their equals. Sailors and soldiers working for European trade companies used the concept of the (premodern) nation to imagine their co-nationals—even co-nationals of a higher rank—as equal to themselves. In nineteenth-century German territories, the idea of the nation gained even more prominence as a point to reference for imaging equals, as Helmut Walser Smith shows. In the nineteenth century, however, 'nation' was a concept invoked primarily by elite voices, while in Antje Flüchter's premodern examples, it was an instrument of empowerment from below. For the French Revolution, Lynn Hunt makes the point that the visualization in popular prints of 'society' as one entity instead of numerous estates made it possible for people to imagine themselves as all being equals. By looking at such prints and realizing that similarities (not differences) predominated, a civic society became thinkable.

There is a certain fluidity in the imagining of others as equals or unequals. Not only is the choice of *tertia* crucial, it is equally crucial how the *tertia* are understood. The choice and the understanding of the *tertium* shape the *comparata*: Is it descent (Antje Flüchter) or rather class (Helmut Walser Smith) that make others appear equal or unequal? Is a minority determined by language, religion, or race (Ulrike Davy)? Is caste defined by descent, which would imply that caste is a form of racial discrimination (David Keane)? Before the UN Committee on the Elimination of All Forms of Racial Discrimination, India has rejected that equation for many years, as it stigmatizes India by equating caste and race. It also seems important who is talking about caste: The understanding of Dr. Ambedkar, a Dalit himself, differed from the understanding of Shri Mohanlal Saksena, who came from a higher caste. Gautam Bhatia, in turn, understands caste as axis of social inequality and sees it closer to class, highlighting social, cultural, and economic disadvantages instead of descent or race. On a more global level, Malika Mansouri analyzes how the imagining of equals was entangled with debates about racial discrimination and the attempts to eliminate racial discrimination. Moreover, Mansouri traces the changing, consolidating, and shifting of notions of equality in the context of the work of the UN Committee on the Elimination of All Forms of Racial Discrimination.

The reading of Bhatia's and Keane's contributions discloses another aspect of the imagining of the relevant *comparata*: When making their arguments, do

Bhatia and Keane imagine individuals or groups? While Keane is thinking of groups when talking about caste, Bhatia discusses backwardness as relating to individuals, even if the Indian regime of affirmative action addresses groups in order to support individuals. The tension between individual right holders and groups holding rights is also present in Ulrike Davy's analysis regarding the minority regimes under the League of Nations. Davy understands these regimes as an "important turning point in conceptualizing equality," because by granting special rights to minorities, the regimes challenged the vision of granting "the same rights for all." Granting special rights to defined groups implies a concept of equality that is particular, not universal. Also, more recent conceptions of equality move beyond the focus on individuals by taking structural discrimination into account, such as in-built discrimination in the judicial system or poverty, as Malika Mansouri shows in her contribution.

*Equality and Inequality.* Concepts of equality tend to imply that equality can become an all-encompassing reality of life. However, such a concept fails to understand that equality is necessarily linked to inequality. The increase of legal equality in one field, for example citizenship rights, can lead to increasing social discrimination and thus to more inequality. We conceptualize equality as a relational phenomenon. Equality can only be understood in its relation to inequality.[29] "Being equal" creates a boundary with regard to those who are not equal. The exclusion of others is the flipside of 'equality' among those included: The equality of citizens is connected to difference vis-à-vis other nationals. Pre-modern social differences according to rank created equality among the members of each social stratum. In other words, members of the nobility felt equal with members of their own rank, because they all felt that they differed from the peasants. Antje Flüchter and Lynn Hunt describe the interplay between equality and inequality in detail. Flüchter concentrates on the attitudes of European travelers from the upper class in premodern India. These travelers, she argues, were outraged when faced with the social mobility in the Mughal Empire, because they felt morally superior to the classes deemed 'lower.' The relevant *tertium* for these travelers was morals. In Hunt's contribution, morals are still important for separating equals from unequals, yet here it is nobility that appears vulgar and immoral. It is rather implicit, but still observable in Hunt's contribution that the new equal society in revolutionary France needed the distancing vis-à-vis the old nobility and elite for

---

29    André Béteille, Homo hierarchicus, homo equalis, in: *Modern Asian Studies* 13 (4/1979), 529–548, see 532–534.

their identity-building and imaging themselves as equals. In Helmut Walser Smith's contribution, the relevant *tertium* changes from morals to capital: The bourgeoisie (as a class) had more money than the poor, and its members felt equal to one another because they were all unequal in relation to the poor. More pointedly, modern Western democracies link their concept of equality to a meritocratic system which necessarily creates economic inequality. Another interplay between equality and inequality is present in the policy of affirmative action, as described by Gautam Bhatia in his contribution. In the late 1940s, Nehru justified a policy of affirmative action (favoring scheduled castes and tribes) by arguing that to achieve a certain kind of equality (substantive equality), the state needed to violate another (formal equality).

*Contested Equality—formal versus substantive equality.* Since the first appearance of equality clauses in law, the clauses have considerably changed in outlook. Clearly, the promise that a specified class of people (such as the country's inhabitants, its nationals, or indeed everyone) was to be treated "equally before the law" remained remarkably stable. Variations with regard to the specified categories of people notwithstanding, the clause was always about "equality before the law" at both the national and international levels. Yet that promise came with varying add-ons. In the nineteenth century, additional clauses rejected all privileges as illegitimate that had, in former times, mirrored societal hierarchies. No one was meant to occupy a superior position in law simply because of his or her position in a social hierarchy. In the twentieth century, additional clauses declared that "equality before the law" meant equality "without distinction" or "without discrimination" of any kind, such as race, nationality, gender, or the like. In the second half of the twentieth century, no one was meant to be left behind in an inferior position, simply because of race, nationality, gender, or the like. Still, the meaning of the core of the promise—"equality before the law"—was blurred from early on. One reading of the promise held that it obliged lawmakers and the executive branch to not differentiate among members of the specified class. In other words, the reading held that all who belonged to the specified class (nationals, citizens, human beings, as the case may be) were supposed to have the same rights, unless different treatment (and different rights) could be justified by objective reasons. According to that reading, equality before the law meant 'formal' equality. Everyone was, in a formal manner, to be treated the same. Another reading stressed that having the same rights might still imply advantages for some and disadvantages for others, particularly in situations where social inequalities hampered the equal enjoyment of the same rights. In other words, a second reading held that rights might be universal, but some right holders might not be in a position to make use of their rights. The second reading further held that, under these circumstances, 'formal' and 'substantive' equality were not congruent with one another, or, to put it in stronger terms, that 'formal' equality missed an important aspect of 'equality.'

Three contributors to our edited volume deal with the tensions between 'formal' and 'substantive' equality. Ulrike Davy analyzes an advisory opinion of the Permanent Court of International Justice, given in 1935, which introduced the notion of "genuine equality" in an early attempt to define what is now called "substantive" equality. The Permanent International Court of Justice not only identified the problem—a lack of equality in fact—but also came up with a remedy: the obligation of the state to grant specific rights to the disadvantaged minority, rights that were not granted to the advantaged majority. Gautam Bhatia traces the idea of substantive equality in the Indian context. The Indian constitution allows for "reservations," i.e., the granting of preferential access to public employment or universities, based on a quota system, for scheduled castes and tribes. Yet even if there can be no doubt that quota-based reservations are permissible under the Indian constitution, courts find themselves at odds when they have to identify the beneficiaries of the affirmative action policies and when they try to balance 'formal' and 'substantive' equality. The concept underlying the Indian constitution is an ambiguous compromise, and courts continue to struggle with finding an unambiguous answer. Malika Mansouri elaborates on how the idea of substantive equality evolved and eventually took shape in the hands of the Committee on the Elimination of All Forms of Racial Discrimination. Like the distress that affects a minority confronting a hostile majority in the 1930s or the lower castes in India in the present day, racial discrimination often feeds on practices that are entrenched in the daily routines of individuals or institutions. Such routines often perpetuate what is no longer sanctioned by law. That is why the Committee on the Elimination of All Forms of Racial Discrimination moved beyond the concept of 'formal' equality early on. Against the background of the wide variety of facts and situations it deals with, the Committee prefers a flexible—i.e., non-doctrinal—approach. Unlike the courts, the Committee is to some extent free to mold 'equality' according to its preferences and priorities. The Committee thus contributes to an international concept of equality that may, at some point, have an impact on the jurisdiction at the national level.

*Practices of Comparing.* The contributions to our edited volume show that concepts of equality interact with practices of comparing—and how. First, practices of comparing trigger and shape the imagining of others as unequal and, hence, incomparable. While *tertia* and *comparata* may change over time, asserting insurmountable differences regularly draws on comparisons that, eventually, cement social boundaries, such as the boundaries between nobility and peasants, men and women, rich and poor, civilized and backward people, Whites and Blacks. Second, practices of comparing shape and consolidate the imagining of others as being equal and, hence, kith and kin. In revolutionary France, painting the deputies of the French parliament in the way kings were portrayed in the Ancien Régime prepared the ground for a new concept of equality. In nineteenth-century Germany, describing the poor in a certain manner—as people of honest *Haltung* (attitude, demeanor)—opened the door to developing empathy with the poor as human beings equally deserving respect. Feeling empathy again was an important prerequisite for accepting the idea of a "deep horizontal comradeship" linking the poor and the wealthy. Third, practices of comparing may invalidate the assumption that others are equal to oneself. In the aftermath of World War I, an internationally and constitutionally embedded concept of equality (equality without distinction as to language, religion, or race) was willfully disregarded when practices of comparing (allegedly) furnished proof of how disloyally minorities behaved or of how majorities undermined the minority regime established by the League of Nations. Minorities and majorities—deemed equal by law—turned into unequals not deserving respect. Fourth, practices of comparing may be used to scandalize social inequality and thus to spur politics into action, for example, in order to mitigate the plight of the poor. Similarly, practices of comparing may be used to undermine socially accepted equality as a response to successful processes of emancipation. Fifth, from a legal perspective, practices of comparing may disclose unequal treatment that is prohibited by law, such as all forms of racial discrimination, and may have legal consequences. Finally, practices of comparing may bolster the belief that some groups—for instance, groups deemed backward or disadvantaged—deserve to be granted particular rights in order for them to overcome what is seen as backwardness or disadvantage. The Indian policy of reservations favoring scheduled castes and tribes is one example, the minority regime promoted by the League of Nations is another. And clearly practices of comparing may help to ascertain or reject the assertation that caste is a form of racial discrimination.

*History and Law.* Our edited volume is based on a collaboration between scholars from the fields of history and law. We think that such an interdisciplinary effort is worthwhile for both sides. The doctrinal arguments advanced by lawyers can profit from well-founded insights in the genealogy of the various concepts of equality and their cultural situatedness. And the narratives offered by historians can benefit if and when historians have a fair understanding of how (political) concepts of equality were incorporated into law and how they operate in practice, both in international law and at the domestic level. Still, when reflecting on the contributions to our edited volume, we also detect some tensions between the disciplines involved. In law, 'equality' is also an aspirational norm, i.e., a norm that proclaims an aim that needs to be furthered in order to be achieved in the future—in other words, an aim that still needs to be concretized and then brought to life. Practitioners as well as scholars of law participate in this struggle. Historians may find their questions in contemporary problems relating to equality; however, their methods demand a (distant) analyzing of how equality or inequality is constructed, produced, and related to empirical phenomena, of finding out and dissecting the contexts, the actors, and the narratives involved in the process. Moreover, legal scholars seem to focus on individuals or groups when dealing with questions involving equality or inequality; they focus on the *tertia* employed to detect inequalities and the fields of life that are prone to discrimination (public and private services, education, the workplace). Historians share these perspectives, but tend to go further. Historians are equally interested in the way people dress or behave, because this is the way how people perform equality or inequality. Moreover, historians are interested in territories, states, or economies. Against that background, our edited volume is not only about concepts of equality, but, at the same time, about two disciplines dealing with and contributing to the evolution of these concepts.

## References

Anderson, Elizabeth S., What is the Point of Equality?, in: *Ethics* 109 (2/1999), 287–337.

Arrow, Kenneth/Bowles, Samuel/Durlauf, Steven (eds.), *Meritocracy and Economic Inequality*, Princeton 2000.

Atkinson, Anthony B., *Inequality: What Can Be Done?*, Cambridge 2015.

Atkinson, Anthony B./Piketty, Thomas (eds.), *Top Incomes: A Global Perspective*, Oxford 2010.

Bell, Mark, *Anti-Discrimination Law and the European Union*, Oxford 2002.

Béteille, André, Homo hierarchicus, homo equalis, in: *Modern Asian Studies* 13 (4/1979), 529–548.

Dann, Otto, *Gleichheit und Gleichberechtigung. Das Gleichheitspostulat in der alteuropäischen Tradition und in Deutschland bis zum ausgehenden 19. Jahrhundert*, Berlin 1980.

Dann, Otto, Gleichheit, in: Brunner, Otto/Conze, Werner/Koselleck, Reinhart (eds.), *Geschichtliche Grundbegriffe. Historisches Lexikon zur politisch-sozialen Sprache in Deutschland (Studienausgabe)*, Bd. 2, E-G, Stuttgart 2004, 997–1046.

Davy, Ulrike, Asylum Seekers' Dignity—Elusive in Europe and Lost in Crisis. At the Threshold of Universality, in: Arel, Stephanie/Cooper, Levi/Hellmann, Vanessa (eds.), *Probing Human Dignity. Exploring Thresholds from an Interdisciplinary Perspective*, Berlin 2022 (in print).

Davy, Ulrike, Refugee Crisis in Germany and the Right to a Subsistence Minimum: Differences That Ought Not Be, in: *Georgia Journal of International and Comparative Law* 47 (2/2019), 367–450.

Davy, Ulrike, Wenn Gleichheit in Gefahr ist. Staatliche Schutzpflichten und Schutzbedürftigkeit am Beispiel des Minderheitenschutzes und des Schutzes vor rassischer Diskriminierung, in: *Zeitschrift für öffentliches Recht* 74 (4/2019), 773–844.

Davy, Ulrike/Grave, Johannes/Hartner, Marcus/Schneider, Ralf/Steinmetz, Willibald, Grundbegriffe für eine Theorie des Vergleichens. Ein Zwischenbericht, in: *Praktiken des Vergleichens. Working Paper 3 des SFB 1288*, Bielefeld 2019, <https://pub.uni-bielefeld.de/record/2939563> [last accessed: October 30, 2021].

Descola, Philippe, *Beyond Nature and Culture*, Chicago, London 2013.

Devyver, André, *Le sang épuré, les préjugés de race chez les français de l'Ancien Régime (1560–1720)*, Brüssel 1973.

Duberman, Martin/Vicinus, Martha/Chauncey Jr., George (eds.), *Hidden from History: Reclaiming the Gay and Lesbian Past*, London 1991.

Dworkin, Ronald, What is Equality? Part 1: Equality of Welfare, in: *Philosophy & Public Affairs* 10 (3/1981), 185–246.

Dworkin, Ronald, What is Equality? Part 2: Equality of Resources, in: *Philosophy & Public Affairs* 10 (4/1981), 283–345.

Eibach, Joachim, Versprochene Gleichheit—verhandelte Ungleichheit. Zum sozialen Aspekt in der Strafjustiz der Frühen Neuzeit, in: *Geschichte und Gesellschaft* 35 (H 4/2009), 488–533.

Ellis, Evelyn/Watson, Philippa, *EU Anti-Discrimination Law*, Oxford Scholarship online 2013.

Engels, Friedrich, *Die Lage der Arbeitenden Klasse in England. Nach eigner Anschauung und authentischen Quellen*, 2nd ed., Stuttgart 1892.

Epple, Angelika, Inventing White Beauty and Fighting Black Slavery. How Blumenbach, Humboldt, and Arango y Parreño Contributed to Cuban Race Comparisons in the Long Nineteenth Century, in: Epple, Angelika/Erhart, Walter/Grave, Johannes (eds.), *Practices of Comparing. Towards a New Understanding of a Fundamental Human Practice*, Bielefeld 2020, 295–328.

Epple, Angelika/Erhart, Walter, Practices of Comparing. A New Research Agenda Between Typological and Historical Approaches, in: Epple, Angelika/Erhart, Walter/Grave, Johannes (eds.), *Practices of Comparing. Towards a New Understanding of a Fundamental Human Practice*, Bielefeld 2020, 11–38.

Epple, Angelika/Flüchter, Antje/Müller, Thomas, Praktiken des Vergleichens: praxistheoretische Fundierung und heuristische Typologien. Ein Bericht von unterwegs, in: *Praktiken des Vergleichens. Working Paper 6 des SFB 1288*, Bielefeld 2020, <https://pub.uni-bielefeld.de/record/2943010> [last accessed: October 30, 2021].

Eudell, Demetrius Lynn, *The Political Languages of Emancipation in the British Caribbean and the US South*, Chapel Hill 2002.

Farahat, Anuscheh, Rechtsunsicherheiten beim Zugang zur Gesundheitsversorgung von Migranten, in: *Zeitschrift für europäisches Arbeits- und Sozialrecht* 13 (2014), 269–278.

Farahat, Anuscheh, Solidarität und Inklusion. Umstrittene Dimensionen der Unionsbürgerschaft, in: *Die Öffentliche Verwaltung* 69 (2/2016), 45–55.

Fisch, Jörg, *Europa zwischen Wachstum und Gleichheit 1850–1914*, Stuttgart 2002.

Freeman, Marsha A./Chinkin, Christine/Rudolf, Beate (eds.), *The UN Convention on the Elimination of All Forms of Discrimination against Women. A Commentary*, Oxford 2012.

Fries, Michaela, *Die Bedeutung von Artikel 5(f) der Rassendiskriminierungskonvention im deutschen Recht: Diskriminierung durch Private beim Zugang zu Gaststätten*, Berlin 2003.

Gagné, Renaud, Introduction: Regimes of Comparatism, in: Gagné, Renaud/Goldhill, Simon/Lloyd, Geoffrey E.R. (eds.), *Regimes of Comparatism*, Leiden 2019, 1–17.

Gerhard, Ute (ed.), *Differenz und Gleichheit. Menschenrechte haben (k)ein Geschlecht*, Frankfurt 1990.

Hanchard, Michael G., *The Spectre of Race. How Discrimination Haunts Western Democracy*, Princeton and Oxford 2018.

Henn, Elisabeth Veronika, *International Human Rights Law and Structural Discrimination: The Example of Violence against Women*, Berlin 2019.

Hofmann, Claudia, *Jenseits von Gleichheit. Gleichheitsorientierte Maßnahmen im internationalen, europäischen und nationalen Recht*, Tübingen 2019.

Honegger, Claudia, *Die Ordnung der Geschlechter. Die Wissenschaft vom Menschen und das Weib, 1750–1850*, Frankfurt 1991.

Huster, Stefan, *Rechte und Ziele. Zur Dogmatik des allgemeinen Gleichheitssatzes*, Berlin 1993.

Janda, Constanze, *Migranten im Sozialstaat*, Tübingen 2012.

Jehne, Martin/Müller, Winfried/Fässler, Peter E., *Ungleichheiten: 47. Deutscher Historikertag in Dresden 2008: Berichtsband*, Göttingen 2009.

Keane, David, *Caste-Based Discrimination in International Human Rights Law*, Aldershot 2007.

Keane, David, Mapping the International Convention on the Elimination of All Forms of Racial Discrimination as a Living Instrument, in: *Human Rights Law Review* 20 (2/2020), 236–268.

Kessel, Martina, *Gewalt und Gelächter. "Deutschsein" 1914–1945*, Stuttgart 2019.

Kingreen, Thorsten, *Das Sozialstaatsprinzip im Europäischen Verfassungsverbund. Gemeinschaftsrechtliche Einflüsse auf das deutsche Recht der gesetzlichen Krankenversicherung*, Tübingen 2003.

Klinger, Cornelia/Knapp, Gudrun-Axeli/Sauer, Birgit, *Achsen der Ungleichheit: Zum Verhältnis von Klasse, Geschlecht und Ethnizität*, Frankfurt 2007.

Kocher, Eva, § 5 Arbeitsrechtlicher Diskriminierungsschutz, in: Schlachter, Monika/Heinig, Hans Michael (eds.), *Europäisches Arbeits- und Sozialrecht*, Baden-Baden 2016, 219–292.

Kuznets, Simon, Economic Growth and Income Inequality, in: *The American Economic Review* 45 (1/1955), 1–28.

Lerner, Natan, *The U.N. Convention on the Elimination of All Forms of Racial Discrimination. A Commentary*, Leyden 1970, reprint 2015.

Martínez, María Elena/Nirenberg, David/Torres, Max-Sebastián Hering, *Race and Blood in the Iberian World*, Münster 2012.

McCrudden, Christopher/Prechel, Sacha, *The Concepts of Equality and Non-Discrimination in Europe: A Practical Approach*, Brussels 2009.

Michaels, Axel, Notions of Nature in Traditional Hinduism, in: Ehlers, E./ Gethmann, C.F. (eds.), *Environment across Cultures. Wissenschaftsethik und Technikfolgenbeurteilung*, Heidelberg 2003, 111–121.

Milanovic, Branko, *Global Inequality: A New Approach for the Age of Globalization*, Cambridge, MA 2016.

Nagel, Thomas, *Equality and Partiality*, New York 1991.

Piketty, Thomas, *Capital in the Twenty-First Century*, Cambridge, MA and London 2017.

Pöschl, Magdalena, *Gleichheit vor dem Gesetz*, Wien 2008.

Rawls, John, *A Theory of Justice*, Cambridge, MA 1971.

Reidy, Joseph P., *Illusions of Emancipation: The Pursuit of Freedom and Equality in the Twilight of Slavery*, Chapel Hill 2019.

Roemer, John E., *Equality of Opportunity*, Cambridge, MA 1998.

Salverda, Wiemer/Nolan, Brian/Smeeding, Timothy M. (eds.), *The Oxford Handbook of Economic Inequality*, Oxford 2009.

Scheffler, Samuel, What is Egalitarianism?, in: *Philosophy and Public Affairs* 30 (1/2003), 5–39.

Schiek, Dagmar/Lawson, Anna (eds.), *European Union Non-Discrimination Law and Intersectionality: Investigating the Triangle of Racial, Gender and Disability Discrimination*, Surrey 2011.

Sen, Amartya, *Equality of What? The Tanner Lecture on Human Values. Delivered at Stanford University*, May 22, 1979, <https://www.ophi.org.uk/wp-content/uploads/Sen-1979_Equality-of-What.pdf> [last accessed: October 30, 2021].

Sen, Amartya, *Inequality Reexamined*, Oxford 1995.

Sen, Amartya, *On Economic Inequality*, Oxford 1997.

Somek, Alexander, *Engineering Equality: An Essay on European Anti-Discrimination Law*, Oxford Scholarship online 2011.

Somek, Alexander, *Rationalität und Diskriminierung*, Wien 2001.

Sørensen, Aage B., The Structural Basis of Social Inequality, in: *American Journal of Sociology* 101 (5/1996), 1333–1365.

Spivak, Gayatri, The Rani of Simur, in: Barker, Francis/Hulme, Peter/Iverson, Margaret/Loxley, Diana (eds.), *Europe and Its Others*, vol. 1, Colchester 1985, 54–67.

Steinmetz, Willibald, *Europa im 19. Jahrhundert*, Frankfurt 2019.

Therborn, Göran, *The Killing Fields of Inequality*, Cambridge 2013.

Thornberry, Patrick, Confronting Racial Discrimination: A CERD Perspective, in: *Human Rights Law Review* 5 (2/2005), 239–269.

Thornberry, Patrick, *The International Convention on the Elimination of All Forms of Racial Discrimination. A Commentary*, Oxford 2016.

Tilly, Charles, *Durable Inequality*, Berkeley, Los Angeles 1998.

Tobin, James, On Limiting the Domain of Inequality, in: *Journal of Law and Economics* 13 (2/1970), 263–278.

Ulbrich, Claudia, Ständische Ungleichheit und Geschlechterforschung, in: Füssel, Marian/Weller, Thomas (eds.), *Soziale Ungleichheit und ständische Gesellschaft. Theorien und Debatten in der Frühneuzeitforschung (Zeitensprünge 15)*, 2011, 85–104.

Verbist, Valérie, *Reverse Discrimination in the European Union. A Recurring Balancing Act*, Cambridge, Antwerp, Portland 2017.

Wehler, Hans-Ulrich, Vorüberlegung zur historischen Analyse sozialer Ungleichheit, in: Wehler, Hans-Ulrich (ed.), *Klassen in der europäischen Sozialgeschichte*, Göttingen 1979, 9–32.

Wehler, Hans-Ulrich, *Deutsche Gesellschaftsgeschichte, Bd. 1: Vom Feudalismus des Alten Reiches bis zur Defensiven Modernisierung der Reformära 1700–1815*, 2nd ed., Munich 1989.

Weller, Thomas, Soziale Ungleichheit und ständische Gesellschaft. Stand und Perspektiven der Forschung, in: *Zeitsprünge. Forschungen zur Frühen Neuzeit* 15 (1/2011), 3–23.

Wenzlhuemer, Roland/Juneja, Monica, *Die Neuzeit 1789–1914*, Konstanz 2013.

# Hierarchy as Order—Equality as Chaos? [1]
## The Mughal Empire through the Eyes of Early Modern European Travelers

Antje Flüchter

**Abstract**

*The contribution asks how equality and inequality were conceptualized and legitimized in early modern Europe. Equality is not an abstract concept but to a large extent dependent on social and cultural context. First, the conception of equality and inequality in the Holy Roman Empire is described, considering both its Christian origin and its implementation into social and political structures. This subchapter serves as a foil to analyze the relevance of equality in early modern accounts by travelers to the Indian Mughal Empire: How did these travelers assess questions of equality and ordered hierarchy in terms of social mobility and legal equality? Analyzing the perception and misunderstandings of dimensions of equality in India reveals how much Europeans valued inequality as an aspect of order. They just could not estimate many dimensions of equality in the India Mughal Empire or translate these dimensions for their European readers. This changed in the late eighteenth and particularly the nineteenth century: When Europe started imagining itself as liberal, socially mobile, and even equal, the Mughal Empire was cast as despotic, and all hints of elements of equality were written out of the discourse.*

1    This contribution draws on research conducted in the Collaborative Research Center "Practices of Comparing. Ordering and Changing the World" (SFB 1288).

## Introduction

Equality is a central value in our world—demanding and fighting for equality is one of the driving forces of modernity and processes of modernization. The early proclamations of human equality in the French and American Revolutions referred only to white men, and well-off white men at that.[2]

But after the three Revolutions in the eighteenth century (America, Haiti, and France) equality became—at least over time—a global demand, fueling movements for decolonization, gender equality, and much more. It was and continues to be adopted by women, Jews, people of color; other groups like the LGBT movement have raised their voices in recent years.

Even though we may question since when modern Western societies have been equal in a political sense—not to mention other dimensions of equality—the claim for equality is deeply embedded in the modern, Western self-image. The narrative of equality was so powerful that it assumed the role, in public discourse, of an anthropological constant, a universal *comparatum* or *tertium* held to be the normal and natural state for a society.[3] Societies and cultures that demand equality were seen as the standard, while others were declared deficient or not (yet) civilized, i.e., they had yet to reach the state of equality.

Yet the concept of equality was not invented by Enlightenment thinkers. The call for equality has been heard throughout human history, and by no means only in Europe. However, these demands came mostly as rather marginal voices. If we consider the structures before the aforementioned revolutions, those of the European-Christian *Ancien Régime*, the demand for equality was not yet hegemonic. On the contrary: The Christian social order was explicitly hierarchized in the *Ancien Régime*, in which a hierarchized order, rather than the notion or imagination of equality, was the social rule and guideline.

---

2    Willibald Steinmetz, *Europa im 19. Jahrhundert*, Frankfurt 2019, 34. According to Stein-metz, the nineteenth century can be characterized by growing equality and at the same time increasing heterogeneity, which he analyzes in fascinating detail along the criteria of gender, age, and class, Steinmetz, *Europa*, 428–488. See also Lynn Hunt, Envisioning Equality in the French Revolution; and Ulrike Davy, Minority Protection under the League of Nations: Universal and Particular Equality, *in this volume*.

3    Angelika Epple, *Doing Comparisons*. Ein praxeologischer Zugang zur Geschichte der Globalisierung/en, in: Angelika Epple/Walter Erhart (eds.), *Die Welt beobachten. Praktiken des Vergleichens*, Frankfurt/New York 2015, 161–199, see 166–167.

The central question of this article concerns the role and relevance of the concepts of order and equality in the early modern era. How were equality and inequality conceptualized, assessed, and legitimized—and, above all, related to each other? By asking this question, this article seeks not only to explain the prehistory of modern society or the triumphal march of equality: Instead, it follows the idea that equality is a relational phenomenon that can only be understood in relation to inequality. Therefore, this article asks about the interplay between equality on the one hand and inequality, hierarchy, or order on the other.[4] Consequently, the transition from early modern to modern times is understood not just as a development from the Ancien Régime to modern democracy. Instead, it is argued that the demand for equality led not just to more equality, but to a different conceptualization of equality.[5]

For this reason, because it is morally charged and a value deeply anchored in our times, 'equality' cannot serve as an analytical tool here. To apply 'equality' to premodern sources means using an anachronism—a mortal sin for historians.[6] Yet we are nonetheless interested in the limits and potential of this term. Therefore, I will use 'equality' as a "controlled anachronism."[7] The concept of anachronism implies that there is a right and a wrong time for a concept like 'equality.' Using a controlled anachronism can help us to understand

---

4    André Béteille holds that in every society, even in the most equal, inequalities exist. Every society needs a concept of merit, and merit can apply only if some are better off than others. André Béteille, Homo hierarchicus, homo equalis, in: *Modern Asian Studies* 13 (4/1979), 529–548, see 532–534.

5    Moreover, increasing equality led to a rearrangement of difference and also to the solidification and stabilization of some fundamental categories of difference, like race and gender. In her seminal article, Joan Scott explained that social revolutions often led to a stabilization of traditional gender roles, Joan W. Scott, Gender. A Useful Category of Historical Analysis, in: *American Historical Review* 91 (5/1986), 1053–1075. Similar arguments apply regarding increasing antisemitism, Steinmetz, *Europa*, 428–429, and thus the construction of white supremacy on the foundation of demands for equality.

6    Lucien Febvre, *Das Problem des Unglaubens im 16. Jahrhundert. Die Religion des Rabelais*, Stuttgart 2002, 17.

7    A new conceptualization of anachronism was developed by Jacques Rancière. My conceptual framing builds on the operationalization of Rancière by Caroline Arni. Caroline Arni, Zeitlichkeit, Anachronismus und Anachronien. Gegenwart und Transformationen der Geschlechtergeschichte aus geschichtstheoretischer Perspektive, in: *L'Homme* 18 (2/2007), 53–76; Caroline Arni, "Moi seule", 1833: Feminist Subjectivity, Temporality, and Historical Interpretation, in: *History of the Present: A Journal of Critical History* 2 (2/2012), 107–121.

if a term is understood in its respective context or if it is being used as part of a narrative deriving from Western modernization theory. Using 'equality' as a controlled anachronism thus helps us to comprehend its premodern understanding and to develop a deeper understanding of the many senses in which it has been understood across cultural and temporal contexts.

'Equality' has been differently conceptualized, understood, and evaluated over the course of time.[8] Otto Dann has traced the conceptual history of the term *Gleichheit* (equality). He connected equality closely to practices of comparing by asking what criteria were at the base of every claim of equality or similarity (*Gleichheits- oder Gleichartigkeitsbehauptung*). To focus on practices of comparison is therefore a promising approach to historicizing and contextualizing equality.[9] Practices of comparing create and affirm comparability in that they start from the assumption of at least one aspect of comparability, with subsequent comparisons creating either equality or difference. Moreover, they create the groups into which a society or culture is divided and at the same time set the criteria by which members of one group are equal. The elements of a comparison are not given. The choice of a specific *tertium* defines the *comparatum*—in this case, a social group.

In this article the focus is on concepts of equality encompassing males. The classic master narrative of increasing equality describes the rise of male political rights and equality, more precise those of white, Christian, and well-off males.[10] Of course equality is closely linked to intersectional questions, but

---

8    Otto Dann, Gleichheit, in: Otto Brunner/Werner Conze/Reinhart Koselleck (eds.), *Geschichtliche Grundbegriffe. Historisches Lexikon zur politisch-sozialen Sprache in Deutschland (Studienausgabe)*, Bd. 2, E–G, Stuttgart 2004, 997–1046.

9    On the conceptual framing of practices of comparing developed under the aegis of the SFB 1288 Practices of Comparing, see Angelika Epple/Walter Erhart, Practices of Comparing. A New Research Agenda Between Typological and Historical Approaches, in: Angelika Epple/Walter Erhart/Johannes Grave (eds.), *Practices of Comparing. Towards a New Understanding of a Fundamental Human Practice*, Bielefeld 2020, 11–38; Ulrike Davy/Johannes Grave/Marcus Hartner/Ralf Schneider/Willibald Steinmetz, Grundbegriffe für eine Theorie des Vergleichens. Ein Zwischenbericht, in: *Praktiken des Vergleichens. Working Paper 3 des SFB 1288*, Bielefeld 2019; Angelika Epple/Antje Flüchter/Thomas Müller, Praktiken des Vergleichens: Praxistheoretische Fundierung und heuristische Typologien. Ein Bericht von unterwegs, in: *Praktiken des Vergleichens. Working Paper 6 des SFB 1288*, Bielefeld 2020.

10    It is only after more than sixty pages, for instance, that Pierre Rosanvallon acknowledges that he has been only writing about males so far, Pierre Rosanvallon, *Die Gesellschaft der Gleichen*, Berlin 2017.

here I will focus on the equality of male human beings.[11] Including women would add a complication to this story: Women did not only attain equality later, they also lost some aspects of equality through the enforcement of modern bourgeois gender roles.[12]

Among the central criteria defining the different dimensions of equality are political, social, or economic factors.[13] Otto Dann concentrated on social and political 'equality,' which he took to be the most relevant.[14] This is indeed the kinds of equality most often discussed in political theory. Another aspect of equality, however, is economic or wealth equality. In classic Western political and philosophical thought, this aspect is rather neglected. Property becomes an important *tertium* to differentiate social groups at the turn of modernity and at the same time is loses its relevance as relevant *tertium* to assess equality. In the thought of John Locke and the American Revolutionary tradition, equality was closely connected with individual property and thus economic equality was more or less excluded.[15]

In my attempt at answering this question, I will first elaborate on conceptions of equality and inequality in the Holy Roman Empire (2.). This will be my foil against which I shall analyze the relevance of equality in early modern accounts of travels to the Mughal Empire, one of the great early modern Islamic empires on the Indian subcontinent. What views did travelers and

---

11   The relevance of race and gender is and will be tackled in my ongoing research project, first hypothesis of this project soon in Cornelia Aust/Antje Flüchter/Claudia Jarzebowski (eds.), *Entrechtete Körper. Vergleichen, Normieren, Urteilen, Leben, 1450–1850,* 2022 (in print). The exclusion of people of color, particularly those enslaved and displaced from Africa and their descendants, was analysed and discussed by Demetrius Lynn Eudell at our November 2019 conference. See also Demetrius Lynn Eudell, *The Political Languages of Emancipation in the British Caribbean and the US South,* Chapel Hill 2002; Demetrius Lynn Eudell, "Come on Kid, Let's Go Get the Thing." The Sociogenic Principle and the Being of Being Black/Human, in: Sylvia Wynter (ed.), *On Being Human as Praxis,* Durham 2015, 226–248.

12   On some of these aspects Hedwig Richter, *Demokratie: Eine deutsche Affäre,* Munich 2020, 24-26.

13   Moreover, the act of comparing may relate to different frames of reference. Otto Dann claims that the main frames of reference are society and nature. Dann, Gleichheit, 998. For premodern times, a religious frame of reference has to be taken into account.

14   Dann, Gleichheit, 998.

15   On the changing of regimes of inequality, see Thomas Piketty, *Capital and Ideology,* London 2020.

authors form with regard to equality and ordered hierarchy in terms of social mobility and legal equality (3.)?

My source corpus consists mostly of texts written in or translated into German. There is not one homogenous European discourse, but an entangled network of texts from different linguistic and cultural contexts. Authors translated with their readers and their patterns of evaluation in mind, which is why regional and cultural differences inside of Europe are also relevant. With texts in German as the point of departure, connections with and processes of transfer into other linguistic and cultural discourses will also be traced.

There are two principal reasons why analyzing the perception of equality in German or European discourse about India makes for a promising case study: First, the early modern preference for order instead of equality was so self-evident to contemporaries that they did not reflect too much about it. But describing and explaining things far away from home in travelogues, authors reveal fundamental attitudes that otherwise went without saying. From their assessments of other cultures and phenomena it can be deduced what they thought "normal," right," or as constituting a "good order."[16] Moreover, the authors had to translate their experience into their readers' patterns of evaluation.[17] It is not the aim of this article to judge whether or not these authors reached an accurate understanding of Indian phenomena or not. Indeed, misunderstandings are often even more revealing of authors' own values and patterns of perception.

Secondly, in modern or colonial discourse—that is, since the late eighteenth century—India and in particular its so-called caste system emerged as a foil for new European ideas of equality. It is a disputed question whether the Indian caste system might not be an invention of British Colonialism rather

---

16    Still seminal is Michael Harbsmeier, Reisebeschreibungen als mentalitätsgeschichtliche Quellen. Überlegungen zu einer historisch–anthropologischen Untersuchung frühneuzeitlicher deutscher Reisebeschreibungen, in: Antoni Maczak/Hans J. Teuteberg (eds.), *Reiseberichte als Quellen europäischer Kulturgeschichte. Aufgaben und Möglichkeiten der historischen Reiseforschung*, Wolfenbüttel 1982, 1–31.

17    Susanna Burghartz, "Translating Seen into Scene?" Wahrnehmung und Repräsentation in der frühen Kolonialgeschichte Europas, in: Susanna Burghartz/Maike Christadler/ Dorothea Nolde (eds.), *Berichten—Erzählen—Beherrschen: Wahrnehmen und Repräsentation in der frühen Kolonialgeschichte Europas*, Frankfurt 2003, 161–175.

than an Indian tradition.[18] This article consequently focusses on contemporary early modern India and specifically the Mughal Empire, the most relevant political entity on the Indian subcontinent. In modern colonial discourse, the Mughal Empire was understood as a prototype of "Oriental despotism."[19] If we follow Edward Said's view that the Occident constructed the Orient as its other, then it is not surprising to find that nineteenth-century Europe with its new liberal ideas of equality needed the contrast provided by a static and despotic other. However, how did the Europeans perceive social differentiation and imagined equality or inequality at a time when they themselves appreciated order more than equality and when India was not yet colonized, but an important and in some respects even superior actor?

## Order and Hierarchy in Early Modern Europe

It is a general assumption in the modern West that equality is the best way a society can be organized. However, this valorization of equality has to be historicized. Equality was not always understood as a social or political ideal. In premodern Christian and European social and political theory, it was quite the opposite. Islamic societies may have appreciated equality in premodern times and early modern China had had a meritocratic bureaucracy, but Christian Europe was a highly differentiated society that appreciated and valued difference by birth, nobility, and the dynastic principle.

### Order as an Ideal

In premodern Europe, social and political inequality were seen by most contemporaries as a feature of their society, as a value rather than a flaw.[20] Society was only imaginable as a God-given hierarchy of estates.[21] That inequality

---

18    Nicholas D. Dirks, *Castes of Mind. Colonialism and the Making of Modern India*, Princeton 2001. On Dirks's oeuvre see Christopher J. Fuller, History, Anthropology, Colonialism, and the Study of India, in: *History and Theory* 55 (3/2016), 452–464.

19    Michael Curtis, *Orientalism and Islam. European Thinkers on Oriental Despotism in the Middle East and India*, Cambridge 2009.

20    Wolfgang Reinhard, *Geschichte der Staatsgewalt. Eine vergleichende Verfassungsgeschichte Europas von den Anfängen bis zur Gegenwart*, Munich 2002, 16.

21    Thomas Weller, Soziale Ungleichheit und ständische Gesellschaft. Stand und Perspektiven der Forschung, in: *Zeitsprünge. Forschungen zur Frühen Neuzeit* 15 (1/2011), 3–23, see

should have constituted a positive value may at first seem strange from a modern perspective. We must therefore ask why inequality labelled as order was valued and legitimized. How did the elites achieve acceptance of their position at the top of the social hierarchy?

One important element was the Christian religion. In Christianity all men are created equal and all are equal before God. In early Christendom some of this equality was not only preached, but also practiced, for instance in the form of shared meals. However, this equality is to be understood in a spiritual, not in a social sense. For example, hardly anybody demanded the abolition of slavery in early Christianity.[22] Christian equality was—and is—first and foremost a spiritual equality. Men were created equal, but because of the fall social inequality was established and consequently social hierarchy and inequality were theologically legitimized. Instead of *aequalitas*, the early medieval concepts characterizing God's creation were *diversitas, disparitas, praelatio*.[23] In premodern times, there were catechetical stories about Cain and Abel's descendants who embarked on different careers and acquired different social status because of their morals.[24] This did not change with the Lutheran Reformation. Luther's proverbial title "On the Freedom of a Christian" (*Von der Freiheit des Christenmenschen*) refers explicitly to spiritual freedom. In this world, Luther wanted everybody to keep their social status and to obey their lawful government. And consequently, Luther vehemently preached and ranted against the peasants who were rising up in Germany at that time, demanding a greater degree equality—even, and particularly controversially, economic equality.[25] The position towards social equality was and not really different

---

6. The term "estates" does not only include political corporations, but also hierarchical orders of social groups, in German the *Stände* or *ständische Gesellschaft*.

22  This point was highlighted at our November 2019 conference by Demetrius Lynn Eudell with reference to the connection between slavery and racism. Denise Kimber Buell, Early Christian Universalism and Modern Forms of Racism, in: Miriam Eliav-Feldon/ Benjamin Isaac/Joseph Ziegler (eds.), *The Origins of Racism in the West*, Cambridge/New York 2009, 109–131. See also Jennifer A. Glancy, *Slavery as moral problem: In the early church and today*, Minneapolis 2011.

23  Dann, Gleichheit, 1002. The most relevant point of reference was St. Paul, for example, "But everything should be done in a fitting and orderly way," 1 Corinthians 14:40 (NIV).

24  Paul Münch, Grundwerte der frühneuzeitlichen Ständegesellschaft? Aufriß einer vernachlässigten Thematik, in: Winfried Schulze (ed.), *Ständische Gesellschaft und soziale Mobilität*, Munich 1988, 53–72, see 63.

25  Martin Greschat, Luthers Haltung im Bauernkrieg, in: *Archiv für Reformationsgeschichte–Archive for Reformation History* 56 (1965), 31–47. It does, therefore, not come as

in Calvinism. Johann Heinrich Alsted (1588-1638) was an important reformed preacher who praised order as the Christian fundament of society: "Nothing is as beautiful and fruitful as order. Order gives everything on this great stage that is the world worth and rank."[26]

There seem to be only one place in Christianity where the equality before God is stressed again and again, and that is the Last Judgement. Illustrations of this event symbolize equality: All people are the same, and kings and popes are as threatened by the fires of hell as the common people, maybe even more so. The spiritual equality of all people (even women) was connected to the social inequality or hierarchized order in the here and now.

Of course, there were also opposing currents, voices of groups that demanded full or at least a greater measure of equality. As much as Christian theology legitimized hierarchy and hierarchized order, there were a lot of practices referring to equality in the clerical sphere. Monasteries had abbots, but they were also communities of monks or nuns, understood as brethren and sisters, though hierarchically distinguished from the lay community. Conciliarists like Marsilius of Padua or Nicholas of Cusa tried to overcome the papal monarchy in the fifteenth century. Nevertheless, these instances still prove the equality only of the privileged. Moreover, the gospels could be read differently, and they were: in the movement of apostolic poverty in the Middle Ages (twelfth, fourteenth, fifteenth centuries), for example, or in the German peasant war (1524-1526). But for long such movements were either destroyed with much bloodshed or, like the mendicant orders, integrated into the system.

---

a surprise, that Friedrich Engels understood the peasant war as the first early bourgeois revolution, Friedrich Engels, Der deutsche Bauernkrieg [1850], in: *Karl Marx—Friedrich Engels—Werke, Bd. 7*, Berlin 1960, 327–413.

26   "Nichts ist schöner, nichts ist fruchtbarer als die Ordnung, Die Ordnung verschafft auf dem riesigen Theater dieser Welt allen Dingen Wert und Rang." Quoted by Münch, Grundwerte, 66. Modern Calvinists in South Africa and in the Netherlands both referred to the Bible, the former to legitimize Apartheid the latter to legitimize equality. Günter Kehrer, Über die Religionen und die Ungleichheit unter den Menschen, in: Günter Kehrer (ed.), *"Vor Gott sind alle gleich." Soziale Gleichheit, soziale Ungleichheit und die Religionen*, Düsseldorf 1983, 9–25, see 18.

## Equality and Society: Order

The idea of order was not only relevant in the religious field. Religious, political and social order were tightly interwoven in early modern European Christianity. Whereas concepts of equality were restricted to the afterworld and the spiritual sphere, concepts of order operated in the social world. Consequently, *inaequalitas* and *disparitas* were positive terms, "ordo," order, *Ordnung* were appreciated values. This order was symbolized in so called estate trees (*Ständebäume*).[27] Society had to be socially differentiated, inequality was understood as necessary. Many political tracts praised order and consequently inequality. Gerhard Hagemann, the author of an influential theory about nobility, wrote in the late seventeenth century: "Human society is ruled by inequality. [...] Therefore, inequality between people is necessary for political harmony." Here, inequality is seen as guaranteeing harmony and reasonable rule.[28]

This inequality was connected or even determined by equality inside one's own social group, and this could work only in a hierarchical, unequal social environment. In-group equality was an important reference point for identification. A very important German term, *Standesgenossen*, literally refers to sharing a distinct social status (*Stand* or "estate"), comparable maybe to peer group, but with consequences for most aspects for everyday life and work. Otto Dann even concludes that in premodern times, "equal meant *standesgleich*, equal within one's own status group."[29] Such a concept of equality obviously depended on an unequal context.

The examples cited so far are drawn from the context of the Holy Roman Empire. Yet social distinctions were perhaps even stricter in France. It is said, that during the Estates General of 1614, the third estate addressed the king with the request to be treated as younger brothers to the first two estates. The

---

27    On the critical reception of this visualization in the French Revolution, see Lynn Hunt, Equality, *in this volume*.

28    "Sic humana societas regitur inaequalitate; [...] Ideoque hanc inaequalitatem inter cives harmonica politiarum ratio exegit," Gerhard Hagemann, *De omnigena hominis nobilitate libri IV: queis pretractantur, quae ad usum et utilitatem de nobilitate hominis naturali*, Hildesheim 1693, 480, quoted by Dann, Gleichheit, 1004. On Hagemann and other theoretical tracts legitimizing and explaining nobility, see Klaus Bleeck/Jörn Garber, Nobilitas. Standes- und Privilegienlegitimation in deutschen Adelstheorien des 16. und 17. Jahrhunderts, in: *Daphnis* 11 (1–2/1982), 49–114.

29    Dann, Gleichheit, 1004.

members of the second estate, that is the nobility, were mortally offended. In their opinion, the different estates must not be seen as one family.[30] It must be stressed here that the third estate had not even asked for equality, but for something like acknowledgement of a family resemblance, whereas the second estate had denied any such comparability. Here a regional difference has to be considered: There was a nobility in all European Christian territories, but its legitimization differed. The French nobility of the robe claimed to be of purer blood than the rest of the people in France.[31] The social distinction between the estates thus took on a quasi-'biological' dimension even in pre-modern times.

It may be not particularly surprising that the members of nobility should have sought to legitimize their privileges and thus to endow inequality with rationality and morality. Moreover, the elite passed down most of the sources historians can work with. Therefore, it is very difficult to grasp the voices of the less privileged groups. This dominance should not conceal the fact that there were always opposing currents in which different opinions were voiced—maybe not openly demanding equality, but at least criticizing the hierarchical order. The tracts about noble privilege quoted here, for example, were answered with tracts criticizing nobility and their demands, a genre quite popular in humanist literature.[32]

Nevertheless, this valuing of order had deeper roots in society than the nobility legitimizing its privileges. It was fundamental for everyday political and everyday life. If one looks into the *Ratmannen-Spiegel* (mirror for aldermen), a guidebook for urban councilors written by Johann Oldendorp (1486-1567), the close interweaving of the divine, natural, and human orders in Protestant political theory is obvious.[33] Every order and every government is seen as divine,

---

30   Rosanvallon, *Gesellschaft*, 23–24.

31   The construct of pure blood and race became even stronger when the nobility's political power was restricted by increasing kingly governance (so-called absolutism). See Guillaume Aubert, "The Blood of France." Race and Purity of Blood in the French Atlantic World, in: *The William and Mary Quarterly* 61 (3/2004), 439–478, see 442–446. The reference to "pure blood" resembles the Iberian "limpieza de sangre." But in France, purity of blood was a criterion for social rather than religious difference.

32   For further references, see Bleeck/Garber, Nobilitas, 61.

33   There is a certain irony in the fact that in 1893 Albert Freyne, the editor of Oldendorp's text, felt compelled to defend Oldendorp against the accusation of having held democratic ideas. See Johannes Oldendorp, *Ein Ratmannen-Spiegel* (1530) Faksimile mit einem Vorwort von Albert Freybe, ed. by Dr. der Bärensprungschen Hofbuchdr[ucke-

and every order and body of laws must be guided by God's word. Moreover, the social status one is born into is also ordained by God, and therefore everybody is required to be content with the situation into which they are born and should not strive for social advancement.[34] For premodern city governments, but also for urban political elites, freedom and equality were not the ideals by which they oriented their actions. Traditional values were instead peace, the common good, and justice—with the latter, unlike in later times, not understood as synonymous with equality.

## Inequality and Law

The prerogatives demanded by the nobility and of territorial or city rulers were typical of early modern times. There remains the legal field to be examined. Equality and justice seem to be closely connected: In English, the term "justice" refers not only to the judiciary, but to the value of justness itself. According to the Swiss jurist Hans Nef: "In general, equality has always been considered a constitutive characteristic of justice; it is the immediately obvious yardstick for a legal relationship between persons and groups."[35]

It nevertheless remains to be asked: What kind of justice was depending on what kind of equality? There were biblical references for a just judiciary, condemning corruption and demanding impartiality.[36] A certain degree of

---

rei], Stettin 1893, 15. On Oldendorp's political theory, see Birgit C. Bender-Junker, *Utopia, Policey und Christliche Securitas. Ordnungsentwürfe der Frühen Neuzeit*, Marburg 1992, 155–162.

34   "Jeder/wie gesagt/in seinem Ampt beruffen/lessei sich an deme begnügen. Was ihm Gott darin zu füget/dem einen mehr/dem ander weniger/gedencket/du hast nichts her gebracht/wirst auch nicht in die Gruben mit nehmen/notturfft und teglichs brodt sey dir genug." Oldendorp, *Ratmannen-Spiegel*, 59.

35   "Überhaupt gilt Gleichheit von jeher als ein konstitutives Merkmal der Gerechtigkeit; sie ist der unmittelbar einleuchtende Maßstab für eine rechtliche Beziehung zwischen Personen und Gruppen." Hans Nef, *Gleichheit und Gerechtigkeit*, Zurich 1941, 9–10. The connection between equality and justice can be traced back to antiquity. Peter Koller, Soziale Gleichheit und Gerechtigkeit, in: Hans-Peter Müller/Bernd Wegener (eds.), *Soziale Ungleichheit und soziale Gerechtigkeit*, Opladen 1995, 53–80, see 53.

36   An important point of reference was the Book of Deuteronomy 1:17 & 16:19. Joachim Eibach, Versprochene Gleichheit—verhandelte Ungleichheit. Zum sozialen Aspekt in der Strafjustiz der Frühen Neuzeit, in: *Geschichte und Gesellschaft* 35 (4/2009), 488–533, see 493.

social equality was necessary between parties to conclude a contract.[37] Imagining equality was certainly more frequent in the premodern legal field than in the political or social sphere, but the concept remained ambivalent and was not important enough to overcome differences of social status. As Conrad Van Dijk concludes with regard to the English medieval context: "equity as a legal practice is both a ubiquitous concept (it is invariably paired with justice) and yet is multi-facetted in its meaning."[38] A generally shared idea in premodern times was that every status group had its own laws, courts, and procedure. The best-known cases are church courts, but universities, too, had their own courts, guilds settled most affairs within their own legal bodies, and religious minorities, like Jewish communities, were allowed to administer at least their own civil jurisdiction. This accepted and indeed valued degree of inequality before the law is one of the most relevant differences between premodern and modern societies.[39]

Quite central for this acceptance of inequality was the work of Domitius Ulpian, an ancient Roman jurist thought to have died in 223 or 228 A.D. who was one of the great legal authorities of his time. In premodern times, his injunction to "give each his due" was well known and of particular relevance to the legal sphere. This phrase gives as a very special meaning to equality, for if everybody gets their due, everybody is treated equally in a special sense. The phrase was often quoted to legitimize inequality before the law or in the legal system.[40] "Giving each his due" was also understood as a negotiation between justice, equality, and mercy.[41] Equal treatment cannot always be understood as fair. We are now familiar with the absence or reduction of criminal responsibility (for example, for children). In premodern times, first of all, the phrase certainly stands for privileges for the social elite, meaning, as Wolfgang Reinhard has put it, that "unequal punishments" were handed out "for the same

---

37    Dann, Gleichheit, 1003.

38    Conrad Van Dijk, Giving Each His Due: Langland, Gower, and the Question of Equity, in: *The Journal of English and Germanic Philology* 108 (3/2009), 310–335, see 320.

39    For details, see Barbara Stollberg-Rilinger, *Europa im Jahrhundert der Aufklärung*, Stuttgart 2000, 69–71.

40    Edgar Thaidigsmann, Jedem das Seine. Zum Thema "Gesetz und Evangelium," in: *Neue Zeitschrift für Systematische Theologie und Religionsphilosophie* 35 (3/1993), 237–258, see 239.

41    Van Dijk, Due, 311–312.

offense if the perpetrator came from a different social background."[42] A well-known example for this phenomenon are the different punishments for theft depending on social status as codified in the *Carolina*, the first German criminal code, enacted by the Diet of Augsburg in 1530 and named after emperor Charles V. It is important to note that these are not medieval relics, nor is this a story of progress to more equality. In the *Theresiana*, a criminal code issued under the Habsburg ruler Maria Theresia in 1768, the social status of the perpetrator was even more relevant than it had been 200 years earlier.[43] Even an early attempt to codify one law for all subjects—the *Allgemeine Landrecht*, the first codified Prussian law initiated by Frederick II—still provides for different courts according to rank, as well as different procedures and different punishments depending on social status or gender.

But the idea of "giving each his due" can also be read against the grain of the previous interpretation: In economic terms, it could be understood as giving everybody what they needed. And this is quite an influential concept in premodern times, at least in the economic rather than in the legal realm. A related and highly influential concept was *Gemeinnutz*,[44] a kind of public and common interest: People should get a fair reward for their work, a demand that mixes a social value with Christian *caritas*. One example is the *Allmende*, the German term for a particular kind of common land that belonged to the whole community and which everybody was entitled to use. The poor of the community could, for example, collect wood or graze their animals there. This *Gemeinnutz* can be understood as an opposite to capitalist self-interest, and shared common goods like the *Allmende* were privatized in the eighteenth and nineteenth centuries. A related concept, also very characteristic of premodern times, is that of *gerechte Nahrung*—'fair food and income'—meaning that while

---

42    Wolfgang Reinhard, *Probleme deutscher Geschichte 1495–1806: Reichsreform und Reformation. Deutsche Geschichte 1495–1555*, Stuttgart 2004, 159. Gender also played a role. According to Roman Law, for example, women were punished less severely for adultery because "Mulieres suapte natura in libidinem sint procliviores." Elisabeth Koch, Die Frau im Recht der Frühen Neuzeit: Juristische Lehren und Begründungen, in: Ute Gerhard (ed.), *Frauen in der Geschichte des Rechts*, Munich 1997, 73–93, see 89.

43    Eibach, Gleichheit, 504. Joachim Eibach argues that, in the eighteenth century, growing inequalities were legitimized by nature rather than needing divine sanction.

44    Peter Blickle, Der gemeine Nutzen. Ein kommunaler Wert und seine politische Karriere, in: Herfried Münkler/Harald Bluhm (eds.), *Gemeinwohl und Gemeinsinn. Historische Semantiken politischer Leitbegriffe*, Berlin 2001, 85–107.

it was fair that the nobleman should have more and better food than his peasants, the peasants should certainly have enough and should receive their fair due according to their needs and work. Whereas social equality was repudiated or at least disputed in premodern times, it seemed—interestingly—easier to demand economic justice. Again, it is not equality that was demanded or morally required, but kind of hierarchized distribution that is closer to the ideal of economic equality than modern capitalism, let alone neo-liberalism.

## Equality, Hierarchy and Order in early modern texts describing India

Equality and order are not abstract concepts, but are embedded in local, societal, and cultural world views. The knowledge and worldviews regarding order, hierarchy, and equality described here structure texts about foreign cultures—the knowledge travelers brought with them as well as their readers' knowledge, into which the travelers had to translate their adventures and descriptions.[45] Building on these ideas, this section asks how equality and ordered hierarchy were assessed in travelogues from the Mughal Empire in India and how their interplay and mutual stabilization was understood. To operationalize these questions, two aspects were chosen as the most promising: the travelogues' descriptions and assessment of (first) social mobility and (second) of the way justice was administered.

### Social Mobility in India

The possibility of social mobility is understood here as an indicator of equality. It should be noted that comprehensive social equality is an ideal only in such social experiments as communism. Also, in modern societies, the ideal of social equality is mostly framed in terms meritocratic values, therefore the chances to reach a social status have to be equal, and not the status itself.[46] A regard for social mobility can be considered a central difference between premodern and modern times.[47]

---

45   Burghartz, Translating.

46   Béteille, Homo hierarchicus, 532–34.

47   Winfried Schulze questioned the notion of a static premodern society. Winfried Schulze, Die ständische Gesellschaft des 16./ 17. Jahrhunderts als Problem von Statik und Dynamik, in: Winfried Schulze/Helmut Gabel (eds.), *Ständische Gesellschaft und soziale Mobilität*, Munich 1988, 1–17.

In modern and Orientalist discourse in the West, Indian social structure was understood as a polar opposite to modern Western equality and its inherent social mobility. India is (or was) most frequently associated with a petrified caste structure, where birth was destiny and inequality the accepted standard.[48] This opposition between India and the West culminated in Louis Dumont's famous comparison between *homo hierarchicus* and *homo equalis*.[49] Postcolonial scholars have very plausible argued that the actual petrification of caste in India happened because of British rule and the colonialist impulse to impose order on Indian diversity.[50]

Though it forms a central aspect in modern images of India, caste was much less often mentioned in early modern times. Missionaries in particular wrote about caste, which they saw as a crucial obstacle to their Christianizing efforts.[51] But it was not a topic that interested many secular early modern travelers. Travelogues wanted to inform and to entertain, and familiar phenomena were not as interesting as those assumed to be exotic and different. Early modern European travelers, as we have seen, knew quite strict social differentiation at home, as we have seen. Only the aspect that different social groups could not eat with each other was interesting enough to be mentioned in many travelogues.[52]

Instead, seventeenth century's travelogues often described the social system of the Islamic Mughal Empire. The Mughal Empire was one of the three

---

48    The supposed petrified structure of the caste system puts the category of caste close to race. Barbara Celarent, Caste and Race in India by G. S. Ghurye, in: *American Journal of Sociology* 116 (5/2011), 1713–1719. See also the differing positions presented by David Keane, India, the UN and Caste as a Form of Racial Discrimination: Resolving the Dispute; and Gautam Bhatia, Equality under the Indian Constitution, *in this volume*.

49    Louis Dumont, *Homo hierarchicus. Le système des castes et ses implications*, Paris 1979.

50    Dirks, *Castes*. See also Fuller, History.

51    Abraham Rogerius, *Offne Thür zu dem verborgenen Heydenthum [...]*, Nürnberg 1663, 3–4; Francis X. Clooney, Yes to Caste, No to Religion? Or Perhaps the Reverse: Re-Using Roberto de Nobili's Distinctions among Morality, Caste, and Religion, in: Chockalingam Joe Arun (ed.), *Intercultural of Religion: Critical Perspectives on Robert de Nobili's Mission in India*, Bangalore 2007, 158–174.

52    Es "sol keine Secte mit der andern weder essen noch trincken." Jürgen Andersen/ Volquard Iversen (eds.), *Orientalische Reise-Beschreibung Jürgen Andersen aus Schleßwig [...]*, Hamburg 1696, 204; "Die Benianen essen mit keinem der nicht ihres Glaubens ist." Johann Albrecht von Mandelslo, *Des Hoch-Edelgebohrnen Johann Albrechts von Mandelslo Morgenländische Reise-Beschreibung*, Hamburg 1696, 78. See also the formulation in Jean Baptiste Tavernier, *Vierzig-Jährige Reise-Beschreibung. [...]*, Nürnberg 1681, 70.

great Islamic Empires in the sixteenth and seventeenth centuries beside the Ottoman Empire and the Safavid Empire in Persia. The Mughals came from central Asia, conquered the Delhi Sultanates (themselves Islamic) in 1526 and expanded from there. In the seventeenth century it stretched from modern Pakistan to Bangladesh as well as far into the south of India.[53]

The following analysis relies mostly on the accounts contained in two travelogues, those of Johann Albrecht von Mandelslo (1616-1644) and François Bernier (1620-1688). Their texts are among the most relevant points of reference for Mughal India in the seventeenth century. As British power in India grew after 1757, the discourse changed and different points came to be emphasized. This marked, as Thomas R. Trautmann has noted, "a titanic shift of authority." The scholars of the newly founded Asiatic Society "were fashioning a new claim of authority over that of the older Orientalism, a claim that largely succeeded."[54]

Mandelslo and Bernier were fascinated and a bit repulsed by the social mobility, maybe even the meritocratic elements inherent in the structure of the elites in the Mughal Empire. Apparently, this was so foreign to them that they chose different comparative framings to translate the structure of the Mughal elite for their readers. François Bernier explains that the Mughal elites could not be compared with European nobility, since the Emirs and princes at the Mughal court were not sons of noble houses as in France. In the Mughal empire there were no dukedoms no margraviates.[55] This statement that there

---

53   On the historic context Muzaffar Alam/Sanjay Subrahmanyam (eds.), *The Mughal State, 1526–1750*, Delhi 1998; Stephen Dale, India under Mughal Rule, in: David Morgan/Anthony Reid (eds.), *The New Cambridge History of Islam, Bd. 3: The Eastern Islamic World, Eleventh to Eighteenth Centuries*, Cambridge 2010, 266–314.

54   Thomas R. Trautmann, *Aryans and British India*, New Delhi 2004, 30. On the topics, narratives, and authors of the older, pre-British India discourse, see Antje Flüchter, *Die Vielfalt der Bilder und die eine Wahrheit: Die Staatlichkeit Indiens in der deutschsprachigen Wahrnehmung (1500–1700)*, Affalterbach 2020; Sanjay Subrahmanyam, *Europe's India. Words, People, Empires, 1500–1800*, Cambridge, MA 2017; Kim Siebenhüner, *Die Spur der Juwelen. Materielle Kultur und transnationale Verbindungen zwischen Indien und Europa in der Frühen Neuzeit*, Cologne 2017.

55   The French original reads: "ni duchés, ni marquisats." François Bernier, *Un libertin dans l'Inde moghole. Les voyages de François Bernier (1656—1669)*, Paris 2008, 207. The German translation reads "daß die Omrahs oder grosse Herren an des Mogols Hof/Söhne der Geschlechter wie in Franckreich sind." In the Mughal Empire, there are "weder Herzogtümer noch Marckgrafschafften noch sonsten reiche Geschlechter in Landen und Gütern." Bernier, Letter to Colbert, François Bernier, *Sonderbare Begebnuß oder Erzehlung*

was no inherited nobility hints at an equal character of the Mughal society, or at least at a society that was much more dynamic than that of France. However, Bernier's text should not be understood as praising this state of affairs. Bernier continued to argue that the elite of the Mughal court were common and brutish people, unreasonable slaves; the courtiers were people who had risen from the dirt and dust to claim the dignity of lords.[56]

Quite similar was the attitude in the report ascribed to the young nobleman Johann Albrecht von Mandelslo, who travelled in the early seventeenth century via Moscow and Persia to India. His posthumously published travelogue[57] recounts that at the Mughal court as well as in the whole Empire, the *Rashis* or dukes are not born as such, but were made dukes by the king. Because of this structure, a craftsman or stable-boy could hope to get a principality.[58] First Mandelslo states the comparability or equality of the Indian *Rashis* with the European dukes, by giving *duke* as a translation for *Rashi*. Thus, there was an elite in the Mughal Empire. However, in the next step, he argues that the members of the elite were started out in life no different from other people, but equal. Mandelslo thus believed that equal social mobility obtained in the Mughal Empire.

This supposed lack of inherited status or nobility was not due merely to a misunderstanding on the writer's part. Compared to the hierarchically ordered society found in the Holy Roman Empire or (similarly) in most Western European Christian societies in the sixteenth and seventeenth centuries, a career at the Mughal court certainly had meritocratic aspects. Early modern Islamic societies were generally more structured by equality than Christian

---

*dessen was sich nach funffjährigen Krieg in denen Landen des Grossen Mogols begeben und zugetragen hat*, Frankfurt 1673, 125–192, see 144. See also Jean Chardin, *Voyages du Chevalier Chardin, en Perse, et autres lieux de l'Orient : Enrichis de Figures en Taille-douce, qui représentent les Antiquités & les choses remarquables du Pais [...]*, Brussels 1973, 312.

56  They are "nichtswürdige Leute/Sclaven/unverständige viehische Menschen/und solche Höflinge/die sich aus dem Staub zu den Würden erhoben haben." Bernier, *Begebnuß*, 145.

57  Mandelslo was for a long time considered an expert on the Mughal court. However, many details of his travelogue were not written by him, but added by his editors or translators. Antje Flüchter, Johann Albrecht von Mandelslo, in: David Thomas/John Chesworth (eds.), *Christian-Muslim Relations. A Bibliographical History*, Amsterdam 2017, 869–885.

58  Mandelslo, *Reise-Beschreibung*, 66.

ones, and most of all there was no dynastic nobility beside the imperial dynasty itself as in Christian Europe.[59] Mughal elite formation originated in the central Asian tradition of military organization, in which everybody had to start low and work his way up. There was a sophisticated system of ranking, with procedures of promotion and demotion.[60]

Some travelers just ignored these dynamic aspects and simply (mis-)translated the terms for offices into European concepts.[61] Both Bernier and Mandelslo, however, recognized the social mobility, and their texts even display some awareness of meritocratic elements. Mandelslo wrote that the dukes were made dukes because they were especially chivalrous and brave, or because they exposed themselves to great dangers.[62] Bernier's formulation suggests an even more formalized career path: "It is a general custom here that you move from humble duties to the prestigious ones."[63] However, these meritocratic elements were mostly misunderstood or assessed negatively. Bernier was scornful of such social climbers: They were only foreigners, gamblers, and unworthy serfs, lacking any aptitude for the job.[64] The ideal of inequality or social hierarchy is deeply written into both texts. Mandelslo and

---

59    Raj Kumar, *Essays on Legal Systems in India*, New Delhi 2003, 43. Of course, this equality referred to men; women were, similar to Christian doctrine, equal only before God.

60    On the *mansabdar system*, see Muhammad Athar Ali, *The Mughal Nobility under Aurangzeb*, rev. ed., New Delhi 2001. See also Christoph Dartmann/Antje Flüchter/Jenny Rahel Oesterle, Eliten im transkulturellen Monarchienvergleich, in: Wolfram Drews/Antje Flüchter (eds.), *Monarchische Herrschaftsformen der Vormoderne in transkultureller Perspektive*, Berlin 2015, 33–173, see 71–86.

61    Christian Burckhardt, soldier of the Dutch East India Company, translated the *mansabdars* as "Hertzog" (duke) or "Reichsfürsten" (imperial princes). Christian Burckhardt, *Ost-Indianische Reise-Beschreibung oder Kurtzgefaßter Abriß von Ost-Indien und dessen angränzenden Provincien*, Halle/Leipzig 1693, 156–157. The German version of the travelogue of the French traveler Tavernier translates *omrahs* as "Prinzen von Geblüt" (princes of the blood). Tavernier, *Reise-Beschreibung*, 98–99.

62    "Wenn sie nemlich durch Ritterliche Thaten/und grosse Gefahr sich darzu würdig gemachet." Mandelslo, *Reise–Beschreibung*, 66.

63    "Massen es fast eine allgemeine Gewohnheit ist/daß man von den geringen Bestall- und Amtsverwaltungen zu den Grossen gelangen." Bernier, *Begebnuß*, 145.

64    "Diese Omrahs sind solchem nach gemeiniglich nur blosse Glücks-Leute und Fremdlinge/wie ich gesagt habe/welche einander an diesen Hoff befördern und hinziehen/theils nichtswürdige Leute/und Leibeigene/der meiste Theil sonder Wissenschafft/die der Mogol solchergestalt nach seinem Belieben zu den Ehrenstellen erhebet/unnd gleichfalls wieder absetztet." Bernier, *Begebnuß*, 145.

Bernier understood social mobility as an expression of the ruler's arbitrary power.

Social mobility, as Winfried Schulze has already highlighted, means not only the ascent to riches of some common person, but also the decline of family or a person.[65] The latter is also described in several travelogues. Some authors explained that as a rule, the sons and grandsons of important office-holders at the Mughal court became less and less important and were unable to attain their father's and grandfather's rank. Thus, each generation lost social status.[66] Moreover, there are several anecdotes in which an office holder, important general, or someone of comparable rank lost his status because he fell out of the Mughal's favor.[67]

Social mobility and equal access to social advancement was nothing the travelers Bernier and Mandelslo considered admirable. On the contrary they saw it is a fault or flaw in the system of the Mughal court. The order embodied in a hierarchized social system was their ideal, and thus inequality. Against the backdrop of the European idea of a well-ordered inequality, this is not astonishing. Both Mandelslo and Bernier belonged to the social elite; members of the elite mostly have a rather positive perception of inequality, unlike lower-status people, the so-called common man. For early modern times, we rarely have sources giving the subaltern a voice. In the German discourse about India, however, we have a special source genre: German-speaking men who signed on with the Dutch East India Company (VOC) as sailors or soldiers.[68] Several of them wrote travelogues. Therefore, we have travelogues by a group of people with a shared stock of narratives whose voices are normally not heard. Unfortunately, they did not write about social mobility in the Mughal Empire.

---

65   Schulze, Gesellschaft, 14–16.

66   Bernier plainly framed such decline from generation to generation as a rule linked to skin color, arguing that 'white' people from central Asia got good positions, but their children and grandchildren became more and more brown and where consequently less valued. François Bernier, *Auffgezeichnete Beobachtungen was sich in dem Reich des Grossen Mogols Begeben und zugetragen hat [...]*, Frankfurt 1673, 139.

67   Jürgen Andersen, for example, describes the cruel execution of a general who surrendered a besieged city to the enemy. Andersen/Iversen, *Reise-Beschreibung*, 39.

68   Roelof van Gelder, *Das ostindische Abenteuer. Deutsche in Diensten der Vereinigten Ostindischen Kompanie der Niederlande (VOC). 1600–1800*, Hamburg 2004; Jan Lucassen, A Multinational and its Labor Force: The Dutch East India Company, 1595–1795, in: *International Labor and Working-Class History* 66 (2004), 12–39.

However, there is one indicator that they saw social distinction in a different light than the more learned and high-status travelers: Authors of travelogues placed the people they met in an order and located themselves in this order by comparing themselves. The chosen groups or *comparata* indicate which aspects or *tertia* were seen as relevant for social differentiation, which criteria were necessary to imagine equality or difference. For members of the European elite, like Mandelslo or Sir Thomas Roe, the first British ambassador to the Mughal court, their comparability with the Indian elite was most relevant. They ranked themselves in the court hierarchy, whereas at the same time their own servants were seen as the other and as unequal.[69] For these actors and authors, social status was of much higher importance than ethnic or proto-national origin. The employees of the VOC, however, referred a nation-oriented order instead.[70] That is, they labelled themselves as German or Dutch and compared themselves with the French and English, sometimes with Persians and Indians. Yet to describe oneself as member of a nation and labelling oneself as English or German or Dutch, is very rare in texts by learned and socially higher standing authors travelling in India. Belonging to a nation implied a certain equality with other members of this nation across social boundaries. This idea of national community was rather foreign to or at

---

69  On integration into court society and diplomatic ceremonial, see Antje Flüchter, Diplomatic Ceremonial and Greeting Practice at the Mughal Court, in: Wolfram Drews/ Christian Scholl (eds.), *Transkulturelle Verflechtungsprozesse in der Vormoderne*, Berlin/ Boston 2016, 89–120.

70  For further references, see Antje Flüchter, Handling Diversity in Early Modern India? Perception and Evaluation in German Discourse, in: *The Medieval History Journal. Special Issue: Handling Diversity. Medieval Europe and India in Comparison (13th–18th Century)* 16 (2/2013), 297–334. Early modern nations are obviously not the same as modern nations. The term "nation" is much older than modern nationalism as a political movement or the concept of the nation state. In early modern times, "nation" was a term in the political field, as for example in the term "Holy Roman Empire of the German Nation." "Nationes" (Latin) were an important topic for Renaissance humanists. The main difference between premodern and modern notions of the nation is that premodern "nationes" were only *one* way to distinguish people, but by far not the principal one. Religion, denomination, social status (*Stand*), family, or dynasty were much more relevant for the individual identity than the nation. Caspar Hirschi, *The origins of nationalism: an alternative history from ancient Rome to early modern Germany*, Cambridge 2011; Herfried Münkler/Hans Grünberger, Nationale Identität im Diskurs der Deutschen Humanisten, in: Helmut Berding (ed.), *Nationales Bewußtsein und kollektive Identität*, Frankfurt 1996, 211–247.

least not considered useful by the premodern elite.[71] With 'nation,' however, the VOC's employees, mostly soldiers and sailors, chose a point of comparative reference that claimed a greater degree of similarity or even equality with their higher-ranking compatriots. Whether one chose nation or social status (*Stand*) as *comparata* quite clearly showed the different mechanisms of inclusion and exclusion depending on the category of equality.

The use of nation by the VOC's employees testifies to an implicit imagining of equality, at least in terms of national affiliation. More explicit demands were not possible; and above all more explicit claims for equality could not be made public in this genre and for this audience. It must be remembered that the intended audience of the published travelogues were mostly the premodern equivalent of the bourgeoisie. They wanted to read about India, but not about equality or the inversion of their social order.

Descriptions of Mughal society and its dynamics changed in the course of the eighteenth century. At the same time that social mobility and equality became modern European values, they were written out of the discourse about India. Instead of acknowledging some kind of social mobility and some meritocratic elements, now the hegemonic narrative to explain the Mughal Empire became that of *oriental despotism*. Although this concept can be traced back to antiquity and Aristotle, in the cohesive form that we have come to know it, it was developed in the context of criticizing European absolutism in the seventeenth and eighteenth centuries.[72]

The concepts presence is palpable in later report in the sample analyzed for this paper, namely that of Jemima Kindersley. In her travelogue, translated into German 1777, she declares the Mughal Empire to be despotic government

---

71    On early nationalism and the idea of a brotherly bond between the wealthy and the poor in nineteenth-century Prussia, see Helmut Walser Smith, "A Deep, Horizontal Comradeship?" Early Nineteenth-Century German Nationalism and the Problem of Poverty, *in this volume*.

72    Werner Kogge/Lisa Wilhelmi, Despot und (orientalische) Despotie—Brüche im Konzept von Aristoteles bis Montesquieu, in: *Saeculum* 69 (2/2019), 305–342; Melvin Richter, Despotism, in: Philip P. Wiener (ed.), *Dictionary of the History of Ideas. Studies of Selected Pivotal Ideas*, New York 1974, 1–18. On the interplay of political theory and travelogues for the development of the concept, see Joan-Pau Rubiés, Oriental Despotism and European Orientalism. Botero to Montesquieu, in: *Journal of Early Modern History* 9 (2/2005), 109–180.

where rule is exercised by a few and all the others are slaves.[73] Whereas for the earlier elite, the lack of a hereditary nobility had been against the God-given order, the perspective changed with the rise of so-called absolutism in Europe, which limited the power of the nobility. The lack of a hereditary group like the European nobility became now the symbol for unrestricted power and a characteristic of the oriental despotism.[74] This is one aspect of the "titanic shift" described by Trautmann.[75] It concerned not only changing authority or knowledge production, but also entailed a re-selection of topics and a re-assessment of India and the Mughal Empire.

This shift, however, was prepared in the way European texts processed information gathered by travelers. Certain phrases and sentences—concerning, for instance, the aspect of the Mughal ruler's arbitrariness for the rise and fall of individuals and families, mentioned before— were now highlighted and put into the foreground in modern encyclopedias like Krünitz's *Oeconomische Encyclopädie* (1803).[76] The narrative of oriental despotism became even more dominant in texts that processed information from the travelogues to make philosophical points. In his *Grundriss der Geschichte der Menschheit* (Outline of the History of Mankind), Christoph Meiners left no doubt that the characteristics of despotism were the lack of a hereditary nobility and the sudden rise of low, often foreign adventurers. The possibility of rising in a merito-cratic system was now seen as another exercise of arbitrary power by the Mughal despot, whose subjects were little more than slaves. Meiners drew largely on Bernier for his argument, quoting him quite selectively.[77] When

---

73    "Eine despotische Regierung hat nur einige wenige Große, die übrigen sind Sclaven." Jemima Kindersley, *Briefe von der Insel Teneriffa, Brasilien, dem Vorgebirge der guten Hoffnung und Ostindien*, Leipzig 1777, 147.

74    Curtis, *Orientalism*, 40.

75    Trautmann, *Aryans*, 30.

76    "Das ist das Ende eines Herrscherstammes, dessen Gewalt so despotisch war, dass er über das Leben und Vermögen seiner Untertanen ganz unumschränkt schaltete. Sein Wille war ihr einziges Gesetz. Dieser entschied auch über alle Rechtshändel, ohne daß jemand bey Lebensstrafe etwas dagegen einwenden durfte. Auf seinen Befehl wurden die Größesten des Reiches hingerichtet, ihre Lehngüter, Ländereyen und Bedienungen entweder verändert oder weggenommen." Johann Georg Krünitz, Mogul, in: Johann Georg Krünitz (ed.), *Oeconomische Encyclopädie oder Allgemeines System der Staats-, Stadt-, Haus- und Landwirtschaft*, Bd. 92, Berlin 1803, 595–607, see 596.

77    Christoph Meiners, *Grundriß der Geschichte der Menschheit*, Lemgo 1785, 154.

Europe started imagining itself as liberal, mobile, and even equal, India became despotic, and its elements of equality were no longer acceptable or even discernible.

## Equality and Justice in the Legal System

In early modern travelogues, social equality was thus mostly imagined as obtaining only among people who imagined themselves as equal in social status and not in a broader, more encompassing sense. The second topic chosen here to analyze the imagination of equality and inequality in the perception of the Mughal Empire is the relation between equality and justice, or rather the judiciary. In our modern understanding equality as an ideal is closely connected with "equality before the law" or "equal rights for all."[78] In early modern times, there were some aspects of equality, but different courts, laws and procedures were accepted and valued for different social groups or corporations. The analysis of how the judiciary in India was perceived by early modern European travelers promises to trace and unravel seemingly self-evident notions about the relation of judiciary and equality that were otherwise not seen as noteworthy. The legal field is a topic often tackled and even admired in early modern travelogues as well as in the earlier discourse about India.

Joseph Stöcklein, editor of a collection of Jesuit letters, the *Neue Welt-Bott* (1726),[79] explained that by reading his work, "scholars of the law (*Rechtsgelehrte*)

---

78    Ulrike Davy/Johannes Grave/Marcus Hartner/Ralf Schneider/Willibald Steinmetz, Grundbegriffe, 7. In modern times, however, this proclaimed equality and even more so the way to overcome inequality were also highly disputed. On the right to equality granted to minorities, see Davy, Minority Protection under the League of Nations, *in this volume*; on caste-based inequality in India and affirmative action Bhatia, Equality under the Indian Constitution, *in this volume*.

79    The *Neue Welt-Bott* is the German equivalent to the *lettres édifiantes et curieuse*, consisting partly of material translated from the French collection, but also collecting and translating letters not included there. Renate Dürr, Der "Neue Welt-Bott" als Markt der Informationen? Wissenstransfer als Moment jesuitischer Identitätsbildung, in: *Zeitschrift für Historische Forschung* 34 (2007), 441–466; Adrien Paschoud, Apologetics, Polemics and Knowledge in Jesuit French Culture: The Collection of the Lettres édifiantes et curieuses (1702–1776), in: Markus Friedrich/Alexander Schunka (eds.), *Reporting Christian Missions in the Eighteenth Century: Communication, Culture of Knowledge and Regular Publications in a Cross Confessional Perspective*, Wiesbaden 2017, 57–72; Isabelle Vissière/Jean Louis Vissière, *Lettres édifiantes et curieuses des jésuites de l'Inde au dix-huitième siècle*, Saint-Etienne 2000.

could gain knowledge about the way how justice was done amongst the pagans without inequality."[80] Thus Stöcklein assumed equality to be crucial for administering justice.

The legal system and the relation between justice and rule were considered relevant topics in learned comparisons between Europe and Asia. Johann Heinrich Gottlob von Justi (1720-1771), a leading cameralist (i.e., a political economist) in the eighteenth century,[81] compared non-European with European governments for the betterment of policy and governance in the German-speaking territories.[82] For Justi, the Mughals' governance was closely connected with justice.[83] He found it particularly praiseworthy that the Mughal emperor administered justice himself every day.[84]

---

80   Readers learn that "auch unter denen Heyden offtmal die Gerechtigkeit ohne Ungleichheit/ohne eigenmüthige Umschweiff/ohne langweilige Verschübe und ohne unerschwingliche Gerichts-Kosten verwaltet werde." Joseph Stöcklein (ed.), *Der Neue Welt-Bott oder Allerhand so lehr-als geist-reiche Brief, Schrifften und Reis-Beschreibungen […]*, Augsburg/Graz 1726, introduction, unpaginated. Stöcklein elaborated on the qualities that made this kind of justice equal, namely that it was "straightforward without long digressions and delay, and without exorbitant costs." Stöcklein, *Welt-Bott*, introduction, unpaginated.

81   On Johann Heinrich Gottlob von Justi, see Erik S. Reinert, Johann Heinrich Gottlob von Justi—The Life and Times of an Economist Adventurer, in: J.G. Backhhaus (ed.), *The Beginnings of Political Economy: Johann Heinrich Gottlob von Justi: The European Heritage in Economics and the Social Sciences*, Berlin 2009, 33–74. Focusing on Justi's comparison with China, see Susan Richter, Reform as Verbesserung. Argumentative Patterns and the Role of Models in German Cameralism, in: Susan Richter/Thomas Maissen/Manuela Albertone (eds.), *Languages of Reform in the Eighteenth Century: When Europe Lost Its Fear of Change*, New York 2019, 153–180.

82   Jürgen Osterhammel, *Die Entzauberung Asiens. Europa und die asiatischen Reiche im 18. Jahrhundert*, Munich 1998, 75.

83   Johann Heinrich Gottlob von Justi, *Vergleichung der europäischen mit den asiatischen und andern vermeintlich barbarischen Regierungen. In drei Büchern verfaßt*, Berlin/Stettin/Leipzig 1762, 41–42.

84   "Eben diese Monarchen von Indostan pflegen fast alle Tage so lange sie gesund sind, ihren Unterthanen in eigner Persohn Recht zu sprechen." Justi, *Vergleichung*, 42. Later, in a similar vein: "Auch die Kaiser von Indostan, oder die großen Moguls sind sehr umgänglich. Sie zeigen sich dreymal des Tages öffentlich; indem sie gemeiniglich zweymal des Tages öffentlich halten; und einmal in eine große Gesellschaft aller ihrer ansehnlichen Bedienten kommen." Justi, *Vergleichung*, 85. In the paragraph where Justi described the punishments in various systems, he mentions that the Mughal examined all death sentences. Justi, *Vergleichung*, 252.

Many authors of travelogues described the Mughal Empire as an example of functioning rule.[85] Very often the general accessibility of the Mughal ruler as the highest judge was mentioned. General accessibility can be understood as a special form of equality, because all subjects had—at least in theory—equal access to the ruler's justice.

Many authors described the public trials held by the Mughal emperors themselves, often several times a week. It should be noted that the ruler's ceremonial appearance and his administration of justice converged in these events.[86] Interest in any ceremonial event was great in early modern discourse. Where the Mughal Empire is concerned, that interest can be deduced because the respective information was absorbed into other German and Dutch texts, most importantly those by the renowned Dutch collector Olfert Dapper, the geographer and director of the Dutch West India Company Joannes de Laet, and the German Polymath Erasmus Francisci.[87] The aforementioned Justi praised the Mughal emperor for administering justice himself every day.[88] The daily appearance was even mentioned in such encyclopedias as those by Zedler and Krünitz, albeit with a more negative accent in the latter.[89] This accessibility was apparently something that astonished German and European authors and readers. In Western European

---

85    Regarding the functioning system, the travelers praised the Mughal system above all because it was a safe country in which to travel. See, for example, Tavernier, *Reise-Beschreibung*, 83. This information was so interesting and maybe noteworthy that it found its way into ethnographic texts, like the famous description of Asia by the Dutch geographer and collector Olfert Dapper, Olfert Dapper, *Asia, oder: Ausführliche Beschreibung Des Reichs des Grossen Mogols Und eines grossen Theils Von Indien [...]*, Nürnberg 1681, 150. Still more praise is to be found in Justi, *Vergleichung*. Justi describes Surat, the most important port of the Mughal Empire, as matchless regarding its safety. In Europe, the rule was that the bigger the town, the higher the incidence of theft, fraud, and murder, Justi, *Vergleichung*, 253.

86    The Mughal emperor Akbar (1542–1605) for example is said to have shown himself at least twice a day and to have administered justice himself several times a week. See Johann Theodor de Bry (ed.), *Der zwölffte Theil der Orientalischen Indien [...]*, Frankfurt 1628, 4–5.

87    Erasmus Francisci, *Ost- und West-Indischer wie auch Sinesischer Lust- und Statsgarten [...]*, Nürnberg 1668, 1464; Johannes De Laet, *The Empire of the Great Mogol. A Translation of De Laet's "Description of India and Fragment of Indian History,"* Taraporevela/Bombay 1928 (reprint New Delhi 1975), 97–98.

88    See footnote 84.

89    Krünitz, Mogul, 597–598.

culture, access to kings, dukes and other ruler was a privilege granted largely to the already privileged.[90] Access to courts was a different matter: The *Reichskammergericht* in the Holy Roman Empire was accessible to everybody, and in England it could be claimed since Magna Carta.[91]

Travelers not only mentioned the Mughal emperor's accessibility *per se*. Many travelogues also deploy a particularly impressive narrative in their description of the so-called *chain of justice*. The Mughal Emperor Jahangir, who ruled from 1569 to 1627, hung a chain with golden bells from the outer door of his palace to his own rooms. Everybody who had been judged or treated wrongly could pull this chain and thus bring his case before the emperor. Jahangir wrote in his memoirs: "After my accession, the first order that I gave was for the fastening of the Chain of Justice, so that if those engaged in administration of justice should delay or practice hypocrisy in the matter of those seeking justice. The oppressed might come to this chain and shake it so that its noise might attract attention."[92] The chain with the bells symbolized the accessibility of the emperor as the 'fountain of justice'.[93] By means of this chain, the emperor underscored his claim to being the highest judge, bridging all social and religious difference in his empire. Jahangir has left an ambivalent image in the European discourse, for which Corinne Lefevre has accounted in a very plausible way. She describes Jahangir as a ruler for whom

---

90   Norbert Elias offers a very striking depiction of hierarchized access to the French king in court ceremonial. Norbert Elias, *Die höfische Gesellschaft. Untersuchung zur Soziologie des Königtums und der höfischen Aristokratie*, Frankfurt 1990, 126–129. On ceremonial practice and access to the court in Vienna, see Barbara Stollberg-Rilinger, *Maria Theresia. Die Kaiserin in ihrer Zeit. Eine Biographie*, Munich 2017, 332–349.

91   Michael Tugendhat, *Liberty Intact: Human Rights in English Law*, Oxford 2017, 66; Rita Sailer, *Untertanenprozesse vor dem Reichskammergericht: Rechtsschutz gegen die Obrigkeit in der zweiten Hälfte des 18. Jahrhunderts*, Cologne 1999.

92   Jahangir mentioned the chain in his own memoirs. Jahangir, *The Tūzuki-i-Jahāngīrī or Memoirs of Jahāngīr*, New Delhi 1994 (1909), 7. Monica Juneja explained, that this motive became something of a leitmotif in the *Badshahnama*, an illustrated chronicle of Shah Jahan's reign. Monica Juneja, On the Margins of Utopia. One More Look at Mughal Painting, in: *Medieval History Journal* 4 (2001), 203–240, see 225–226.

93   The Mughal emperor understood himself as the "fountain of justice," corresponding to rulers' virtues in the Islamic discourse. Kumar, *Essays*, 52; Mohammad Siddiqui, *Administrative History of Mughal India*, Delhi 1996, 126–127. On justice as an ideal for an Islamic ruler, see also Linda Darling, "Do Justice, Do Justice, For That is Paradise:" Middle Eastern Advice for Indian Muslim Rulers, in: *Comparative Studies of South Asia, Africa and the Middle East* 22 (1&2/2002), 3–19.

justice was both important as well as a central instrument in ruling his multicultural empire. The balance between the different religious and social groups was crucial, which is why he not only administered justice himself, but underlined the need for impartiality with regard to the rank and religion of the litigants. There is a quality of equality ascribed to his practice and his attitude towards his subjects.[94]

European authors seem to have found Jahangir's attitude and his proclaimed accessibility both remarkable and difficult to grasp. There are different strands of tradition regarding the chain of justice. For one, there is a Jesuit tradition, for example the Jesuit Fernão Guerreiro wrote: "He—that is Jahangir—displayed so great love for justice that, calling to mind what one of the ancient kings of Persia had done, he gave orders that a silver bell with a chain twenty cubits long should be suspended close to his own apartments, so that all who felt that they had grievances and were unable to obtain redress at the hands of the law or the officers of the State, might pull this chain, when the King would immediately come forth and deliver justice verbally."[95] But for the material—silver rather than gold—his description is very close to the one Jahangir wrote himself in his memoirs. It is interesting that the Jesuit knew (or assumed) that Jahangir had got this idea from a Persian tradition—an aspect that can be found in recent literature,[96] but is not mentioned in other European sources of that time. Guerreiro's text and the information it contains were not received in early modern European discourse beyond the Iberian and Catholic or Jesuit discourse.[97]

---

94  Corinne Lefèvre, Recovering a Missing Voice from Mughal India: The Imperial Discourse of Jahangir (R. 1605–1627) in his Memoirs, in: *Journal of the Economic and Social History of the Orient* 50 (2007), 452–489.

95  Fernao Guerreiro, *Jahangir and the Jesuits*, übers. v. C. H. Payne, London 1930, 13.

96  Lefèvre, Voice, 470. Moreover, the chain of justice seems to have been a travelling concept. Monica Juneja showed the transcultural character of the 'real' chain, which combined 'Hindu' and Islamic traditions. Juneja, Margins, 225–226. Rudolf Wagner discussed the drum or bell of justice in China, <https://www.soas.ac.uk/china-institute/events/26may2016-the-drum-or-bell-of-justice-and-remonstrance-the-transcultural-adaptation-of-a-political-i.html> [last accessed: September 30, 2021].

97  Guerreiro's text was translated into Spanish in 1614 and the information about the chain of justice was incorporated by Pierre du Jarric in his *Histoire des choses plus memorables advenes tant ez Indes Orientales [...]*, Bordeaux 1608–1614. Interestingly in the modern edition and translation of Jahangir's memoirs, Guerreiro is referred to in explaining the chain of justice.

The image of the chain of justice, however, was of interest to the western and northern European as well as Iberian discourse. Another line of tradition comes from the account of William Hawkins, who in the early seventeenth century was sent by the British East India Company to the Mughal Court. Hawkins mentioned the chain of justice: "He—Jahangir—is severe enough, but all helpeth not, for his poore Riats and Clowns complain of Iniustice done them, and cry for Iustice at the Kings hands. They come to a certaine place, where a long rope is fastened full of Bels, plated with gold, so that the rope beeing shaken, the Bels are heard by the King: who sendeth to know the cause, and doth his Iustice accordingly."[98] Unlike that of Guerreiro, Hawkins' description has a critical or at least ironic undertone. In the early seventeenth century, when the British East India Company was less successful than its Dutch and Portuguese competitors, their reports about the Mughal court were the most negative—perhaps its agents felt compelled to explain their failure. Hawkins' text was published in the famous compilation by Purchas, but not much referred to in continental discourse about the Mughal Empire. Only later on, since the second half of the eighteenth century, when the British colonial regime in India was established, did English sources become primary points of reference regarding India and the Mughal Empire.

Of particular relevance for European discourse was a passage from Johann Albrecht von Mandelslo's travelogue: "On the opposite side [to the place where only the chancellor and the vizier had access— AF], there hang small golden bells. They are touched and rang by such people who obtained personal access to the king and thus can bring their complaints before him."[99] This information was probably added by his editor Adam Olearius, drawing on a Dutch travelogue by Johan van Twist, which states: "Tegen over de plaets hangen Goude klockjens/de welcke geenen lupden/ die eenigh ongelijck geleden hebben/ ende worde so toegelaten den Koninck te sprecken."[100] Olearius incorporated a very close translation of the Dutch text, but he left out a meaningful half-sentence about why people should pull the chain in the first place: Whereas Twist explained—like Hawkins and Guerreiro—that this bell was for people who had experienced injustice, Olearius left this part out. In

---

98   Samuel Purchas, *Purchas his Pilgrimes: In Fiue Bookes. [...]*, London 1625, 223.

99   "Gegenüber hangen kleine güldene Glöcklein/welche von denen berühret und geläutet werden/die man zulässet in Person dem König ihre Klagen vorzubringen." Mandelslo, *Reise-Beschreibung*, 82.

100   Johan van Twist, *Generale Beschrijvinge van Indien [...]*, Amsterdam 1648, 28.

Mandelslo's—or rather Olearius's—version, the narrative about the bells is thus stripped of one its central characteristics: the demand to obtain justice for everybody! Moreover, in his text access and thus the implied imagination of equality are limited: Not everyone can ring the bell, but only those granted personal access to the king. Olearius was part of a court society. As has already been explained, access to the king at European courts has always to be seen in a ceremonial context: The more access somebody had to the ruler, the more social capital a person possessed.[101] Mandelslo's text was changed even further in the course of its translation into French by Abraham de Wicquefort. In Wicquefort's version, it is dangerous to pull the chain, thus further limiting universal access.[102] One possible interpretation is that this kind of accessibility regardless the status of a person might have been even less thinkable and writeable in a French discourse.[103] Wicquefort's translation was still known in the eighteenth century and parts of it were integrated into the *Histoire générale des voyages* by Prévost and was thus, re-translated into German, published in Schwabe's *Allgemeine Historie der Reisen*. Prevost added a footnote, which was also added into Schwabe's German translation, in which he indicated that the chain of justice had been described by Thomas Roe.[104] Besides the fact that Thomas Roe did certainly *not* write about the chain of justice, this footnote indicates that the first official English ambassador and English sources in general had become one of the most important points of reference for Ja-

---

101    See for references footnote 90.

102    "Ceux qui ont des plaintes à faire sonnen tune de ces clochettes d'or, qui sont sus-
        pendues en l'air au dessus de la balustrade; mais a moins d'avoir des preuves con-
        vaincantes en main, il ne faut pas se hazarder d'y toucher: car il y va de la vie." Adam
        Olearius/Johann Albrecht von Mandelslo, *Relation du voyage d'Adam Olearius en Moscovie,
        Tartarie et Perse [...]*, Paris 1666, 168.

103    However, the republican Dutch author Joannes de Laet, writing for a Dutch republi-
        can audience, used similar formulations: "On the opposite side of this courtyard hang
        small golden bells which are set in motion by those who complain that the king's sub-
        ordinates have failed to do them justice: [...] but such a proceeding is attended with
        great danger, lest the said subordinates' decision be adjudged well-justified." De Laet,
        *Empire*, 98.

104    Johann J. Schwabe, *Allgemeine Historie der Reisen zu Wasser und Lande oder Sammlung
        aller Reisebeschreibungen, welche bis itzo in verschiedenen Sprachen von allen Völkern her-
        ausgegeben worden*, Leipzig 1753, 83; Antoine-Francois Prévost D'Exiles, *Histoire générale
        des voyages [...]*, La Haye 1755, 163.

hangir's court.[105] This gives another indication of Trautmann's proclaimed "titanic shift" of authority in discourse about India.

The chain of justice is one of the rather few items of information or narrative that other authors like Olfert Dapper repeated in their ethnographic work.[106] Moreover, although the chain of justice is also mentioned in the article "Mogul" in *Zedlers Universal-Lexicon*, the wording did not change much compared to that of Mandelslo, quoted above.[107]

It is quite remarkable that this fairly short narrative element should have been selected for more generalizing texts. It was obviously thought to be an important and interesting story. The misunderstandings and misinterpretations, the changes during the transfer from one text to the other prove how difficult it was to translate the equality practiced at the Mughal court or to believe in equal access for everyone.

And again, the narrative of the accessible Mughal emperor and his personal administration of justice was fundamentally re-interpreted in the course of the eighteenth century: Accessibility was no longer thought to be positive if rule was despotic. Instead of praising his accessibility, the emperor's judgements were now described as cruel and arbitrary.[108]

---

105   It is also worth mentioning, that Prevost did not refer to Hawkins' report, who had actually written about the bell. The main reason—besides academic inaccuracy—might be, that Thomas Roe, as a member of the English high nobility, seemed to be a better point of reference. Social background was a highly relevant criterion in determining whether a text was included in the acknowledged inventory of knowledge.

106   Dapper, *Asia*, 271. Erasmus Francisci quoted both Mandelslo and de Laet. Francisci, *Lust- und Statsgarten*, 1438 and 1439.

107   "Wofern jedoch jemand von den Unterthanen, die Unter-Obrigkeiten zu verklagen hat, oder appelliret, so ist ihm erlaubet an einem langen Faden eine in des Königs Zimmer hängende Glocke anzuziehen, da sie so dann vor den Groß-Herren kommen, und nach Befinden ihren Beschwerungen abgeholfen wird. Ist aber ihre Sache schlimm, so wird ihnen übel gelohnet." Johann Heinrich Zedler, Mogul, in: Johann Heinrich Zedler (ed.), *Grosses vollständiges Universal-Lexicon aller Wissenschafften und Künste, welche bißhero durch menschlichen Verstand und Witz erfunden und verbesset worden [...]*, Halle/Leipzig 1739, 816–826, see 829.

108   Krünitz, Mogul, 603. Moreover, Krünitz stressed that only very few people had access to the Mughal. Krünitz, Mogul, 597–598. The cruelty of the Mughal's judgments is also highlighted by Meiners, *Grundriß*, 153, 160, and 194. The assertion that the Mughal's justice system was arbitrary because decision-making depended on the ruler's mood can already be found in early modern times. Francisci, for example, writes that Jahangir was much tougher in his judgments when he was drunk, Francisci, *Lust- und Statsgarten*, 1439–1440.

## Conclusion

This contribution began with the hypothesis that the concepts of equality and inequality are related to each other, even determining each other in their interplay. Equality is not an abstract concept, but depends on time, on its social and cultural context. This article asked how equality and inequality were conceptualized and legitimized in early modern Europe.

The Holy Roman Empire and other early modern European Christian societies were highly hierarchized. This hierarchy was not seen as a flaw, and equality was demanded only seldom and from the margins of society. Hierarchy was mostly understood as a God-given order and valued because it ensured social harmony. It was legitimized in terms of Christian doctrine and had migrated from the religious sphere into politics and society. Nevertheless, the inequality between the *Stände* or social classes was structured by an internal equality. Inclusion and equality within a class were determined by the exclusion of other social groups.

This early modern understanding of equality and inequality came into sharper focus by analyzing travelogues about the early modern Mughal Empire. This empire displayed some dimensions of equality—for instance, social mobility and the access to the ruler—that were different from the European or German context. The misunderstandings and misinterpretations in both examples showed just how much inequality within the sense of order was not only accepted, but highly valued. The possibility of social rise was disapproved of or simply ignored. The general approachability of the Mughal ruler as a judge was limited to special circumstances or described as a dangerous endeavor. There are, however, differences in the European discourse. European discourse about India is entangled and far from homogeneous. The paths of transmission between different linguistic and cultural discourses inside Europe and their relevance for the perception of Mughal India is a topic still in need of further research.

Most of the texts analyzed here were written by elite and educated travelers, that is, by the beneficiaries of social inequality. However, even the texts written by rather subaltern VOC employees appreciated social mobility no more than did those by middle- and upper-class authors. Of course, there were boundaries of what was sayable, and the interests of the intended buyers and readers had to be considered. Nevertheless, that is not enough to explain this silence. The only implicit difference and perhaps tentatively articulated claim to greater equality can be seen in the different self-labeling and thus the different categories by which society was structured. Whereas elite travelers differentiated according to social status, the VOC's employees used nation-oriented categories and thus claimed equal status to their superiors in this respect.

The difference between the Mughal society as modern studies present it and early modern descriptions increased with the processing of information from travelogues into European discourse, with every transfer from one text to another. This was a rather gradual change. However, in the late eighteenth and nineteenth centuries we can observe a much more fundamental shift in understandings of the Mughal Empire. Now the concept of oriental despotism became the hegemonic lens and sometimes completely reversed the interpretation. This suggests that when Europe started imagining itself as liberal, mobile, and even equal, the Mughal Empire became despotic in European eyes. Its elements of equality, of which there had been at least partial awareness, were no longer acceptable or credible as far as modern, dominant Europe was concerned.

## References

Alam, Muzaffar/Subrahmanyam, Sanjay (eds.), *The Mughal State, 1526–1750*, Delhi 1998.

Andersen, Jürgen/Iversen, Volquard (eds.), *Orientalische Reise–Beschreibung Jürgen Andersen aus Schleßwig [...]*, Hamburg 1696.

Arni, Caroline, Zeitlichkeit, Anachronismus und Anachronien. Gegenwart und Transformationen der Geschlechtergeschichte aus geschichtstheoretischer Perspektive, in: *L'Homme* 18 (2/2007), 53–76.

Arni, Caroline, "Moi seule," 1833: Feminist Subjectivity, Temporality, and Historical Interpretation, in: *History of the Present: A Journal of Critical History* 2 (2/2012), 107–121.

Athar Ali, Muhammad, *The Mughal Nobility under Aurangzeb*, rev. ed., New Delhi 2001.

Aubert, Guillaume, "The Blood of France:" Race and Purity of Blood in the French Atlantic World, in: *The William and Mary Quarterly* 61 (3/2004), 439–478.

Aust, Cornelia/Flüchter, Antje/Jarzebowski, Claudia (eds.), *Entrechtete Körper. Vergleichen, Normieren, Urteilen, Leben, 1450–1850*, 2022 (in print).

Bender–Junker, Birgit C., *Utopia, Policey und Christliche Securitas. Ordnungsentwürfe der Frühen Neuzeit*, Marburg 1992.

Bernier, François, *Auffgezeichnete Beobachtungen was sich in dem Reich des Grossen Mogols Begeben und zugetragen hat [...]*, Frankfurt 1673.

Bernier, François, *Sonderbare Begebnuß oder Erzehlung dessen was sich nach funffjährigen Krieg in denen Landen des Grossen Mogols begeben und zugetragen hat*, Frankfurt 1673.

Bernier, François, *Un libertin dans l'Inde moghole. Les voyages de François Bernier (1656—1669)*, Paris 2008.

Béteille, André, Homo hierarchicus, homo equalis, in: *Modern Asian Studies* 13 (4/1979), 529–548.

Bleeck, Klaus/Garber, Jörn, Nobilitas. Standes und Privilegienlegitimation in deutschen Adelstheorien des 16. und 17. Jahrhunderts, in: *Daphnis* 11 (1–2/1982), 49–114.

Blickle, Peter, Der gemeine Nutzen. Ein kommunaler Wert und seine politische Karriere, in: Münkler, Herfried/Bluhm, Harald (eds.), *Gemeinwohl und Gemeinsinn. Historische Semantiken politischer Leitbegriffe*, Berlin 2001, 85–107.

Buell, Denise Kimber, Early Christian Universalism and Modern Forms of Racism, in: Eliav-Feldon, Miriam/Isaac, Benjamin/Ziegler, Joseph (eds.), *The Origins of Racism in the West*, Cambridge/New York 2009, 109–131.

Burckhardt, Christian, *Ost-Indianische Reise-Beschreibung oder Kurtzgefaßter Abriß von Ost-Indien und dessen angränzenden Provincien*, Halle/Leipzig 1693.

Burghartz, Susanna, "Translating Seen into Scene?" Wahrnehmung und Repräsentation in der frühen Kolonialgeschichte Europas, in: Burghartz, Susanna/Christadler, Maike/Nolde, Dorothea (eds.), *Berichten—Erzählen—Beherrschen: Wahrnehmen und Repräsentation in der frühen Kolonialgeschichte Europas*, Frankfurt 2003, 161–175.

Celarent, Barbara, Caste and Race in India by G. S. Ghurye, in: *American Journal of Sociology* 116 (5/2011), 1713–1719.

Chardin, Jean, *Voyages du Chevalier Chardin, en Perse, et autres lieux de l'Orient: Enrichis de Figures en Taille-douce, qui représentent les Antiquités & les choses remarquables du Pais [...]*, Brussels 1973.

Clooney, Francis X., Yes to Caste, No to Religion? Or Perhaps the Reverse: Re-Using Roberto de Nobili's Distinctions among Morality, Caste, and Religion, in: Arun, Chockalingam Joe (ed.), *Interculturation of Religion: Critical Perspectives on Robert de Nobili's Mission in India*, Bangalore 2007, 158–174.

Curtis, Michael, *Orientalism and Islam. European Thinkers on Oriental Despotism in the Middle East and India*, Cambridge 2009.

Dale, Stephen, India under Mughal Rule, in: Morgan, David/Reid, Anthony (eds.), *The New Cambridge History of Islam, Bd. 3: The Eastern Islamic World, Eleventh to Eighteenth Centuries*, Cambridge 2010, 266–314.

Dann, Otto, Gleichheit, in: Brunner, Otto/Conze, Werner/Koselleck, Reinhart (eds.), *Geschichtliche Grundbegriffe. Historisches Lexikon zur politisch-sozialen Sprache in Deutschland (Studienausgabe), Bd. 2, E-G*, Stuttgart 2004, 997–1046.

Dapper, Olfert, *Asia, oder: Ausführliche Beschreibung Des Reichs des Grossen Mogols Und eines grossen Theils Von Indien [...]*, Nürnberg 1681.

Darling, Linda, "Do Justice, Do Justice, For That is Paradise:" Middle Eastern Advice for Indian Muslim Rulers, in: *Comparative Studies of South Asia, Africa and the Middle East*, 22 (1&2/2002), 3–19.

Dartmann, Christoph/Flüchter, Antje/Oesterle, Jenny Rahel, Eliten im transkulturellen Monarchienvergleich, in: Drews, Wolfram/Flüchter, Antje (eds.), *Monarchische Herrschaftsformen der Vormoderne in transkultureller Perspektive*, Berlin 2015, 33–173.

Davy, Ulrike/Grave, Johannes/Hartner, Marcus/Schneider, Ralf/Steinmetz, Willibald, Grundbegriffe für eine Theorie des Vergleichens. Ein Zwischenbericht, in: *Praktiken des Vergleichens. Working Paper 3 des SFB 1288*, Bielefeld 2019, <https://pub.uni-bielefeld.de/record/2939563> [last accessed: October 30, 2021].

De Bry, Johann Theodor (ed.), *Der zwölffte Theil der Orientalischen Indien [...]*, Frankfurt 1628.

De Laet, Johannes, *The Empire of the Great Mogol. A Translation of De Laet's "Description of India and Fragment of Indian History"* Taraporevela/Bombay 1928 (reprint New Delhi 1975).

Dirks, Nicholas D., *Castes of Mind. Colonialism and the Making of Modern India*, Princeton 2001.

Dumont, Louis, *Homo hierarchicus. Le système des castes et ses implications*, Paris 1979.

Dürr, Renate, Der "Neue Welt-Bott" als Markt der Informationen? Wissenstransfer als Moment jesuitischer Identitätsbildung, in: *Zeitschrift für Historische Forschung* 34 (2007), 441–466.

Eibach, Joachim, Versprochene Gleichheit - verhandelte Ungleichheit. Zum sozialen Aspekt in der Strafjustiz der Frühen Neuzeit, in: *Geschichte und Gesellschaft* 35 (4/2009), 488–533.

Elias, Norbert, *Die höfische Gesellschaft. Untersuchung zur Soziologie des Königtums und der höfischen Aristokratie*, Frankfurt 1990.

Engels, Friedrich, Der deutsche Bauernkrieg [1850], in: *Karl Marx—Friedrich Engels - Werke, Bd. 7*, Berlin 1960, 327–413.

Epple, Angelika, *Doing Comparisons*. Ein praxeologischer Zugang zur Geschichte der Globalisierung/en, in: Epple, Angelika/Erhart, Walter (eds.), *Die Welt beobachten. Praktiken des Vergleichens*, Frankfurt/New York 2015, 161–199.

Epple, Angelika/Erhart, Walter, Practices of Comparing. A New Research Agenda Between Typological and Historical Approaches, in: Epple, Angelika/Erhart, Walter/Grave, Johannes (eds.), *Practices of Comparing. Towards a New Understanding of a Fundamental Human Practice*, Bielefeld 2020, 11–38.

Epple, Angelika/Erhart, Walter/Grave, Johannes (eds.), *Practices of Comparing. Towards a New Understanding of a Fundamental Human Practice*, Bielefeld 2020.

Epple, Angelika/Flüchter, Antje/Müller, Thomas, Praktiken des Vergleichens: Praxistheoretische Fundierung und heuristische Typologien. Ein Bericht von unterwegs, in: *Praktiken des Vergleichens. Working Paper 6 des SFB 1288*, Bielefeld 2020.

Eudell, Demetrius Lynn, *The Political Languages of Emancipation in the British Caribbean and the US South*, Chapel Hill 2002.

Eudell, Demetrius Lynn, "Come on Kid, Let's Go Get the Thing:" The Sociogenic Principle and the Being of Being Black/Human, in: Wynter, Sylvia (ed.), *On Being Human as Praxis*, Durham 2015, 226–248.

Febvre, Lucien, *Das Problem des Unglaubens im 16. Jahrhundert. Die Religion des Rabelais*, Stuttgart 2002.

Flüchter, Antje, Handling Diversity in Early Modern India? Perception and Evaluation in German Discourse, in: *The Medieval History Journal. Special Issue: Handling Diversity. Medieval Europe and India in Comparison (13th–18th Century)* 16 (2/2013), 297–334.

Flüchter, Antje, Diplomatic Ceremonial and Greeting Practice at the Mughal Court, in: Drews, Wolfram/Scholl, Christian (eds.), *Transkulturelle Verflechtungsprozesse in der Vormoderne*, Berlin/Boston 2016, 89–120.

Flüchter, Antje, Johann Albrecht von Mandelslo, in: Thomas, David/Chesworth, John (eds.), *Christian-Muslim Relations. A Bibliographical History*, Amsterdam 2017, 869–885.

Flüchter, Antje, *Die Vielfalt der Bilder und die eine Wahrheit: Die Staatlichkeit Indiens in der deutschsprachigen Wahrnehmung (1500–1700)*, Affalterbach 2020.

Francisci, Erasmus, *Ost- und West-Indischer wie auch Sinesischer Lust- und Stats-garten [...]*, Nürnberg 1668.

Fuller, Christopher J., History, Anthropology, Colonialism, and the Study of India, in: *History and Theory* 55 (3/2016), 452–464.

Gelder, Roelof van, *Das ostindische Abenteuer. Deutsche in Diensten der Vereinigten Ostindischen Kompanie der Niederlande (VOC). 1600–1800*, Hamburg 2004.

Glancy, Jennifer A., *Slavery as moral problem: In the early church and today*, Minneapolis 2011.

Greschat, Martin, Luthers Haltung im Bauernkrieg, in: *Archiv für Reformationsgeschichte-Archive for Reformation History* 56 (1965), 31–47.

Guerreiro, Fernao, *Jahangir and the Jesuits*, übers. v. C.H. Payne, London 1930.

Hagemann, Gerhard, *De omnigena hominis nobilitate libri IV: queis pretractantur, quae ad usum et utilitatem de nobilitate hominis naturali*, Hildesheim 1693.

Harbsmeier, Michael, Reisebeschreibungen als mentalitätsgeschichtliche Quellen. Überlegungen zu einer historisch-anthropologischen Untersuchung frühneuzeitlicher deutscher Reisebeschreibungen, in: Maczak, Antoni/Teuteberg, Hans J. (eds.), *Reiseberichte als Quellen europäischer Kulturgeschichte. Aufgaben und Möglichkeiten der historischen Reiseforschung*, Wolfenbüttel 1982, 1–31.

Hirschi, Caspar, *The origins of nationalism: an alternative history from ancient Rome to early modern Germany*, Cambridge 2011.

Jahangir, *The Tūzuki-i-Jahāngīrī or Memoirs of Jahāngīr*, New Delhi 1994 (1909).

Jarric, Pater Piérre du, *Histoire des choses plus memorables advenes tant ez Indes Orientales [...]*, Bordeaux 1608–1614.

Juneja, Monica, On the Margins of Utopia. One More Look at Mughal Painting, in: *Medieval History Journal* 4 (2001), 203–240.

Justi, Johann Heinrich Gottlob von, *Vergleichung der europäischen mit den asiatischen und andern vermeintlich barbarischen Regierungen. In drei Büchern verfaßt*, Berlin/Stettin/Leipzig 1762.

Kehrer, Günter, Über die Religionen und die Ungleichheit unter den Menschen, in: Kehrer, Günter (ed.), *"Vor Gott sind alle gleich." Soziale Gleichheit, soziale Ungleichheit und die Religionen*, Düsseldorf 1983, 9–25.

Kindersley, Jemima, *Briefe von der Insel Teneriffa, Brasilien, dem Vorgebirge der guten Hoffnung und Ostindien*, Leipzig 1777.

Koch, Elisabeth, Die Frau im Recht der Frühen Neuzeit: Juristische Lehren und Begründungen, in: Gerhard, Ute (ed.), *Frauen in der Geschichte des Rechts*, Munich 1997, 73–93.

Kogge, Werner/Wilhelmi, Lisa, Despot und (orientalische) Despotie–Brüche im Konzept von Aristoteles bis Montesquieu, in: *Saeculum* 69 (2/2019), 305–342.

Koller, Peter, Soziale Gleichheit und Gerechtigkeit, in: Müller, Hans-Peter/ Wegener, Bernd (eds.), *Soziale Ungleichheit und soziale Gerechtigkeit*, Opladen 1995, 53–80.

Krünitz, Johann Georg, Mogul, in: Krünitz, Johann Georg (ed.), *Oeconomische Encyclopädie oder Allgemeines System der Staats-, Stadt-, Haus- und Landwirtschaft*, Bd. 92, Berlin 1803, 595–607.

Kumar, Raj, *Essays on Legal Systems in India*, New Delhi 2003.

Lefèvre, Corinne, Recovering a Missing Voice from Mughal India: The Imperial Discourse of Jahangir (R. 1605–1627) in his Memoirs, in: *Journal of the Economic and Social History of the Orient* 50 (2007), 452–489.

Lucassen, Jan, A Multinational and its Labor Force: The Dutch East India Company, 1595–1795, in: *International Labor and Working-Class History* 66 (66/2004), 12–39.

Mandelslo, Johann Albrecht von, *Des Hoch-Edelgebohrnen Johann Albrechts von Mandelslo Morgenländische Reise-Beschreibung*, Hamburg 1696.

Meiners, Christoph, *Grundriß der Geschichte der Menschheit*, Lemgo 1785.

Münch, Paul, Grundwerte der frühneuzeitlichen Ständegesellschaft? Aufriß einer vernachlässigten Thematik, in: Schulze, Winfried (ed.), *Ständische Gesellschaft und soziale Mobilität*, Munich 1988, 53–72.

Münkler, Herfried/Grünberger, Hans, Nationale Identität im Diskurs der Deutschen Humanisten, in: Berding, Helmut (ed.), *Nationales Bewußtsein und kollektive Identität*, Frankfurt 1996, 211–247.

Nef, Hans, *Gleichheit und Gerechtigkeit*, Zurich 1941.

Oldendorp, Johannes, *Ein Ratmannen-Spiegel (1530) Faksimile mit einem Vorwort von Albert Freybe* ed. by Dr. der Bärensprungschen Hofbuchdr., Stettin 1893.

Olearius, Adam/Mandelslo, Johann Albrecht von, *Relation du voyage d'Adam Olearius en Moscovie, Tartarie et Perse [...]*, Paris 1666.

Osterhammel, Jürgen, *Die Entzauberung Asiens. Europa und die asiatischen Reiche im 18. Jahrhundert*, Munich 1998.

Paschoud, Adrien, Apologetics, Polemics and Knowledge in Jesuit French Culture: The Collection of the Lettres édifiantes et curieuses (1702–1776), in: Friedrich, Markus/Schunka, Alexander (eds.), *Reporting Christian Missions in the Eighteenth Century: Communication, Culture of Knowledge and Regular Publications in a Cross Confessional Perspective*, Wiesbaden 2017, 57–72.

Piketty, Thomas, *Capital and Ideology*, London 2020.

Prévost D'exiles, Antoine-Francois, *Histoire générale des voyages [...]*, La Haye 1755.

Purchas, Samuel, *Purchas his Pilgrimes: In Fiue Bookes. [...]*, London 1625.

Reinert, Erik S., Johann Heinrich Gottlob von Justi - The Life and Times of an Economist Adventurer, in: Backhhaus, J.G. (ed.), *The Beginnings of Political Economy: Johann Heinrich Gottlob von Justi: The European Heritage in Economics and the Social Sciences*, Berlin 2009, 33–74.

Reinhard, Wolfgang, *Geschichte der Staatsgewalt. Eine vergleichende Verfassungsgeschichte Europas von den Anfängen bis zur Gegenwart*, Munich 2002.

Reinhard, Wolfgang, *Probleme deutscher Geschichte 1495–1806: Reichsreform und Reformation. Deutsche Geschichte 1495–1555*, Stuttgart 2004.

Richter, Hedwig, *Demokratie: Eine deutsche Affäre*, Munich 2020.

Richter, Melvin, Despotism, in: Wiener, Philip P. (ed.), *Dictionary of the History of Ideas. Studies of Selected Pivotal Ideas*, New York 1974, 1–18.

Richter, Susan, Reform as Verbesserung. Argumentative Patterns and the Role of Models in German Cameralism, in: Richter, Susan/Maissen, Thomas/Albertone, Manuela (eds.), *Languages of Reform in the Eighteenth Century: When Europe Lost Its Fear of Change*, New York 2019, 153–180.

Rogerius, Abraham, *Offne Thür zu dem verborgenen Heydenthum [...]*, Nürnberg 1663.

Rosanvallon, Pierre, *Die Gesellschaft der Gleichen*, Berlin 2017.

Rubiés, Joan-Pau, Oriental Despotism and European Orientalism. Botero to Montesquieu, in: *Journal of Early Modern History 9* (2/2005), 109–180.

Sailer, Rita, *Untertanenprozesse vor dem Reichskammergericht: Rechtsschutz gegen die Obrigkeit in der zweiten Hälfte des 18. Jahrhunderts*, Cologne 1999.

Schulze, Winfried, Die ständische Gesellschaft des 16./17. Jahrhunderts als Problem von Statik und Dynamik, in: Schulze, Winfried/Gabel, Helmut (eds.), *Ständische Gesellschaft und soziale Mobilität*, Munich 1988, 1–17.

Schwabe, Johann J., *Allgemeine Historie der Reisen zu Wasser und Lande oder Sammlung aller Reisebeschreibungen, welche bis itzo in verschiedenen Sprachen von allen Völkern herausgegeben worden*, Leipzig 1753.

Scott, Joan W., Gender. A Useful Category of Historical Analysis, in: *American Historical Review 91* (5/1986), 1053–1075.

Siddiqui, Mohammad, *Administrative History of Mughal India*, Delhi 1996.

Siebenhüner, Kim, *Die Spur der Juwelen. Materielle Kultur und transnationale Verbindungen zwischen Indien und Europa in der Frühen Neuzeit*, Cologne 2017.

Steinmetz, Willibald, *Europa im 19. Jahrhundert*, Frankfurt 2019.

Stöcklein, Joseph (ed.), *Der Neue Welt-Bott oder Allerhand so lehr- als geist-reiche Brief, Schrifften und Reis-Beschreibungen [...]*, Augsburg/Graz 1726.

Stollberg-Rilinger, Barbara, *Europa im Jahrhundert der Aufklärung*, Stuttgart 2000.

Stollberg-Rilinger, Barbara, *Maria Theresia. Die Kaiserin in ihrer Zeit. Eine Biographie*, Munich 2017.

Subrahmanyam, Sanjay, *Europe's India. Words, People, Empires, 1500–1800*, Cambridge, MA 2017.

Tavernier, Jean Baptiste, *Vierzig-Jährige Reise-Beschreibung. [...]*, Nürnberg 1681.

Thaidigsmann, Edgar, Jedem das Seine. Zum Thema "Gesetz und Evangelium," in: *Neue Zeitschrift für Systematische Theologie und Religionsphilosophie* 35 (3/1993), 237–258.

Trautmann, Thomas R., *Aryans and British India*, New Delhi 2004.

Tugendhat, Michael, *Liberty Intact: Human Rights in English Law*, Oxford 2017.

Twist, Johan van, *Generale Beschrijvinge van Indien [...]*, Amsterdam 1648.

Van Dijk, Conrad, Giving Each His Due: Langland, Gower, and the Question of Equity, in: *The Journal of English and Germanic Philology* 108 (3/2009), 310–335.

Vissière, Isabelle/Vissière, Jean Louis, *Lettres édifiantes et curieuses des jésuites de l'Inde au dix-huitième siècle*, Saint-Etienne 2000.

Wagner, Rudolf, The Drum or Bell of Justice and Remonstrance. The Transcultural Adaptation of a Political Installation across Eurasia, London 2016, https://www.soas.ac.uk/china-institute/events/26may2016-the-drum-or-bell-of-justice-and-remonstrance-the-transcultural-adaptation-of-a-political-i.html [last accessed: September 30, 2021].

Weller, Thomas, Soziale Ungleichheit und ständische Gesellschaft. Stand und Perspektiven der Forschung, in: *Zeitsprünge. Forschungen zur Frühen Neuzeit* 15 (1/2011), 3–23.

Zedler, Johann Heinrich, Mogul, in: Zedler, Johann Heinrich (ed.), *Grosses vollständiges Universal-Lexicon aller Wissenschafften und Künste, welche bißhero durch menschlichen Verstand und Witz erfunden und verbesset worden [...]*, Halle/Leipzig 1739, 816–826.

# Envisioning Equality in the French Revolution

Lynn Hunt

**Abstract**

*Without denying the importance of a conceptual history of equality, the main focus here is the emotional and aspirational aspects of equality that developed during the French Revolution. These aspects can be traced in visual practices, especially those associated with popular prints. Prints exploded in number and offered contemporaries new ways of seeing and thereby taking distance from their society and customary social relations. The space created by visualization provided an impetus to equality without which the ideal might have remained a dead letter. Envisioning social relationships is more than a simple mirroring of social life.*

## Equality as Concept and Social Practice

Equality is not only an idea, that is, a mental construct used to organize the social and political world; it is also an aspiration, that is, something with strong emotions attached to it [Figure 1]. The ideas and emotions surrounding equality coalesced explosively during the French Revolution, in part because the eighteenth-century Enlightenment had prepared the way with dramatic and controversial discussions of equality as a concept. Without denying the importance of a conceptual history of equality, the main focus here will be on its emotional and aspirational aspects as they developed during the French Revolution. These aspects will be traced in practices that are at once the most evident and the most obscure: popular prints. Prints are the most direct forms of witness in the sense that they often depicted naturalistically the inequality of social relations and in so doing brought into question that inequality. At the same time, prints are obscure in the sense that little is known about their creators or their intentions. Prints did not produce equality all on their own, but they did offer contemporaries a way of seeing and thereby taking distance from their society and customary social relations. The space created by visualization provided an impetus to equality without which the ideal might have remained a dead letter.

Figure 1. *The Aspiration for Equality, 1789. Anonymous hand-colored etching probably from 1789, 28.5 x 25 cm, titled "J' savois ben qu' jaurions not tour: vive le roi, vive la nation" (I knew we would have our turn: long live the king, long live the nation).*

Source: Bibliothèque Nationale de France (hereafter BNF).

Although it may seem that questions of equality and inequality have always bedeviled humans, a pair of Google n-grams (however crude or schematic) shows that discussion of equality is not a constant of human behavior.

*Figure 2. Google n-gram of French term égalité from 1700 to 2019*

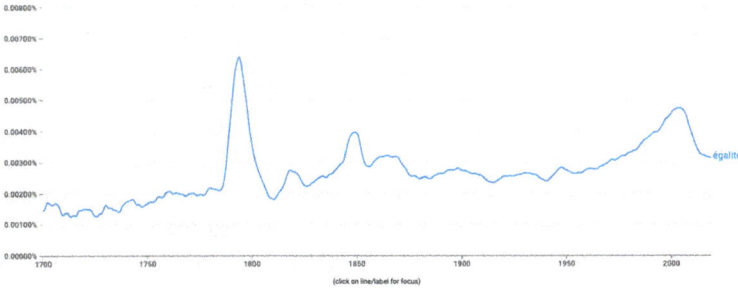

Source: Google n-gram viewer at https://books.google.com/ngrams (accessed October 13, 2020).

*Figure 3. Google n-gram of "equality" in English, 1700–2019*

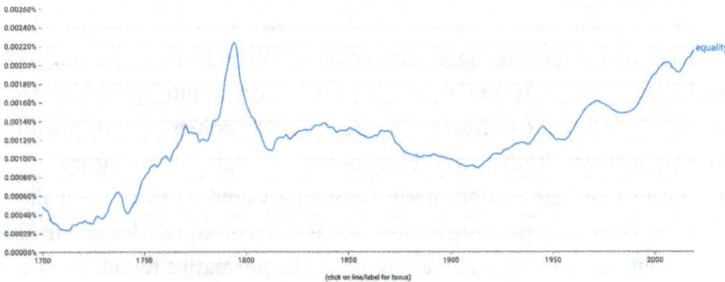

Source: Google n-gram viewer at https://books.google.com/ngrams (accessed October 13, 2020).

Leaving aside the difference in scale, since references in French are much more common than in English, it is apparent that in both languages the period of the French Revolution marks a distinct departure. The database for French literature FRANTEXT gives a similar result.

*Figure 4. FRANTEXT: Relative frequency of égalité, 1700–1850, by decades*

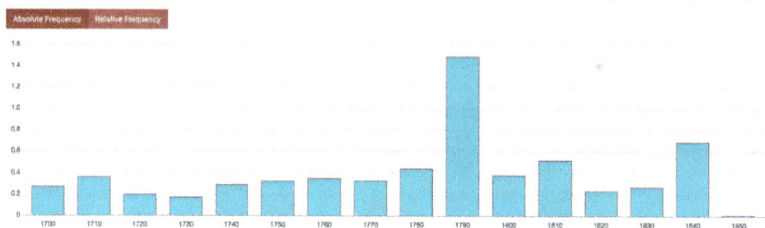

Source: The graph was derived by doing a time series search for the relative frequency of *égalité*, 1700–1850, in ten-year intervals at https://artfl-project.uchicago.edu/content/artfl-frantext (accessed October 13, 2020).

Because the upturn that occurs in the 1790s is so sharp and sudden, it follows that the political crisis in France galvanized thinking about equality and not just in France. The steady diffusion of Enlightenment ideas over the decades cannot explain this sudden surge in concern with equality. Without the French Revolution equality would not have gained this traction in either French or English.

Yet the sudden increase might not have taken place if the conceptual ground had not been prepared, so the conceptualization of equality does matter. The idea of equality has been thoroughly excavated in the work of intellectual historians, especially Siep Stuurman. He rightly avoids focusing too narrowly on the late eighteenth century, for he begins with the ancient Greeks and goes up to the present and considers a mind-bending array of the world's different cultures, religions, and philosophies. Yet, even with this broadest of views, Stuurman still argues that the eighteenth-century Enlightenment invented the modern notion of equality (and its twin, inequality). It did so, he asserts, by positing individuals as free and equal, theorizing liberty and equality as natural, and making them the normative foundations of the social and political order.[1]

How did these ideas penetrate society? Stuurman emphasizes that equality is not the default position. "Common humanity and equality are not

---

1    Siep Stuurman, *The Invention of Humanity: Equality and Cultural Difference in World History*, Cambridge, MA 2017, 258–259, 557. See also Devin Vartija, *The Colour of Equality: Race and Common Humanity in Enlightenment Thought*, Philadelphia 2021.

primeval facts," he insists: "We should rather conceive of them as inventions of novel and potentially disruptive ways of looking at human relationships."[2] Those "ways of looking" can be approached in more than one manner. Stuurman assumes that formal texts can disrupt ways of looking at human relationships, and that is surely true, though it is far from the whole story. Hierarchy long seemed the natural condition of the political and social order. Figure 1, for example, references that expectation while overturning it; the humorous charge of the image comes from its visual reversal of traditional expectations. The peasant is now on top, riding on the back of the aristocracy. Ways of looking are not just conceptual, that is, in the mind's metaphorical eye. Ways of looking are in the first instance visual.

In previous work on the equality of human rights, I tried to broaden the textual basis by drawing attention to less highbrow writings, such as epistolary novels, that enabled people to imagine the equality of others, especially those of lower social standing. Novels, autobiographies of slaves, and eyewitness accounts of brutal executions worked through narrative strategies that provoked strong emotions, and through emotions incited empathy and identification. This is not to say that more formal political or philosophical tracts did not trigger emotional responses, but the aim of such tracts was not to stimulate empathy and identification with others. One very striking example of the intensity of reaction that can be inspired by formal texts is the dramatic spread of rights language in response to the French Declaration of the Rights of Man and Citizen of August 1789. As soon as a very abstract formulation of "the rights of man" passed into law, all kind of rights came up for discussion even though they had not been explicitly mentioned in the Declaration: the rights of religious minorities, actors and executioners, men without property, free blacks and slaves, and women. All of these groups, except women, gained political rights during the French Revolution. They would not have done so without a declaration of rights that drew their attention to the possibilities of rights and that left open the question of just who qualified as a man and citizen. There would have been no declaration if the Enlightenment had not cleared the path with pointed discussions of natural rights and the rights of man.[3]

When reconstructing this history of human rights, I concentrated for the most part on the ways people of the middle and upper classes learned to em-

---

2     Stuurman, *Invention of Humanity*, 1.

3     Lynn Hunt, *Inventing Human Rights*: A History, New York 2007.

pathize with those of lower social station but largely left to the side the converse: the aspirations of those habitually excluded from equality. Getting at the hopes and desires of the lower orders is very difficult since peasants, servants, day workers, laundresses and the like rarely committed their thoughts to paper. Evidence abounds, nonetheless, for the egalitarianism of the militants of the popular classes in Paris between 1792 and 1794. The experience of political participation in an atmosphere of growing crisis sharpened the militants' perceptions of social difference and gave a largely negative cast to their identity. As Haim Burstin explains, the "sans-culotte" was neither an aristocrat nor an unemployed vagrant; he was a worker with family, neighborhood, and work connections. He did not live off his investments but rather depended on his daily labor for his existence. Looking at their society in the heat of the political moment, popular militants developed very clear dislikes for aristocrats, the rich, and those who profited from the needs of those who worked with their hands. It is the way they learned to look that is at issue here.[4]

One way to approach the question of looking is to consider it on the most abstract level, as William Sewell does in his fascinating attempt to rehabilitate Marxist thinking about commodity capitalism.[5] Sewell argues that eighteenth-century commercial capitalism fostered an abstract understanding of social relations and in the process made civic equality thinkable. It did this through consumption, or what he calls the abstracting logic of capitalism. Sewell focuses on the public promenade in Paris because in that space new forms of fashionable consumption enabled participants to "abstract their public personas from their given social stations." People did not walk in the streets of Paris, needless to say (because of the mud), but they did promenade, either in carriages or on foot, in sites such as the Tuileries garden or the Palais Royal. As a consequence, Sewell argues, "Parisians became accustomed to sharing public space on an anonymous basis with persons of diverse social status."[6] This anonymity and social diversity helped foster abstract ideals of equality.

---

4    The obvious starting point is Albert Soboul, *Les Sans-culottes parisiens en l'an II: Mouvement populaire et gouvernement révolutionnaire, 2 Juin 1793-9 Thermidor An II*, Paris 1958. See also Haim Burstin, *L'invention du sans-culotte: regards sur Paris révolutionnaire*, Paris 2005, 61.

5    William H. Sewell, Jr., Connecting Capitalism to the French Revolution: The Parisian Promenade and the Origins of Civic Equality in Eighteenth-Century France, in: *Critical Historical Studies* 1 (1/2014), 5–46.

6    Sewell, Jr., Connecting Capitalism to the French Revolution, 17 and 40.

It was not enough, however, to share public space on an anonymous basis. Looking and being looked at had to take new forms that were prompted by the commodification of fashion. These new ways of looking generated the distance required to give the notion of society a new salience. Rather than being a term that referred to good company, as it had in the past, society came to mean the organized substructure of social relations. In that sense, we might say that without the commodification of fashion, there would have been no Karl Marx. Conflictual social relations only gained theoretical relevance when society emerged as an object of perception, and society became visible in part through the commentary, visual and textual, on fashion.

The new ways of looking were first uncovered by Daniel Roche in his pioneering work on clothing in eighteenth-century Paris. He showed how the consumption of lighter and more colorful fabrics, especially printed cottons, and the commercialization of fashion changed what he called "the perception of the social scene." Buying second-hand clothing, servants could imitate their masters. Individual choices could take precedence over the staging of traditional social status. Appearances no longer coincided with social rank. Fashion became, in Roche's words, "the frivolous schoolteacher of liberty and equality."[7]

Even before Roche pointed to the political significance of fashion in eighteenth-century France, a British psychologist, J.C. Flügel, had drawn attention to the "Great Masculine Renunciation," his term for "the sudden reduction of male sartorial decorativeness which took place at the end of the eighteenth century." The psychologist tended to insert intention into his account: "men gave up their right to all the brighter, gayer, more elaborate, and more varied forms of ornamentation." Flügel saw this as "one of the most remarkable events in the whole history of dress": "Man abandoned his claim to be considered beautiful. He henceforth aimed at being only useful."[8] Concretely, this meant that upper class men in Europe began to abandon their knee breeches in favor of trousers, previously worn only by working men. They also progressively threw off their wigs in favor of powdered then natural hair and left makeup to women.

Flügel attributed the transformation to the French Revolution. The new social order, based on the common humanity "of all men," required a greater

7    Daniel Roche, *La culture des apparences: une histoire du vêtement (XVIIe–XVIIIe siècle)*, Paris 1989, 480 and 492.
8    J.C. Flügel, *The Psychology of Clothes*, London 1950 [1930], 110–111.

uniformity and simplification of dress that had to take place by leveling down, not up. The "democratisation in clothes" was not completed all at once and was still proceeding, in Flügel's view. As far as he was concerned, however, the gender consequences were obvious: "in sartorial matters, man has a far sterner and more rigid conscience than has modern woman [...]; modern man's clothing abounds in features which symbolise his devotion to the principles of duty, of renunciation, and of self-control." While we may question Flügel's judgment that women's narcissism and sexual competition kept them from adopting the same changes in costume, he did predict correctly that as women played a more active role in social life, they "are themselves tending to adopt a more uniform and less decorative costume, at any rate for the working hours of life."[9]

Film and literary scholars have used Flügel's analysis of the history of dress to buttress a theory of the "male gaze," which is the idea that since the eighteenth century, and especially in cinema and modern painting, men do the looking and women are simply looked at.[10] In what follows, I will present evidence that men were still intently observed, by both men and women, even as their dress codes changed. Nevertheless, the virtue of these psychoanalytically-informed analyses of the gaze (Flügel was a leading British psychoanalyst) is that they draw attention to the complexities of looking, albeit from a point of view that emphasizes Freudian categories (e.g., fear of castration, narcissism) rather than the cultural and social ones that I will highlight. Looking is not a straightforward process.

## Conceptualizing Society

People on promenades, buyers of second-hand clothing, or men choosing trousers were not looking at society. It is impossible to visualize society as a whole since society is an imaginary construct. Society is not the sum of social relationships. Society is the set of rules that shapes social relationships

---

9    Flügel, *The Psychology of Clothes*, 113–117.

10    Kaja Silverman argues that we should understand "the Great Masculine Renunciation in terms of the female subject it constructs—a female subject who is the mirror reflection not only of the male subject's castration, but of his specularity, exhibitionism, and narcissism." Kaja Silvermann, *The Acoustic Mirror: The Female Voice in Psychoanalysis and Cinema*, Bloomington 1988, 27.

and configures the ways that people look at each other and at themselves. Society in this sense has always existed, but its existence only becomes an issue at certain moments in history. In both English and French, the use of the terms "society" and "social" took off after the mid-1700s, though here, too, the frequency is greater in French than in English.

*Figure 5. Google n-gram of "society" and "social" in English, 1700–1850*

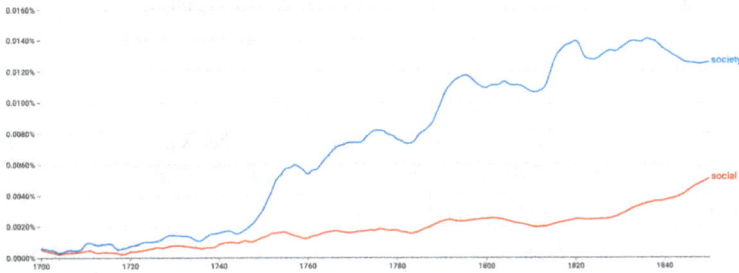

Source: Google n-gram viewer at https://books.google.com/ngrams (accessed October 13, 2020).

*Figure 6. Google n-gram of "société" and "social" in French, 1700–1850*

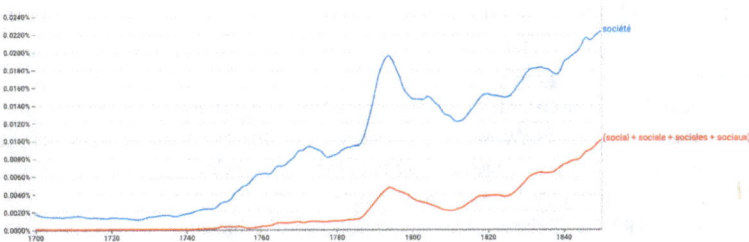

Source: Google n-gram viewer at https://books.google.com/ngrams (accessed October 13, 2020).

Enlightenment writers such as Jean-Jacques Rousseau and Denis Diderot put society on the intellectual agenda in the second half of the 1700s, and then the French Revolution of 1789 convinced leading intellectuals that society required a new kind of scientific study called "social science" ("sociology" as a term first appeared in the 1840s).[11] The advent of social science in France in the 1790s signaled a new, more systematic, interest in society and social relations.

The increasing use of the terms "society," "social," and "social science" signals a new attention to the social body, and this awareness both stimulates and is reinforced by the yearning for equality. Equality becomes thinkable when people recognize that they are part of a social body whose rules are not fixed. "Social science" is particularly significant as a term and a discipline because it did not exist before the French Revolution; society might be thought to exist ever since humans lived in groups, but social science clearly did not. Early appearances of the term "social science" in French can be traced to the writings between 1792 and 1794 of the mathematician and political visionary Nicolas de Caritat, Marquis de Condorcet. It had been used earlier (but only once) in 1789 in Abbé Sieyès's sensational anti-noble pamphlet *What is the Third Estate?* and also figured here and there in other writings of the period 1789–1794, often linked to the moral and political sciences.[12]

The idea of a social science took root after 1795 among the followers of Condorcet (he had committed suicide in 1794 when faced with the prospect of the guillotine) who were members or associates of the newly established National Institute. The Institute included a section for the moral and political sciences, one of whose subsections was titled "social science and legislation." The term "social science" and invocations of Condorcet occur repeatedly, for example, in the works of the Institute associate Antoine Destutt de Tracy in the late 1790s and early 1800s. Born a nobleman like Condorcet, Destutt de Tracy took a leading role in setting the foundation for social science in France

---

11    According to the Oxford English Dictionary, "sociology" appeared for the first time in English 1842. <https://www.oed.com/view/Entry/183792?redirectedFrom=sociology#eid >. Auguste Comte introduced the term in French as a neologism in 1839 in his *Cours de philosophie positive*, vol. 4, Paris: Bachelier, 1839, 252.

12    ARTFL-FRANTEXT <https://artfl-project.uchicago.edu/content/artfl-frantext> gives the first appearance in French as 1789. On early appearances of the term in the French Revolution and crucial developments after 1795, see Robert Wokler, From the Moral and Political Sciences to the Sciences of Society by Way of the French Revolution, in: *Jahrbuch für Recht und Ethik / Annual Review of Law and Ethics*, Vol. 8, Themenschwerpunkt: Die Entstehung und Entwicklung der Moralwissenschaften im 17. und 18. Jahrhundert / The Origin and Development of the Moral Sciences in the Seventeenth and Eighteenth Century (2000), 33–45. The term "social science" in English only took hold in the 1840s when John Stuart Mill took up the writings of Auguste Comte.

in the 1790s. He coined the term "ideology," by which he meant the science of ideas. In 1798 Destutt de Tracy argued that social science required "recognized and systematized principles" in order to become truly scientific, and that with them "we would be able to explain and even predict the good fortune and misfortune of diverse societies."[13] From the beginning, the scientific study of the social was tied to comparisons between societies. Such comparisons only became significant when people began to believe that the principles organizing society could be altered by conscious decision.

For society to become an object of systematic study in a social science, it had to be susceptible to conceptualization, and visualization was critical to that conceptualization. There cannot be a science of the social until the social gains visibility, literally in terms of apprehending the density, complexity, and general significance of social relations. Meaning has to be constructed in social terms; the "sociality" of life has to become visible.[14] Society was on view in fashion and promenades, but social relations came into sharpest focus in the prints produced during the French Revolution. By their nature as visual depictions, the various forms of printmaking called on viewers to think about what they were seeing and thus to see differently, that is, with attention.

## Prints and the Crisis of Meaning

Two general aspects of the prints produced during the decade 1789–1799 merit consideration: the impact of the explosion in the sheer number of visual productions, and the ways prints generated a kind of second order of representation that facilitates abstraction, that is, the derivation of general principles from concrete portrayals. That abstraction could serve the goal of civic equality (all individuals are alike and should enjoy equal rights) but in the form of

---

13    The references to Condorcet and social science by Destutt de Tracy were derived from a search of ARTFL-FRANTEXT. For the definition of social science see Antoine Destutt de Tracy, Mémoire sur la faculté de penser, Extrait du procès-verbal de la classe des sciences morales et politiques de L'Institut national, du 22 germinal an VI, in: *Mémoires de L'Institut national des sciences et arts*, vol. 1, Paris: Baudoin Thermidor an VI [1798], 389. The series of papers on the subject were first read in 1796 and then reformulated in 1798.

14    Brian C.J. Singer, *Society, Theory, and the French Revolution: Studies in the Revolutionary Imaginary*, Houndmills, Basingstoke, Hampshire 1986. Singer was interested in visibility but not visualization.

social science it could also serve the goal of stabilizing rather than further equalizing social relations. The emphasis here will be on the former.[15]

The printing of images in France was increasing before the French Revolution but expanded dramatically as the political crisis unfolded after 1787.

Figure 7. *"Images Produced in France by Decade, 1749–1798"*[16]

## Images in French Collections

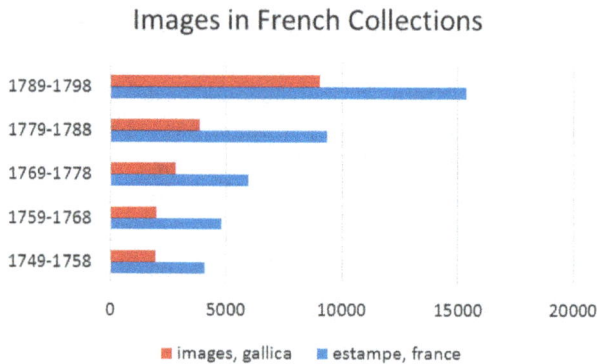

Source: The number of "images" for each decade was determined using the search engines of the general catalogue of the BNF (using the categories "estampe" and "France") and the catalogue for Gallica, the digital arm of the BNF (using the category "image" which could not be further refined). The catalogues are available at https://catalogue.bnf.f r/index.do and https://gallica.bnf.fr/accueil/en/content/accueil-en?mo de=desktop (accessed October 10, 2020).

The increase in prints between the 1780s and the 1790s was almost entirely due to the making of prints related to the revolutionary rupture. Although the number of prints concerned with the revolution cannot be precisely determined, a comparison of various collections in Paris yields about 6-7000 images related in some way to those events. The largest single collection, known

---

15    Much has been written about the efforts of leading intellectuals who hoped to stabilize the revolution. See, for example, Martin S. Staum, *Cabanis: Enlightenment and Medical Philosophy in the French Revolution*, Princeton 1980, and Brian Head, *Ideology and Social Science: Destutt de Tracy and French Liberalism*, Dordrecht 1985.

16    These figures can only be considered generally representative as the numbers keep fluctuating with changes in the catalogues.

as the De Vinck collection after the collector, Belgian Baron Eugène de Vinck de Deux-Orp (1859–1931), includes some 5700 images for the period 1789–1799 but nearly 500 of these are duplicates.[17]

Prints were not the only visual forms increasing dramatically in number. With the loosening of censorship, the figures for newspapers and pamphlets skyrocketed. A few included illustrations, many of which appear in the De Vinck collection. After the National Assembly abolished theatrical monopolies, the number of theaters in Paris rose from nine before 1789 to 50 different ones during the revolutionary decade.[18] Similarly, when the deputies opened the annual art exhibition known as the Salon to all comers, the Salon of 1791 included twice as many works as 1789 and three times as many exhibitors.[19] With the reorganization of government, official letters with new seals and vignettes and in particular the introduction of paper money put untold numbers of images into circulation.[20]

Although the relaxing of censorship certainly facilitated this outpouring of images, the frenzy of image-making also reflected an underlying crisis of meaning. Would the traditional monarchical and aristocratic regime give way to a different political and social order? What would the new regime look like,

---

17    I compared prints within and among different collections using Excel sheets. The 8 volumes of the printed catalogue of the De Vinck collection are listed under a maddening variety of titles because their completion required decades and collaboration by many different people. Bibliothèque nationale (France). Cabinet des estampes. Collection de Vinck, *Un siècle d'histoire de France par l'estampe, 1770–1871*, 8 vols., Paris: Imprimerie nationale, 1909–1969. For the purposes of this study, volumes 2–4 are the relevant ones: *La Constituante* (1914), *La Législative et la Convention* (1921), and the first part of *Napoléon et son temps* (1969). The other major collection is that of Michel Hennin (also in the BNF): Georges Duplessis, *Inventaire de la collection d'estampes relatives à l'histoire de France, léguée en 1863 à la Bibliothèque nationale par M. Michel Hennin*, 5 vols., Paris: H. Menu; H. Champion 1877–1884. The Musée Carnavalet also has many prints but its collection has not been organized in the same fashion. Some of the prints in these collections were produced outside of France but the vast majority are French.

18    John Lough, *Paris Theatre Audiences in the Seventeenth and Eighteenth Centuries*, London 1957, 157; Emmet Kennedy/Marie-Laurence Netter/James P. McGregor/Mark V. Olsen, *Theatre, Opera, and Audiences in Revolutionary Paris: Analysis and Repertory*, Westport, Connecticut 1996, 379.

19    Tony Halliday, *Facing the Public: Portraiture in the Aftermath of the French Revolution*, Manchester 1999, 30.

20    Richard Taws, *The Politics of the Provisional: Art and Ephemera in Revolutionary France*, University Park 2013.

figuratively and literally? Images had been used to buttress the monarchy but they could also undermine it once the floodgates opened. While newspapers and pamphlets gave verbal expression to the hopes and fears prompted by rapidly escalating events, prints necessarily approached those hopes and fears in a different fashion; the visual form compressed and abstracted them and gave them an edge that might or might not be consciously grasped by the viewer. Print makers thus responded to the crisis of meaning and at the same time deepened it. Visualization heightened the sense that the political and social orders were changing in unexpected ways.

*Figure 8: Portrait of Deputy Michel Gérard. Aquatint by C. Lefebvre and Antoine Sergent, 1789, 23.5 x 18 cm.*

Source: BNF

*Figure 9: Portrait of Louis XVI. Aquatint by Antoine Ser-*
*gent, 1789, 23.5 x 18 cm.*

Source: BNF

A fuller discussion of the prints would include attention to the significance of different techniques (etching, line engraving, aquatint, etc.) and the
use of hand coloring, the chronology of print production (very vexed because
so many are undated and unsigned), the differentiation by themes, and any
evidence as to reception, to mention only the most obvious. Many of these aspects of the prints have to be left to the side here in favor of a general overview
followed by a consideration of evidence from two remarkable eyewitnesses.[21]

21    For another kind of overview, see Rolf Reichardt/Hubertus Kohle, *Visualizing the Revolution: Politics and Pictorial Arts in Late Eighteenth-Century France*, London 2008.

The large number of prints testifies, in itself, to the astonishment and uncertainty created by rapid changes in the political order and the social transformations implied by those changes. Everything had to be depicted in order to be more fully comprehended: the personalities involved (about one third of the images in the French Revolution Digital Archive are portraits, the biggest single category), the unfolding events (a quarter are "scènes historiques"), the places, and the changing social customs.[22] The prints did not just describe persons or events; they helped establish the significance of personalities and events.

The supposedly anodyne genre of portraits provides an excellent example of the ways in which visualization could shape political understanding and therefore political outcomes. As Amy Freund has shown, the collections of portraits of deputies that were rushed into print in the summer of 1789 made the implicit but nonetheless potent argument that the deputies represented the nation as much as the king did [Figures 8 and 9].

They did this visually by framing the deputies in the same way as they framed the king. The portrait of the deputy in Figure 8 shows the kinds of changes in dress and appearance that were coming in; unlike most of the deputies, he does not wear a wig or a cravat in the opening of his coat. By offering a series of portraits of the deputies to the public, the engravers and print merchants helped establish their collective importance.[23] In various ways, then, the prints helped undermine the semiotic stability of the monarchical regime and laid out, less explicitly to be sure, the possible bases of a new one. They did this through the process of portrayal by asking viewers to focus their attention and take the moment to reflect.

## Eyewitness Accounts

Evidence concerning how people felt when they viewed such prints is difficult to find, but there are two contemporary commentators of note, one from the

---

22    For portraits I combined the figures for the dates 1789–1799 for "portraits," "portraits en médaillon," "portraits satiriques," and "portraits-18e siècle" in the French Revolution Digital Archive (FRDA), available at <https://frda.stanford.edu/?locale=en> (accessed October 28, 2020). The current version of the FRDA has 4623 images for the period 1789–1799, all derived from the collections of the Bibliothèque Nationale de France (BNF). The categories are those of the BNF.

23    Amy Freund, *Portraiture and Politics in Revolutionary France*, University Park 2014, 49–80.

political right and one from the political center left. Both of them referred to specific images. The first historian of revolutionary caricatures, Jacques-Marie Boyer-Brun, wrote out of anti-Protestant fervor; he was a Catholic royalist from Nîmes, a city in southern France where more than 300 people died in street fighting between Catholics and Protestants in June 1790. His religious bias enhanced his appreciation of the power of images which no doubt also derived from his career as a journalist. Boyer had founded his own journal in Nîmes in 1786 and was at first favorable to the Revolution. He accepted election as deputy attorney general for the city in March 1790, but after publishing anti-revolutionary and anti-Protestant writings in reaction to the massacres of 1790, he fled to Paris where he continued to work as a journal editor and collected caricatures that formed the source for his 1792 book about them. In May 1794 the revolutionary court in Paris condemned him to death on the grounds that he had encouraged violence against patriots in Nîmes.[24]

Although he had not commissioned illustrations for his journal in Nîmes, Boyer came to see prints as "the thermometer that registers the degree of public opinion," and therefore "those who know how to master their variations also know how to master public opinion."[25] [Figure 10] The prospectus for his book made the aim explicit:

> "the author will demonstrate in the first part of this work that every means was employed to overthrow the altar and the throne and it will be shown that caricatures were one of the means used with the greatest skill, perseverance, and success to mislead and whip up the people."[26]

Boyer showed particular interest in the psychological effects of prints. In his analysis of an anonymous etching with the sardonic legend, "they only wanted what was good for us," he concluded,

---

24   Henri Wallon, *Histoire du Tribunal révolutionnaire de Paris avec le Journal de ses actes*, 6 vols., Paris: Librairie Hachette et cie, 1880–82, IV: 12–13.

25   Jacques-Marie Boyer-Brun, *Histoire des caricatures de la révolte des Français, par M. Boyer de Nîmes, …*, 2 vols., Paris: Impr. du Journal du peuple, 1792, I: 10. See also, Champfleury, *Histoire de la caricature: sous la République, l'Empire et la Restauration*, 2nd ed., Paris: E. Dentu 1877, 170–193.

26   As quoted in Annie Duprat, Le regard d'un royaliste sur la Révolution: Jacques-Marie Boyer de Nîmes, in: *Annales historiques de la Révolution française*, 337 (2004), 21–39, see <https://journals.openedition.org/ahrf/1505>, paragraph 2.

"the man of the people must necessarily feel humiliated when in becoming aware of his own feelings he says to himself: 'like the imbeciles that are being mocked here I had respect and confidence in the clergy, the nobility, and the parlements [high courts], who must not be as respectable as I believed since someone dares to denounce them to public opinion and ridicule them in ways that would be avoided if they did not deserve it.'"[27]

*Figure 10: Hand-colored Original of "They Only Wanted What was Good for Us". Anonymous hand-colored etching, 1789–1790, 22 x 33 cm.*

Source: BNF

While Boyer's assumptions about the humiliation felt by an imagined man of the people are contestable, he makes the important point that etchings like this one engage a process of visual communication that includes the artist's, engraver's, or publisher's intentions (not necessarily identical) and the reactions of viewers. Moreover, he gives pride of place to the emotions (*sensations* in French) triggered in the viewer and the process by which those emotions prompt the development of new attitudes. The humiliation shown presumably provokes the opposite response in its viewers, that is, a kind of revulsion

27    Boyer-Brun, *Histoire des caricatures*, I: 69. Although the legend does not appear on Boyer's reproduction in the book, it does appear in this hand-colored version (Figure 10).

at previous habits of subservience. The portrayal of humiliation by means of the supplicant postures of the lower orders contrasts vividly with the evident grossness of features of the bishop, the aristocrat, and the judge. The vulgarity of the upper classes reinforces the egalitarian charge of the image; if the upper classes are not even more refined, why are the lower classes continuing to think of themselves as lesser?

Boyer abhorred the notion of equality, which is why this image and others like it disturbed him. He believed that Protestants had leagued with the Jansenists (dissident Catholics), Physiocrats (*économistes*), and Freemasons to spur the French to revolt, which was "a necessary consequence of the insubordinate principles of equality set down by *John Calvin* [his emphasis]." Liberty and equality were illusory concepts; liberty really meant "that it was necessary to shake off the yoke of the priests," and equality was trumpeted in order "to insinuate that the king was only a man like any other." The "sublime" equality promised in the declaration of rights ended up being "equality of incoherent and illusory systems, equality of absurdities and extravagances, equality of impiety, apostasy and revolt against those in power."[28] Such caricatures could be found on all the quays of the Seine and in virtually every square and intersection, he complained, and they spoke directly to viewers in a way that the written word could not. Through their manipulation of sentiments, the prints could compel viewers to take stock of themselves and of their place in a system of social relations. In this way, the prints did more than frame events or create personalities; they prompted viewers to think socially, to criticize the status quo, to aspire to equality, and even to reflect about the nature of social relations more generally.

From the very different perspective of a centrist republican, in the late 1790s Louis-Sébastien Mercier expressed ambivalence about popular prints. On the one hand, they could serve valuable purposes by reminding viewers of the horrors of the recent past or criticizing the more outlandish versions of contemporary fashion. On the other hand, they could illustrate obscene books or simply amuse passersby with their renditions of current customs. Like Boyer, Mercier was unusual in his attention to prints, and like his political opposite, his partisan views only intensified his appreciation for the power of such depictions. Unlike Boyer, however, he considered equality to be one of the most important gains of the Revolution. Get rid of "Monsieur" [mister]

---

28    Boyer-Brun, *Histoire des caricatures*, I: 27–28, 70, 71; Boyer-Brun, *Histoire des caricatures*, II: 72.

and those formal closings, the "very humbles," "obedient servants," "profound respects, very profound, the most profound," he expostulated, and just stick with "citizen." It may be associated with recent bloody events, but it is worth preserving: "This word [citizen] is the one that has most pained the aristocracy; but despite all their efforts, their lamentations and their sarcasm, it has become the patronymic of French liberty."[29]

Mercier served as a deputy between 1792 and 1797, and spent more than a year in prison in 1793–94 as a supporter of the Girondins, the moderate republican opponents of Maximilien Robespierre. This political engagement gave Mercier a first-hand view of the constantly changing situation, and he came to that engagement with a reputation already established as a playwright, novelist, and observer of Parisian life before the Revolution. His *Tableau de Paris* [Picture of Paris] (1781) had not suited everyone when it came out; one critic complained that "this is a book conceived in the street and written in the gutter."[30] In those pages Mercier had already drawn attention to the licentious prints that had multiplied along the quays and boulevards.[31] Other than his defense of the Girondins, Mercier failed to establish much of a reputation as a legislator. Marie-Jeanne Roland wrote of Mercier not long before her own execution as a Girondin supporter in 1793: "The good Mercier, facile, amiable in company, more than is common among people of letters, was only a zero in the [National] Convention."[32] Mercier seemed to suffer from an ailment that appeared in his dictionary of neologisms in 1801: "*Scribomanie* [scribbling mania]. Passion for writing. It is sometimes a sickness but at least it makes the one who has it happy."[33]

In his revisiting of Paris after years of revolution, *Le Nouveau Paris* [The new Paris, 1799], Mercier continued to complain about obscene books with their prints that were "equally repellent to modesty and good taste," but now he blamed them on post-revolutionary conditions: counterfeiters who pushed

---

29    Louis-Sébastien Mercier, *Le Nouveau Paris*, Jean-Claude Bonnet, dir., Paris 1994, 278.

30    Samuel Lutz, Quelques échos, in: Hermann Hofer (ed.), *Louis-Sébastien Mercier, précurseur et sa fortune: avec des documents inédits: recueil d'études sur l'influence de Mercier*, München 1977, 285–300, see 289.

31    Louis-Sébastien Mercier, *Tableau de Paris*, 8 vols., Amsterdam 1783, VI: 92. Louis-Sébastien Mercier, *Tableau de Paris*, 2 vols., Jean-Claude Bonnet, dir., Paris 1994, I:1323. Bonnet's team has compared the various editions.

32    Marie-Jeanne Roland de la Platière, *Mémoires de Madame Roland*, Paris 1967, 312.

33    Louis-Sébastien Mercier, *Néologie, ou Vocabulaire de mots nouveaux, à renouveler, ou pris dans des acceptions Nouvelles*, 2 vols., Paris: Chez Moussard, chez Maradan 1801, II: 244.

for an unlimited freedom of the press, the institution of divorce, gluttony, and daily attendance at the theater and dances.[34] Still, in his chapter on "critical prints" he praised the efforts of [Carle] Vernet who satirized the *Incroyables* [incredibles] and *Merveilleuses* [marvelous females], young men and women who affected outrageous costumes, and he argued that the print with the title *Interior of a Revolutionary Committee* could make the viewer relive the horror of the "plots hatched in those lairs of Polyphemus [savage man-eating giant in Greek mythology]," that is, that period of terror and violence in 1793–94 when Mercier himself languished in prison threatened with execution.[35]

Like Boyer, but without an actual illustration reproduced in the text, he offered a psychological reading, in this case of a scene depicting someone accused by their local revolutionary committee:

"Who does not tremble with horror at the look of this livid president? One hears the croaky snoring of the secretary with a red cap, elbows on the table, who is sleeping off his morning wine. The viewing of these bottles whose label establishes the crime of suspicious relations with foreign countries; the fright which grabs hold of the unfortunate accused who repeats in a low voice, *Vin de Hongrie* [Hungarian wine, the Austrian Empire being at war with France]."[36]

The title that Mercier cites is that of a play by Charles-Pierre Ducancel first performed in Paris in April 1795. Mercier probably had in mind an etching that was published in 1797 as an illustration of the final scene of the play [Figure 11].

The etching shows the very staging that Mercier described except that Mercier mistakes the figure under accusation which in the play is the wife, not the husband.

As his rendition of this print shows, Mercier believed in a certain equality but not the radical egalitarianism that had appeared among popular militants in 1793–94. The Jacobin clubs had emerged auspiciously as schools of public spirit but they degenerated into "demagogic fanaticism," and their meetings turned into "hell on earth," Mercier insisted, due to the vile influence of "the women of the rabble," "ugly shrews" who denounced people on the slightest of pretexts.[37] Mercier commended "the good and regenerative equality" that

---

34    Mercier, *Le Nouveau Paris*, 430.
35    Mercier, *Le Nouveau Paris*, 623–625.
36    Mercier, *Le Nouveau Paris*, 625.
37    Mercier, *Le Nouveau Paris*, 75, 453.

*Figure 11: The Interior of a Revolutionary Committee: Last Scene.*
*Aquatint by Boulet (no first name), 1797, 43 x 59.5 cm*

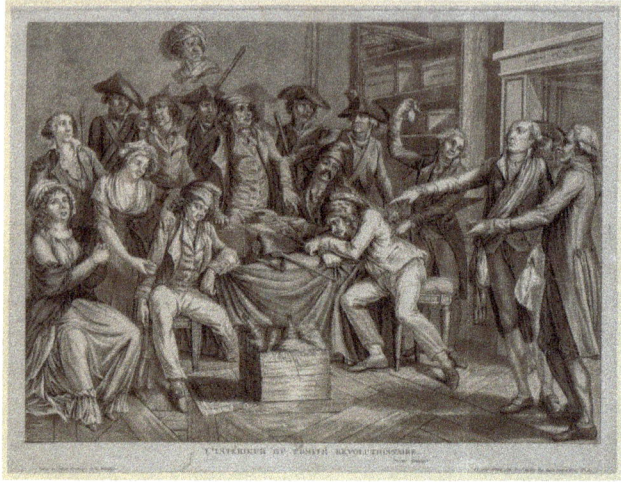

Source: BNF

he found on visiting the veterans' hospital in Paris where officers and ordinary soldiers shared the same food. He did not fault the word "equality" for creating the gross differences between rich and poor that he found in Paris in the late 1790s, for it was difficult to provide a remedy when the two political extremes, "democratic equality" and "despotic equality," were equally dangerous. Mercier threw out the thought but left it there.[38]

Mercier remarked on the proliferation of prints, but he was not entirely sure what to make of them, so even while he vaunted the power of prints to capture the dread of the recent past and applauded Vernet for lampooning extravagant fashions, he could not resist disparaging the caricature vogue. He bemoaned the license that had destroyed the credibility of the political press and reduced to insignificance periodical publications because they could not keep up with fast-moving events. "Caricatures seem to want to replace them [periodicals]," he wrote, "and add to the unlimited liberty of the press. Passersby crowd in front of the print sellers to look at the *Incroyables*, the *Merveilleuses*,

---

38    Mercier, *Le Nouveau Paris*, 688, 826.

the fish vendor, the *rentier* [someone who lives off his investments], the *folie du jour* [folly of the day], anarchy, the danger of wigs." These prints were nothing but "naïve depictions of our ridiculousness, of our follies, of our idiosyncrasies, of our vices" that "only excites a fleeting smile from a fickle people that sizes itself up by weighing its choices of dress [*qui s'étudie dans sa mise*]."[39]

Although Mercier scorned the practice—the constant comparison of appearances—he had nonetheless hit upon something significant about visual images and especially the rendering of fashion: it was a way for people to see their society in a mirror and therefore to understand what they were becoming and even to become something else. He went on, "Who would believe it? The print of the *Incroyables* has spread [the style of] 'dog's ears' [two long curls hanging down the side of the face]: that is how inept newspapers, *frondeurs* [rebellious troublemakers] of republicanism, made a lot of republicans."[40] Mercier meant this sardonically, yet in one of his characteristic reversals, he then lauded the many print portraits of French generals, who "saved all Europe from the horrible system of oppression and slavery that the kings had prepared against the people," and cheerfully reported that black market prints of the deaths of Louis XVI and Marie-Antoinette could be had for little money since no one wanted them.[41]

Mercier worried about the effect of prints, sensed the growing preoccupation with identifying social roles after 1794, and clearly understood that something profound had happened to the social order. "The social system has been shaken down to its foundations," he affirmed, but he was not very optimistic about what was replacing it: "From every part of the social body [*de toutes les parties du corps social*] we have seen the appearance of the newly opulent, and with them, gold and riches."[42] Mercier's use of the adjective "social"—social system, social body, social interest, and social mechanism—reflects the influence on him of Rousseau and to a lesser extent, Condorcet. Mercier helped organize the publication of the collected works of Rousseau (1788–1793) and published a two volume work in 1791, *Jean-Jacques Rousseau Considered as One of the Authors of the Revolution*. He did not write about the philosophical views of Condorcet in the same way, but he learned that he shared many political

---

39   Mercier, *Le Nouveau Paris*, 421.
40   Mercier, *Le Nouveau Paris*, 421–422.
41   Mercier, *Le Nouveau Paris*, 422.
42   Mercier, *Le Nouveau Paris*, 266 and 25.

views with Condorcet when they both sat as deputies to the National Convention and collaborated on the journal, *Chronique du mois*, closely identified with
the Girondins. Mercier defended Condorcet and the Girondins in 1793, went
to prison for objecting to their arrest, and continued to exalt the memory of
Condorcet, in particular, for years afterward.

Alongside other followers of Condorcet, in 1795 Mercier had been named
to the second class of the new National Institute, the class of "moral and political sciences," and to the subsection "morals." His friend Pierre Daunou sat in
the subsection "social science;" Sieyès was named to the subsection "political
economy." Mercier had his doubts, however, about scientific approaches to
analyzing humans or their societies. He understood that "the social mechanism" was still more or less "a secret for the eighteenth century," but he
was not sure that that secret should be unlocked, if unlocking followed from
the "reign of those guilty philosophers who wanted to explain everything by
the bodily senses, who wanted to reduce everything to purely physical opera-
tions."[43] Mercier fretted about the influence of atheism and materialism and
wanted no part of either. Yet at the same time as a close observer of social life,
he found himself speaking the language of social systems and social mechanisms, a language that emerged along with and in part in reaction to the
spread of egalitarianism.

What Mercier did not see, but then no one did, was the way visual imagery
helped make the notion itself of a social order more intelligible.[44] Those supposedly "naïve depictions" of ridiculous behavior, denounced by Mercier, all
had deeper political and social meanings. Although he provides no information about the prints he names and includes no reproductions, it is possible
to identity those titles he lists by searching various print collections. The first
two are the Vernets that he had praised in an earlier chapter. [Figures 12 and
13] The fish vendor [*marchande de merlans*] and *rentier* can be found together on

---

43    Mercier, *Le Nouveau Paris*, 868–9. Mercier did not use the term "social science" himself.

44    Some of the themes of social reconstruction appear in Lynn Hunt, La visibilité du
monde bourgeois, in : Jean-Pierre Jessenne, dir., *Vers un ordre bourgeois? Révolution française et changement social*, Rennes 2007, 371–381. It is worth noting that the Goncourts
attributed criticism of Mercier's stand on the arts in the Conseil des Cinq Cents to the
fact that he "n'a guère voulu voir d'hiérarchie de genre dans l'art." Edmond de Goncourt/
Jules de Goncourt, *Histoire de la société francaise pendant le directoire*, Paris: E. Dentu 1855,
279. In other words, Mercier's views on the arts left him more open than most to considering the impact of that "low" genre, printmaking.

a stippled etching by Laurent-Joseph Julien with the title *Poor Ruined Rentier – Whiting [merlan] to Fry, to Fry.*[45]

*Figure 12: Les Incroyables. Etching with stippling by Carle Vernet and Louis Darcis, 1796, 30.5 x 36 cm*

Source: BNF

The other three—the *folie du jour* [folly of the day], anarchy, and the danger of wigs—can also be quite confidently identified based on similarities of technique and dating to the others. Two different engravers did stippled etchings titled *Folie du jour* based on a painting by Louis-Léopold Boilly.[46] By the

---

45    The engraving was announced in a journal in March 1797. Information can be found at <https://data.bnf.fr/16863819/laurent_joseph_julien_pauvre_rentier_ruine_merlan_a_frire_a_frire___/> (accessed November 4, 2020). The information no longer links to a view of the print itself though it did in the past. It can, however, be visualized at http://arts-graphiques.louvre.fr/detail/oeuvres/1/520925-Pauvre-rentier-ruine-merlan-a-frire-max.

46    According to the British Museum, the print by Salvatore Tresca was registered at the BNF in February 1797. For image and information, see <https://www.britishmuseum.org/collection/object/P_1998-0426-30> (accessed November 4, 2020). The version by J. P. Levilly can be seen at <https://www.parismuseescollections.paris.fr/fr/musee-carnaval et/oeuvres/la-folie-du-jour> (accessed November 4, 2020). Both show the same scene in slightly different formats.

*Figure 13: Les Merveilleuses. Etching with stippling by Carle Vernet and Louis Darcis, 1797, 32 x 36 cm*

LES MERVEILLEUSES.

Source: BNF

"danger of wigs" Mercier no doubt meant the print titled *L'Inconvénient des perruques* [The inconvenience of wigs] because the scene of the woman on a horse is quite precisely described by Mercier in his text. It too is a stippled etching from 1797 based on a drawing by Carle Vernet, engraved by Louis Darcis.[47] If the same line of reasoning is followed (use of stippling, date of 1797), then the most likely *"anarchy"* is a print by Simon Petit titled *L'Anarchiste je les trompe tous deux* [The Anarchist, I fool both of them], which shows a two-faced man appealing on the one side to a woman of the popular classes and on the other to a young man of the middle classes dressed very fashionably. [Figure 14]

Is it accidental that Mercier combined the supposedly critical prints by Vernet and seemingly apolitical prints about fashion with two prints with more obvious political messages? The poor ruined *rentier* is forced to accept charity from a humble fish vendor because the Directory repudiated two-

---

47    A hand-colored version can be seen at <https://www.britishmuseum.org/collection/object/P_1925-0214-11> (accessed November 4, 2020). The British Museum dates it as 1797.

*Figure 14: The Anarchist, I Fool Both of Them. Etching with stippling by Simon Petit, 1797, 32.5 x 38 cm.*

Source: BNF

thirds of the national debt in 1797. *L'Anarchiste* captured perfectly Mercier's visceral dislike of the Jacobins, whom he denounced repeatedly in *Nouveau Paris*. Since Mercier's writing often verged on the slapdash it is hardly surprising that he sometimes contradicted himself from one passage to another; thus the Vernet prints could be models of critical depiction on one page and examples of French ridiculousness on another. In the end, however, it is possible that they were both.

The mania for the socially picturesque had a logic that was not immediately evident. Fashion was a key indicator of social change, especially the new mixing of classes, but it also still signaled social status, as the print *Anarchist* demonstrates. Without the depiction of fashion in this print, there would be no political message: the face turned toward the woman of the popular classes is dark-skinned, dark-haired, and mustachioed, signaling a supposedly lower racial type, and that man wears the short jacket, loose trousers and clogs of the popular classes; the face turned toward the middle-class young man is lighter and smooth-skinned with blond hair, and he wears a fashionable frock coat,

tight pants, and stockings with elegant shoes. The young man he is impor-
tuning is dressed similarly though he wears a hat and ankle boots and sports
the sideburns that developed out of the *Incroyable* fashion of "dog's ears."[48]

The young man is therefore even more fashionable than the "anarchist"
[revolutionary extremist]. Ankle boots with pointed toes were fashionable in
1797 and in late 1798 they still were, according to one of the major fashion journals.[49] Fashion required serious study because it was changing so quickly and
because it carried social and political messages.[50] The young man in *Anarchist*
carries a stick (in contrast to the more vulgar club of the man whose face
is turned toward the woman of the people) because anyone dressing like an
*Incroyable* could find themselves involved in a street fight with republicans.

## Conclusion

The fashion for women of the prosperous classes changed with vertiginous
speed during the French Revolution, but men's appearances were more fundamentally transformed. As Mercier noted, the classic French three-piece outfit
[*habit français*], worn in courts throughout Europe, "no longer dares to show
itself." In its place, "The old man, like the adolescent, puts on the shortened *frac*
[riding-coat or frock coat]."[51] The fashion endured though the *habit français*,
with knee breeches rather than pants, made something of a comeback under
Napoleon who wanted to emulate court finery and who as he got fat found
long pants uncomfortable.[52] While men's hairstyles varied, sometimes from
year to year, wigs fell out of favor and increasingly men wore their own hair

---

48    According to Aileen Ribeiro, ribbon garters were worn over pants [*pantalons*] to create
      the illusion of knee breeches. Aileen Ribeiro, *Fashion in the French Revolution*, New York
      1988, 119.

49    "La mode des pantalons et des bottines se soutient." *Tableau général du gout, des modes,
      et des costumes de Paris*, no. II de Brumaire, an VII [October –November 1798], 108.

50    On the political meanings of fashion in the French Revolution, see the invaluable
      Richard Wrigley, *The Politics of Appearances: Representations of Dress in Revolutionary
      France*, Oxford 2002.

51    Mercier's comment is from a previously unpublished manuscript that is reproduced in
      the Bonnet edition of Mercier, *Le Nouveau Paris*, 1238.

52    On the frac, see Philip Mansel, Monarchy, Uniform and the Rise of the Frac, 1760–1830,
      in: *Past & Present* 96 (1/1982), 103–132.

unpowdered, though women still wore wigs and men did, too, on certain formal occasions. The painters and engravers who collaborated in making images like the ones presented here could barely keep up. Their work shows that people were noticing the changes taking place and trying to make sense of them. Men were moving toward a more uniform style of self-presentation, though not all at once, but they were not as a consequence moving out of the gaze of observers. On the contrary, every little detail mattered, and looking mattered more than ever.[53]

The viewers of prints were studying themselves in the mirror of these images; they were seeing a society experiencing rapid social changes and facing continuing political challenges. People who could not afford the prints nevertheless looked at them in print shops, as Mercier himself complained, so the viewing was not limited to those who could buy them. The prints, even the fashion prints, prompted viewers to think about social types, social relations, and ultimately, society itself as an organism with its own rules. It seems hardly accidental, then, that the term "science sociale" first appeared in the writings of Sieyès and Condorcet early in the Revolution and then took root from the mid-1790s onward in the writings of the intellectuals known as the "Idéologues," associates of Destutt de Tracy. The painters and engravers did not know themselves to be advancing "social science," but their sense of the market for images led them to produce prints that made it possible to visualize society in new ways. Society became an object of study seen to have its own rules of operation.

The eighteenth-century conceptualizations of equality, the rapid political changes of the Revolutionary decade, the vertiginous evolution of fashion in the 1790s, and the market for prints combined in unexpectedly generative ways. Viewers brought an already germinating conceptual seedbox to their experience of rapid political and social change. Those changes then created a kind of hothouse atmosphere, in which the proliferation of prints led to social relations being more extensively and intensively visualized than ever before. Visualization deepened social criticism which then found expression in new conceptualizations, not just of the need for, threat of, and inevitable ambigu-

---

53    Although it is true that the fashion journals paid more attention to women's dress than to men's, I do not agree with Ribeiro's contention that "With regard to the details of men's dress, there are few changes to chronicle in the last years of the eighteenth century." Ribeiro, *Fashion in the French Revolution*, 119.

ities of equality but also of need for, threat of, and inevitable ambiguities of social science.

The work was done in part by intellectuals thinking about what had happened, what had changed, and what those changes meant. But much work was also done by those with no intention of writing a tract. The representations of personalities, events, and social relations enabled viewers to feel new emotions and think new thoughts. Equality is never a given. It is the product of struggle between those used to being on top and those who are not but it is also the product of internal struggles within each person between customary patterns of behavior, long ingrained by force and by habit, and new ways of imagining the social order. Although images, like the life they encapsulate, never have only one message, they do offer a site where emotions and concepts can intersect with sometimes surprising consequences.

## References

Bibliothèque nationale (France). Cabinet des estampes. Collection de Vinck, *Un siècle d'histoire de France par l'estampe, 1770–1871*, 8 vols., Paris: Imprimerie nationale, 1909–1969.

Boyer-Brun, Jacques-Marie, *Histoire des caricatures de la révolte des Français, par M. Boyer de Nîmes, ...* , 2 vols., Paris: Impr. du Journal du peuple, 1792.

Burstin, Haim, *L'invention du sans-culotte: regards sur Paris révolutionnaire*, Paris 2005.

Champfleury [no first name], *Histoire de la caricature: sous la République, l'Empire et la Restauration*, 2nd ed., Paris: E. Dentu 1877.

Comte, Auguste, *Cours de philosophie positive*, vol. 4, Paris: Bachelier 1839.

Destutt de Tracy, Antoine, Mémoire sur la faculté de penser, Extrait du procès-verbal de la classe des sciences morales et politiques de L'Institut national, du 22 germinal an VI, in: *Mémoires de L'Institut national des sciences et arts*, vol. 1, Paris: Baudoin Thermidor an VI [1798].

Duplessis, Georges, *Inventaire de la collection d'estampes relatives à l'histoire de France, léguée en 1863 à la Bibliothèque nationale par M. Michel Hennin*, 5 vols., Paris: H. Menu; H. Champion 1877–1884.

Duprat, Annie, Le regard d'un royaliste sur la Révolution: Jacques-Marie Boyer de Nîmes, in: *Annales historiques de la Révolution française*, 337 (2004), 21–39.

Flügel, J. C., *The Psychology of Clothes*, London 1950.

Freund, Amy, *Portraiture and Politics in Revolutionary France*, University Park 2014.

de Goncourt, Edmond/de Goncourt, Jules, *Histoire de la société francaise pendant le directoire*, Paris: E. Dentu 1855.

Halliday, Tony, *Facing the Public: Portraiture in the Aftermath of the French Revolution*, Manchester 1999.

Head, Brian, *Ideology and Social Science: Destutt de Tracy and French Liberalism*, Dordrecht 1985.

Hunt, Lynn, La visibilité du monde bourgeois, in: Jean-Pierre Jessenne, dir., *Vers un ordre bourgeois? Révolution française et changement social*, Rennes 2007, 371–381.

Hunt, Lynn, *Inventing Human Rights: A History*, New York 2007.

Kennedy, Emmet/Netter, Marie-Laurence /McGregor, James P. /Olsen, Mark V., *Theatre, Opera, and Audiences in Revolutionary Paris: Analysis and Repertory*, Westport, Connecticut 1996.

Lough, John, *Paris Theatre Audiences in the Seventeenth and Eighteenth Centuries*, London 1957.

Lutz, Samuel, Quelques échos, in: Hermann Hofer (ed.), *Louis-Sébastien Mercier, précurseur et sa fortune: avec des documents inédits: recueil d'études sur l'influence de Mercier*, München 1977, 285–300.

Mansel, Philip, Monarchy, Uniform and the Rise of the *Frac*, 1760–1830, in: *Past & Present* 96 (1/1982), 103–132.

Mercier, Louis-Sébastien, *Tableau de Paris*, 8 vols., Amsterdam 1783.

Mercier, Louis-Sébastien, *Néologie, ou Vocabulaire de mots nouveaux, à renouveler, ou pris dans des acceptions nouvelles*, 2 vols., Paris: Chez Moussard, chez Maradan 1801.

Mercier, Louis-Sébastien, *Le Nouveau Paris*, Jean-Claude Bonnet, dir., Paris 1994.

Mercier, Louis-Sébastien, *Tableau de Paris*, 2 vols., Jean-Claude Bonnet, dir., Paris 1994.

Reichardt, Rolf/Kohle, Hubertus, *Visualizing the Revolution: Politics and Pictorial Arts in Late Eighteenth-Century France*, London 2008.

Ribeiro, Aileen, *Fashion in the French Revolution*, New York 1988.

Roche, Daniel, *La culture des apparences: une histoire du vêtement (XVIIe-XVIIIe siècle)*, Paris 1989.

Roland de la Platière, Marie-Jeanne, *Mémoires de Madame Roland*, Paris 1967.

Sewell, William H. Jr., Connecting Capitalism to the French Revolution: The Parisian Promenade and the Origins of Civic Equality in Eighteenth-Century France, in: *Critical Historical Studies* 1 (1/2014), 5–46.

Silverman, Kaja, *The Acoustic Mirror: The Female Voice in Psychoanalysis and Cinema*, Bloomington 1988.

Singer, Brian C.J., *Society, Theory, and the French Revolution: Studies in the Revolutionary Imaginary*, Houndmills, Basingstoke, Hampshire 1986.

Soboul, Albert, *Les Sans-culottes parisiens en l'an II: Mouvement populaire et gouvernement révolutionnaire, 2 Juin 1793-9 Thermidor An II*, Paris 1958.

Staum, Martin S., *Cabanis: Enlightenment and Medical Philosophy in the French Revolution*, Princeton 1980.

Stuurman, Siep, *The Invention of Humanity: Equality and Cultural Difference in World History*, Cambridge, MA 2017.

*Tableau général du gout, des modes, et des costumes de Paris*, no. II de Brumaire, an VII [October–November 1798].

Taws, Richard, *The Politics of the Provisional: Art and Ephemera in Revolutionary France*, University Park 2013.

Vartija, Devin, *The Colour of Equality: Race and Common Humanity in Enlightenment Thought*, Philadelphia 2021.

Wallon, Henri, *Histoire du Tribunal révolutionnaire de Paris avec le Journal de ses actes*, 6 vols., Paris: Librairie Hachette et cie, 1880–82.

Wokler, Robert, From the Moral and Political Sciences to the Sciences of Society by Way of the French Revolution, in: *Jahrbuch für Recht und Ethik / Annual Review of Law and Ethics*, Vol. 8, Themenschwerpunkt: Die Entstehung und Entwicklung der Moralwissenschaften im 17. und 18. Jahrhundert / The Origin and Development of the Moral Sciences in the Seventeenth and Eighteenth Century (2000), 33–45.

Wrigley, Richard, *The Politics of Appearances: Representations of Dress in Revolutionary France*, Oxford 2002.

# "A Deep, Horizontal Comradeship?"
## Early Nineteenth Century German Nationalism and the Problem of Poverty

*Helmut Walser Smith*

**Abstract**

*Benedict Anderson called the fundamental sentiment underlying nationalism "a deep horizontal comradeship." Yet the salience of this idea has not been fully explored in terms of the actual inequalities that existed in the era of early nationalism. Germany, in the first half of the nineteenth century, was essentially a developing economy. It trailed leading nations, like the United Kingdom, and it contained significant economic disparities. This article looks at early nineteenth century Germany through the lens of Friedrich List, a founding figure of development economics, and Bettina von Arnim, who argued for new forms of empathy with the poor. Often overlooked in the literature on nationalism, these figures took seriously the imperative of creating "a deep horizontal comradeship" and understood this imperative in the context of nascent industrial growth and the persistence of significant poverty.*

## "Horizontal Comradeship"

Nationalism, one may have assumed, would have constituted an ideology that set out to combat poverty—after all, nationalism, in the words of Benedict Anderson, is conceived as "a deep horizontal comradeship," and this comradeship is surely difficult to maintain if one part of the social order revels in riches while the other is forced to clothe themselves with rags. In *Imagined*

*Communities*, still a seminal text, Benedict Anderson did not address the issue, but he was certainly aware of it. Consider how he carefully parsed his words:

> "Finally, [the nation] is imagined as a community, because, regardless of the actual inequality and exploitation that may prevail in each, the nation is always conceived as a deep, horizontal comradeship. Ultimately, it is this fraternity that makes it possible, over the past two centuries, for so many millions of people, not so much to kill, as willingly to die for such limited imaginings."[1]

The qualifier—regardless of the actual inequality and exploitation—is a significant one, and in the culturalist moment of the 1980s and 1990s, in which Anderson's book was initially read, it received little commentary, especially in light of Anderson's far greater contribution, which was to take the study of nationalism out of the history of ideas and politics and align it more closely with the investigations of literature and the cultural imaginary.

And yet, it bears recalling that pre-industrial, developing economies typically imparted the actual context for early nationalism, certainly in continental Europe, but also in much of the rest of the world. This relationship was often obscured in much of the canonical literature on nationalism, which posited a close link to industrialization.[2] Given that industrial take-off did not occur outside of the Benelux countries, England, and northern France until the 1860s, this implied one of two corollaries. The first is that nationalism was sociologically thin in the first half of the nineteenth century; the second is that nationalist movements often generated momentum amidst extremely high levels of poverty, especially in the countryside. The first corollary has been amply documented, the second has been less explored. Still less commented upon is the relationship between the two corollaries.

How is it that bourgeois nationalist intellectuals, for this is the class that first articulated nationalist ideas as Anderson understood them, came to even conceive of the peasantry and the poor as somehow kith and kin? Put simply, were ideas of equality important to early nationalism?

The German case would lead one to answer in the negative –at least if one followed the older historiography. Consider the marginal importance of

---

1    Benedict Anderson, *Imagined Communities: Reflections on the Origin and Spread of Nationalism*, 2nd rev. ed., London 1991, 6–7.
2    Ernest Gellner, *Nations and Nationalism*, London 1983; Eric Hobsbawm, *Nations and Nationalism since 1780: Programme, Myth, Reality*, Cambridge 1983.

Friedrich List, often thought of as a founding father of the national school of economics, across generations of studies on German nationalism, from Hans Kohn's *The Mind of Germany* (1960) to Otto Dann's *Nation und Nationalismus in Deutschland* (1993).[3] Both historians were familiar with the works of List, yet he is not so much as mentioned in Kohn and only in passing in Dann. The best of the newer works, like Jörg Echternkamp's *Der Aufstieg des deutschen Nationalismus* (1998) or Mathew Levinger's *Enlightened Nationalism* (2000), are hardly different in this regard.[4] Why might this be the case?

The weight of later developments is likely the principal reason. The unification of Germany, the subsequent ethnicization of nationality, and the twentieth century catastrophe of two world wars and the Holocaust all cast immense backward shadows on nineteenth century contexts and developments. These shadows make certain aspects of early nationalism both difficult to see and hard to narrate as part of a larger story. It is well known, for example, that Ernst Moritz Arndt penned fiery anti-French philippics. Yet the immense scholarship on German nationalism routinely omits that he also wrote a seven-hundred-page treatise on the abolition of serfdom in Pomerania.[5]

The chapter that follows can only offer hints as to how to reconstruct a history of German nationalism that brings the problem of poverty back in.[6] It is, in this spirit, an initial foray into the topic. Pre 1848 Germany, it will be contended, was economically much like a developing nation, and therefore any notion of a "deep, horizontal comradeship," which Benedict Anderson argued was constitutive of nationalist imagined communities, necessarily entailed addressing the question of poverty. By focusing on two thinkers, Friedrich List and Bettina von Arnim, this chapter begins to reinscribe this question into the history of German thinking about the nation. Each thinker was pivotal to the story in different ways: List for strategies to alleviate poverty, von Arnim for developing a "deep, horizontal comradeship" with the poor. Finally, it will be argued that it is necessary to consider more seriously the double

---

3   Hans Kohn, *The Mind of Germany*, New York 1960; Otto Dann, *Nation und Nationalismus in Deutschland*, München 1993.

4   Jörg Echternkamp, *Der Aufstieg des deutschen Nationalismus 1770–1840*, Frankfurt 1998; Matthew Levinger, *Enlightened Nationalism. The Transformation of Prussian Political Culture, 1806–1848*, New York 2000.

5   Ernst Moritz Arndt, *Versuch einer Geschichte der Leibeigenschaft in Pommern und Rügen – Nebst einer Einleitung in die alte teutsche Leibeigenschaft*, Berlin 1803.

6   For the general topic, though one that focuses on the early modern period, Bronislaw Geremek, *Poverty. A History*, Oxford 1994, is indispensable.

meaning of "developing nation," both as a country undergoing a nationalist re-imagining and as a nation struggling to exit the poverty trap.

## Economic Development and Early Nationalism

In the early modern period, scholars who described their own nations did not think of poor people as part of "a horizontal comradeship." When sixteenth-century humanists, like the cosmographer Sebastian Münster, imagined "our Germany," as he put it, "as if in a mirror," he meant something like the cities and towns (not primarily the countryside) of the contiguous space in which German was spoken.[7] Approximating but not quite coterminous with the Holy Roman Empire, that space was the subject of major mapping efforts, geographies, spatially organized cosmographies (ordered according to continents, nations, regions, and cities and towns), humanistic poetry, disquisitions, and lamentations.[8] For Münster, who was central to this tradition of nation describing, the people of the nation also counted—only not as part of a "horizontal comradeship." This was because the people of a nation, the Germans, comprised different estates, with the mass of the people, the peasantry, the lowliest and least important. Rustics might be pitied for their burdens, or examined for their exotic customs, but never celebrated for their virtue. A quarter of a millennium later little had changed. Enlightened travelers either ignored them, studied their shapes (as the physiogamist Johann Caspar Lavater did), or denigrated them. A few reflected on how to ameliorate their miserable lot. But virtually no enlightened thinker wished to step out of his coach and walk among them.

The first glimmers of a shift away from this view did not occur until the second half of the eighteenth century, when a general warming allowed for a series of unbroken and bountiful harvests, allowing a general sense to arise that the rural population was finally winning its battle against what had

---

7    Cited in Helmut Walser Smith, *The Continuities of German History: Nation, Religion, and Race across the Long Nineteenth Century*, Cambridge 2008, 39.

8    On early modern conceptions of the German nation, as well as an extended discussion of how humanists described, measured, mapped, and viewed the nation, see Helmut Walser Smith, *Germany. A Nation in its Time. Before, During, and After Nationalism, 1500–2000*, New York 2020, 1–83.

seemed like an endless string of subsistence crises. As widespread undernourishment visited the countryside less and less, denizens of cities could slowly imagine their rural compatriots as part of the same cultural universe.[9]

The late eighteenth-century claim that the countryside, including the people who inhabited it, made the nation beautiful, worthy of praise, or a reason for pride, was a newer phenomenon than is often supposed. In Germany, it could be seen in the prose and poetry of the writers and poets of *Sturm and Drang* (foremost the philosopher Johann Gottfried Herder), the first wave of German intellectuals who celebrated the common people, including their language and customs, as the very basis for an imagined national community. As is well known, Herder's initial insight was about language, the mother tongue, which he extolled not for its laudable characteristics, or its ancientness, or even because it allowed one to understand the word of God, but rather because it was the language of parents and children, the natural language. Expressing how ordinary people loved and feared, and how they touched, saw, and heard the world around them, this natural language, according to Herder, could lead German poetry and literature back to its essential, original, uncorrupted voice.

Advanced by philosophers and poets employed by courts, this imagined vision of the common people included neither policy prescriptions for the problem of poverty nor a close description of the poor. Slowly, though, poverty would come to be seen as something other than a natural or an inevitable part of the order of things. Even as the poor were still pitied or blamed for their alleged moral deficiencies, the idea arose that poverty could be more than chipped at, and that its amelioration was "the true test of civilization," as Samuel Johnson put it in 1770.[10] In Great Britain, the nascent field of political economy—with its focus on the wealth of nations, or societies, and not just states, as was still the case with the cameralist sciences on the continent—developed in this circumstance. It was in the British context, too, that the first

---

9   Joel Mokyr/Hans-Joachim Voth, Understanding Growth in Europe, 1700–1870: Theory and Evidence, in: Stephen Broadberry/Kevin H. O'Rourke (eds.), *The Cambridge Economic History of Modern Europe*, vol. 1: *1700–1870*, Cambridge 2010, 7–42, see 19; Robert William Fogel, *The Escape from Hunger and Premature Death, 1700–2100*, Cambridge 2004, 6; Wolfgang Hardtwig, *Hochkultur des bürgerlichen Zeitalters*, Göttingen 2005, 176, 186.

10   Cited in Gertrude Himmelfarb, *The Idea of Poverty. England in the early Industrial Age*, New York 1984, 4.

extended descriptions of the poor arose, and in which the first critical surveys of urban blight appeared.

In the German lands, by contrast, economic development took a different turn in the first decades of the nineteenth century. As the British economy expanded, urbanization in the German lands continued to lag behind, and the Napoleonic Wars, the British blockade, and economic depression kept population growth in check. After 1815, when the German Confederation defined the boundaries of what was generally acknowledged to constitute the German nation, slow peacetime economic growth, mainly fueled by increases in agricultural productivity, led to higher levels of per capita consumption. But in the countryside, where the preponderance of people lived, these higher levels of consumption ended up reducing the average age of marriage and widening the window of female fertility, with larger families and regional overpopulation the result. Certain areas of Germany, especially the southwest, the central highlands, and Silesia, suddenly became vulnerable again to the very subsistence crises that had plagued early modern Europe for centuries. Bad harvests, triggered by crop failures and potato blight, created price hikes and led to misery for day laborers and poor artisans, who spent more than seventy percent of their income on food and had little or no cushion to absorb the higher prices. Armies of indigent were suddenly forced to rely on imperfectly organized systems of charity.

Germany was still a developing country, decades behind Great Britain in per capita GDP, and despite regional pockets of incipient industrialization, behind other leading nations in northwestern Europe as well.[11] In this comparative calculation, the data for "Germany" derives from the work of the demographer Ulrich Pfister. Based on extrapolations from smaller samples of a series of cities and towns, it represents the values of places within the territorial boundaries of the German nation state in 1871.

If the shifting historical boundaries of "Germany," and still more the rudimentary collection of statistics, makes the comparison imperfect, major

---

11    Jutta Bolt/Jan Luiten van Zanden, *"GDP per Capita"*. *IISH Data Collection, V1. Data* (2015), <https://hdl.handle.net/10622/8FCYOX> [last accessed: September 30, 2021], also accessible at: Max Roser, *Economic Growth* (2013), <https://ourworldindata.org/economic-growth> [last accessed: September 30, 2021]. For Germany, the pre-1850 data is based largely on Ulrich Pfister, *Economic Growth in Germany, 1500–1850*, paper presented to the Quantifying Long Run Economic Development Conference, University of Warwick in Venice, 22-24 March 2011.

*Figure 1: GDP per capita, 1775 to 1900*

GDP per capita, 1775 to 1900

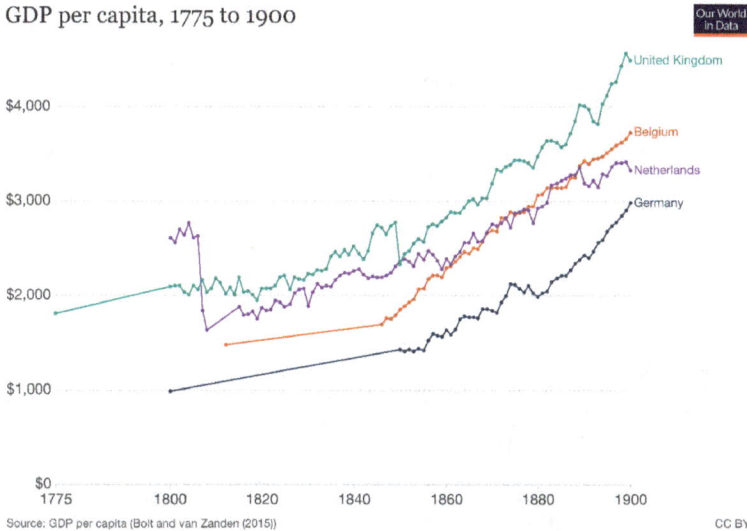

Source: GDP per capita (Bolt and van Zanden (2015))                                    CC BY

Source: Jutta Bolt/Jan Luiten van Zanden, "GDP per Capita". IISH Data Collection, V1. Data (2015), <https://hdl.handle.net/10622/8FCYOX> [last accessed: September 30, 2021], also accessible at: <https://ourworldindata.org/economic-growth>.

economic indicators, like real wages, nevertheless offer a revealing window onto the past.[12] In the 1840s, for example, German construction workers trailed the earnings of similar workers in England and France, were on par with those in northern Italy (and were just beyond what a worker in Tokugawa Japan or the Yangtze Basin in China might earn).[13] Infant mortality, a negative indicator of life chances, tells a similarly bleak story. Germany's rate of infant mortality remained among the highest in western Europe, with nearly thirty percent of German children dying before the age of one, and more than forty percent dying by the age of five.[14] These alarming high

---

12   For a discussion of the method, Pfister, *Growth*, 3.

13   Carole Shammas, Standard of Living, Consumption, and Political Economy over the Past 500 Years, in: Frank Trentman (ed.), *The Oxford Handbook of the History of Consumption*, Oxford 2012, 211–228, see 218–219.

14   Etienne van de Walle, Historical Demography, in: Dudley L. Poston/Michael Micklin (eds.), *Handbook of Population*, New York 2005, 577–600, see 591–592; Loftur Guttorms-

rates also brought down figures for life expectancy, which in 1820 hovered at thirty-three years, placing Germany behind the United States, Great Britain, France, and Sweden, and just ahead of the lands of Italy and Poland.[15]

*Figure 2: Child mortality, 1800 to 1900*

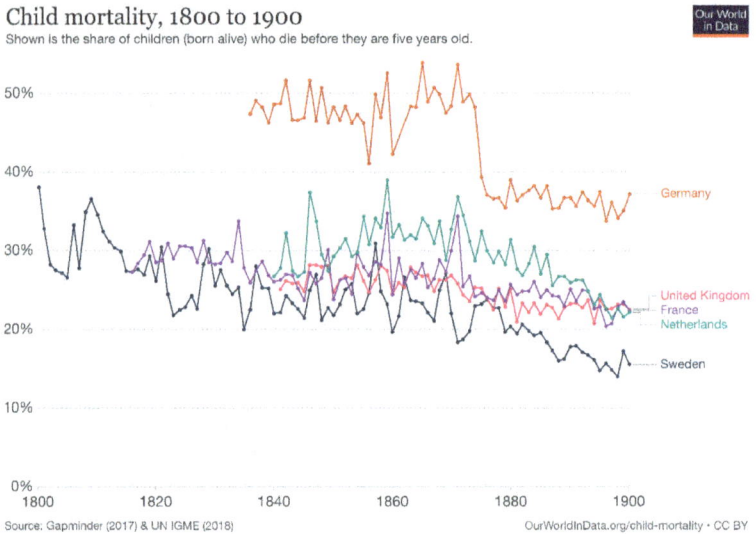

Child mortality, 1800 to 1900
Shown is the share of children (born alive) who die before they are five years old.

Source: Max Roser/Hannah Ritchie/Bernadeta Dadonaite, Child and Infant Mortality (2013), <https://ourworldindata.org/child-mortality> [last accessed: September 30, 2021].

Taken together, central economic indicators for Germany in the early nineteenth century placed it closer to Mexico around 1900, Brazil around 1950, and India around 1990. And as was the case for these developing economies, it was not the absolute levels of poverty so much as the inequality

---

son, Parent-Child Relations, in: David I. Kertzer/Mario Barbagli (eds.), *Family Life in the Long Nineteenth Century: 1789–1913*, New Haven 2002, 251–281, see 254–255; Şevket Pamuk/Jan Luiten van Zanden, Standards of Living, in: Stephen Broadberry/Kevin H. O'Rourke (eds.), *The Cambridge Economic History of Modern Europe*, vol. 1: 1700–1870, Cambridge 2010, 217–234, see 227.

15   Pamuk/Zanden, Standards, 227.

between nations, and between classes within the nation, that sensitized German intellectuals to the disparities between rich and poor.

## Friedrich List

One person who would come to understand the deleterious effects of inequality between nations was Friedrich List. Born in the Württemberg town of Reutlingen in 1789, List led an unremarkable life until 1817, when as an assessor in the employ of his home state he interviewed some two hundred destitute subjects leaving for the Americas.[16] Taking measure of their desperation and its causes, List noted that most of the emigrants were not the dissolute rabble they had been made to appear. Rather, according to List, they comprised "strong men" and their families, eager and willing to work.[17] Only they faltered in the face exorbitant taxes, a cumbersome bureaucracy, corrupt officials, and a lethargic court system.

Initially, List's main focus was the failure of the state of Württemberg to ameliorate a difficult circumstance. There was as yet little structural analysis of the underlying causes, such as the burdens of the Napoleonic Wars, or the abrupt and temporary cooling that occurred in the wake of the eruption of Tambura in 1815, creating failed harvests and higher mortality for livestock throughout the northern hemisphere. Nor did List speculate that population pressure was beginning to develop as more and more people divided the land into ever smaller and less efficient parcels. Instead, he simply implored officials to redress wrongs and in this way reinstate an equilibrium.

List's Memorandum concerning the emigrants of 1817 reminds us that early nineteenth-century Europe was mainly an agricultural world, and the vast majority of wealth creation still had to be eked out from the earth. It also reminds us that states existed in order to augment the glory and power of

---

16    See three letters from Friedrich List to the Württembergische Ministerium des Innern, May 1, May 3, and May 7, 1817, in: Friedrich List, *Schriften, Reden, Briefe*, vol. 8: *Tagebücher und Briefe, 1812–1846*, ed. by Edgar Salin, Berlin 1933, 101–108.

17    List to the Württembergische Ministerium des Innern, May 1, 1817, in: List, *Schriften*, 101. On this episode, Günter Moltmann/Ingrid Schöberl (eds.), *Aufbruch nach Amerika: Friedrich List und die Auswanderung aus Baden u. Württemberg 1816/17: Dokumentation einer sozialen Bewegung*, Tübingen 1979. See also Roman Szporluk, *Communism and Nationalism: Karl Marx versus Friedrich List*, Oxford 1993, 96–97.

dynastic houses, not to care for the welfare of the population, and that over-population did not yet haunt the corridors of power. On the contrary, reigning cameralist doctrine held that states benefitted from population increases, and measured the power of realms by the number of souls in a state's possession.[18]

Slowly, however, the specter of overpopulation began to take hold, and the first country to register its effects was England. In the *Principles of Population*, first published anonymously in 1798, Robert Malthus predicted that while the amount of cultivable land grows at an arithmetic ratio, population expands geometrically, doubling, as indeed it was beginning to do, every twenty-five years. "In two centuries," Malthus calculated, "the population would be to the means of subsistence as 256 to 9."[19] Given this ratio, the ability of agriculture to improve yields would simply never keep up with the increase in population. Instead, the population, which seemed to surge as wealth increased, would always be confined to penury, with few ways out of this viscous cycle. One was birth control, which Malthus discounted given the supposed inability of the laboring classes to discipline themselves. The others—war, famine, and disease—were less pleasant.

In *On the Principles of Political Economy and Taxation*, published in 1817, David Ricardo, the leading economist of the period, proffered a view hardly less bleak.[20] Positing three basic factors—labor, capital, and land—Ricardo envisioned initial progress for the first two, but diminishing returns for the third, as the most fecund land had already been put to plow, and technological innovations only brought limited advantage. It was, paradoxically, the well-situated landowners who stood to benefit the most from this impasse. As industrial capitalism progressed, population increased, and with it the demand for food, driving up the price, leading to misery for the many and pecuniary gain for the few who owned especially fertile land. From the perspective of capital and labor, the solution for Great Britain was international trade, in which Britain possessed a comparative advantage in manufactured goods, which it could exchange for primary products, notably grain. In this exchange, both sides stood to gain: Great Britain received cheaper grain while the other country, with lower agricultural costs, received manufactured items. Conversely, if tariffs, like the infamous Corn Law of 1815, were erected, only the powerful landowners won, and everyone else lost.

---

18    On how states counted, see Smith, *Germany*, 101–103.

19    Thomas Robert Malthus, *An Essay on the Principle of Population*, London 1798.

20    David Ricardo, *On the Principles of Political Economy and Taxation*, London 1817.

Ricardo saw overpopulation as essentially a national problem. But he found a global solution to it—the doctrine of comparative advantage in international trade. List, not yet deeply immersed in what contemporaries referred to as the "dismal science" of economics, saw a local problem, and blamed the mismanagement of the state of Württemberg. Other solutions glimmered only faintly on the horizon. The massive waves of European emigration to the new world had just commenced, and the so-called "great transition" (in which a declining birth rate would follow a reduction in the death rate, as occurred in the second half of the nineteenth century) would not pick up pace for another fifty years.[21] The ideas of Malthus, which List would not begin to reference until 1830, and of Ricardo, which List knew as early as 1820, would soon suggest the complexities of international disparities in wealth in the early phases of northwestern Europe's industrial revolution.[22] Yet if Malthus and Ricardo saw the problem from the vantage of the comparatively rich countries, List would come to see it from the perspective of the poorer nations.

List would first begin to see it this way when exiled in a rapidly developing country: the United States. Displeased with List's suggestions that corruption was in part to blame for the emigrant misfortunes, List's superiors in Württemberg had him arrested, jailed, and eventually banished. List thereafter lived in exile, eventually becoming a citizen of the United States, where he worked as a farmer, businessman, journalist, and political propagandist for Andrew Jackson. In the young republic, List witnessed the benefits of unfettered entrepreneurship, participated in a major railway boom, and saw the sagacity in the protectionism practiced by the first decolonized country in the world (and justified by economists of the "national school" who insisted that young economies need protection in an international environment where the terms of trade were skewed against them).[23] When List returned to the continent in 1832, he made precisely this argument about his own country, which

---

21 On the pace of the transition, George Alter/Gregory Clark, The Demographic Transition and Human Capital, in: Stephen Broadberry/Kevin H. O'Rourke (eds.), *The Cambridge Economic History of Modern Europe*, vol. 1: 1700–1870, Cambridge 2010, 43–69.

22 List, *Schriften*, vol. 8, 215, List to von Cotta, May 1, 1822 (for Ricardo); 385–386, List to President Andrew Jackson, draft, October 19, 1930 (for Malthus).

23 By 1840, it had already surpassed all of Europe, including Great Britain, in track mileage. See Winfried Baumgart/Heinz Duchhardt/Franz Knipping (eds.), *Handbuch der Geschichte der internationalen Beziehungen*, vol. 6, Paderborn 2007, 26; Szporluk, *Communism*, 110.

he now thought of not as Württemberg but as Germany, by which he meant, as was typical of the time, the German Confederation, including Austria.

Germany, List argued, should be safeguarded against the unfair invasion of foreign goods. A customs union was a first step, and List originally conceived of it for Germany's small southern states. But sprawling Prussia pursued it first, eliminating internal tariffs among its provinces, then extending favorable conditions and entry to its neighbors, and eventually uniting, step by step in the 1830s and 1840s, other German states behind a common tariff wall.[24] List thought the wall too low, especially in view of the dominant position of British industry. "It is not yet safe for the lamb to lay with the lion," he wrote in Paris in 1837 in his *Le Système Naturel d'Économie Politique* (*The Natural System of Political Economy*), in which he described for the first time his scheme involving three stages of economic growth: in the first, a country has mainly agriculture with some trade; in the second, it possesses infant industries; and in the third, industry is prevalent throughout the nation.[25] In his celebrated, extended treatise on economic development, *Das nationale System der politischen Ökonomie* (*The National System of Political Economy*), published with its telling new title in 1843, List explicated the concept of stages more fully, and showed how tariff levels should conform to stages of economic development. He also decried "cosmopolitan economics," accused Britain of "smothering in the cradle the infant manufacturers on the continent," and derided the terms of trade that made Germany into a British India.[26]

India was indeed the cautionary tale. As Britain industrialized, India deindustrialized. As manufacturing in Manchester and the Midlands grew, the same activity in Behar and the Ganges river basin declined. But in the 1830s, when List began to write about tariff levels, few saw the degree to which English textile output would ruin India's nascent textile manufacturing sector, undercut its flourishing textile sector, and obliterate India's shared of global manufacturing—reducing it from 25% of world output in 1750 to barely one percent in 1880.[27] Fewer still discerned the mechanism involved, namely that

---

24    James M. Brophy, The End of the Economic Old Order: The Great Transition, 1750–1860, in: Helmut Walser Smith (ed.), The *Oxford Handbook of Modern German History*, Oxford 2011, 169–194.

25    Friedrich List, *Schriften, Reden, Briefe*, vol. 4: *Das nationale System der politischen Ökonomie*, ed. by Edgar Salin, Berlin 1927, 326–327.

26    List, *Schriften*, vol. 4, 182–183.

27    Richard Allen, *Global Economic History. A Very Short Introduction*, Oxford 2011, 6, 8.

that free trade constituted a disincentive for the trailing nation to invest in capital intensive manufacturing, the royal road out of the poverty trap.

The "dismal science," as Thomas Carlyle called economics, was still in its infancy. It remained mired in the assumptions embedded in Adam Smith's *Wealth of Nations*, namely that the division of labor, and not technology coupled with investment in capital intensive industries, was the principal driver of economic growth.[28] Both in Britain and on the continent, economists were only beginning to see just how explosive machinery was in macro-economic terms, or the importance of leading sectors—meaning that it mattered little to England that the impact of technological change was mainly confined to the textile industry. They were also just starting to understand that the higher costs of labor, as existed in Britain, actually encouraged still more investment in research and in capital intensive industries, and therefore had the counter-intuitive effect of being an enormous boost for an economy set to take off. And finally, they only imperfectly understood the degree to which Britain's comparative advantage in a period of rapid technological change and declining shipping costs crippled other countries.

What List did know, however, was that the history of American economic growth diverged significantly from the story of India's decline. Lack of protection, high population, and lower labor costs had stunted India's economic growth. Was it not possible that protection, a low population, and high labor costs, the exact opposite of India's situation, fueled America's incipient take off?

Another advantage America had was its railroads—in List's lifetime, the United States became the world leader in laying down track, and List had tried, unsuccessfully, to capitalize on this nascent industry. He certainly understood its importance. If protective tariffs was one precondition for development, the railroad was the other. In a series of essays, part conception, part plea, List sketched out the grids that would tie diverse parts of Germany closer together, allow its influence to expand, and liberate Europe from "war, national hate, and unemployment, ignorance, and laziness."[29]

Here too List was acutely aware of the international comparisons. In his lifetime, the United States and Great Britain had significant interconnected

---

28    Gareth Stedman Jones, *An End to Poverty. A Historical Debate*, New York 2004, 175.

29    Friedrich List, *Das deutsche National-Transport-System in volks- und staatswirthschaftlicher Beziehung*, Altona 1838, 6.

rail systems, drawing these countries together in national terms but also reducing shipping costs and expanding domestic markets. So too did Belgium and the Netherlands. By contrast, Germany's rails remained sporadic and isolated. They consisted of mainly short, privately financed regional railways in Upper Silesia, the Eifel, along part of the Upper Rhine, in Bavaria (connecting Munich to Augsburg, and Nuremberg to Bamberg), and in Schleswig-Holstein. In this system, only Prussia and Saxony were relatively well connected from south to north, with tracks leading from Crimetschau (the Ore Mountains) and Dresden through Leipzig and to Berlin and Stettin on the North Sea. Increased state investment could help tie the railroads together, List argued, with obvious benefits from the standpoint of unity and defense. As important, improved infrastructure would increase economic development and ameliorate poverty.

The key was closing the gap, creating a convergence. Free trade, while maximizing efficiencies in the abstract, ill-served developing economies trying to enter the world market. Conversely, unifying home markets by the elimination of internal tariffs, erection of external duties against British dominance, and infrastructure investment could all raise Germany to the higher ranks of manufacturing nations. Monetary standardization and stabilization would help as well, as would the liberalization of credit, as these measures would ease the flow of capital to machines in order to increase the value of labor. List also underscored the importance of an educated workforce, and noted that the German lands had pursued a different path in this realm. While Germany had fallen behind in industrial indexes and markers of material well-being, it remained on par in literacy, primary schooling, and book production.

List clearly thought as a nationalist. But his place in the canon of nationalist thinkers has been skewed by focusing on his economic prescriptions that seem to have led to national unification, like customs unions and railway construction, while ignoring the wider spectrum of List's economic insights. Moreover, his nationalism, often evidenced by his anti-English sentiment, was not about German superiority. Rather, it was a nationalism concerned to close an economic gap, to pull the lamb, Germany, closer to the lion, Great Britain. The logic had a global dimension in its time, as it does in our own. And this is that the gap often confines whole populations caught on the wrong side of comparative advantage equations to persistent inequality, including its most enduring and visible marker: poverty.

## Bettina von Arnim

The novelty of a figure like List should not be underestimated. Thinkers throughout the ages have contemplated how to ameliorate the lot of the poor. Absolutist governments had attempted to mitigate the worst of it—Frederick the Great's famous order to plant potatoes rather than rye, for example. But sustained arguments that poverty could be eradicated, that it was not a natural but rather a historical phenomenon, did not occur until circa 1770, when, at least in England, productive potential allowed for the possibility that poverty could be more than scratched at.[30]

In central Europe, the fundamental insight—that poverty and penury were not the warp and woof of the natural order but rather situational and eradicable—followed circuitous routes. Enunciated first by enlightened economists and advice givers, the new attitude followed the heightened optimism of the French Revolution and early utopian socialism, then thickened as a consequence of the panicked discussion of the transmission of Cholera in 1832, and finally became broad-based through religious communities that insisted on this-world improvement in the conditions of life.[31] By the 1840s, hundreds of Christian and Jewish groups dedicated their energies to helping the poor. They collected money, food, clothing and coal for heat, engaged in pedagogical work, and cared for orphaned and neglected children. Books, pamphlets, petitions, and articles on what came to be known as the social question had by this time exploded onto the public sphere. A wide spectrum of writers decried instances of extreme poverty wherever it was found. Ranging from influential Prussian officials to dismayed county commissioners, engaged priests and pastors to rough edged novelists, these authors also included early advocates of state social welfare, political economists, medical doctors, statisticians, and radical school teachers. Their criticisms were often caustic and withering.

Not even the budding capital of Prussia was spared scrutiny. By 1828, according to one calculation, the number of Berlin families below the poverty line had quadrupled since 1815, and stood at sixteen percent of all families.[32]

---

30  See especially Himmelfarb, *Idea*.
31  This section draws on Smith, *Germany*, 224–225.
32  Ilja Mieck, Von der Reformzeit zur Revolution (1815–1848), in: Wolfgang Ribbe (ed.), *Geschichte Berlins, vol 1: Von der Frühgeschichte bis zur Industrialisierung*, München 1987, 407–602, see 495.

Especially alarming were developments near Berlin's Hamburg Gate, where in the slums of the so-called Vogtland a community of some 2000 people were pressed into some 400 rooms in a dismal series of shoddily-built tenement houses. Originally drawing from migrants from the poverty-stricken hills of southern Thuringia, the so-called "family houses" of the Vogtland were increasingly filled with Berlin's own poor.

Fervent Christians were the first do something about the plight of the local poor—even if they often blamed the poor for their own poverty, and chastened them for dissolute lives and excessive drink. By 1827, local Christians had already begun to organize devotional hours on Wednesdays and Sundays in the tenements; by 1831, an Association of Christian Men were dedicating themselves to opening a free school in the tenements; and by 1832, clergymen had begun to hold continual Sunday services in the bleak rows of housing. Within a few years, these arrangements became more permanent. Christians also set up soup kitchens, associations to help the sick and injured, and stations to help the poor find employment, however temporary.

Soon city officials also began to be alarmed by the slums on the outskirts of Berlin. In 1927, a certain Dr. Thümmel, the so-called "*Armenarzt*" of the Berlin Poor Commission, inspected the tenements and found malnourished renters, often suffering from severe ailments, like tuberculosis, dropsy, or pneumonia. Like the Christian reformers, Thümmel placed much of the blame on the poor themselves. In an utterly unsparing report to the Berlin poor Commission, he noted that the men were habitually inebriated, human waste and ordinary garbage (collected in buckets) was frequently left standing in the corridors, and children were often raised in disgusting filth.[33] Although Thümmel's report was roundly and rightly criticized for exaggeration, subsequent events seemed to bear out his opinions. In 1831, Cholera hit Berlin, and while it effected just under one percent of all Berliners, in the Vogtland tenement houses it struck close to ten percent of the people, with a death rate of those who fell ill around 60%.[34]

In this context, it would seem unlikely that a romantic author famous for her childhood letters to Goethe would emerge with a unique voice. Yet Bettina von Arnim was no ordinary person. A vital presence in the Berlin intellectual scene with an important role in the local court society, she was attentive to

---

[33]    The report is reprinted in Johan Friedrich Geist/Klaus Kürvers, *Das Berliner Mietshaus*, vol. 1: *1740–1862*, München 1980, 194–199.

[34]    Geist/Kürvers, *Mietshaus*, 154.

the discussions about the poor and acutely aware of the grim situation on the outskirts of the city. But unlike previous commentators, she focused less on the structure of poverty than the on the individuals who experienced it; and she wrote for the new king, Friedrich Wilhelm IV, in the hope that he would intervene.

She did not conduct her investigations alone. In the tradition of Friedrich Engels, who was guided through the bleak tenements of Manchester by the young Mary Burns, von Arnim engaged and paid for the help of a Swiss schoolteacher, Heinrich Grunholzer, who had moved to Berlin to study at its new university. Having met Grunholzer at the apartment of the Brothers Grimm, von Arnim asked him to make numerous trips—more than thirty in all—to the tenements in order to talk with families, inspect the rooms where they huddled together, and record his impressions. The shaping hand of Grunholzer, who would later return to Switzerland and emerge as a contentious, radical figure in the field of pedagogy, should not be under-estimated. He was her eyes, ears, and to a significant extent her pen. In 1843, Bettina von Arnim was nearly sixty years old, and there is little direct evidence to suggest that she went to the Vogtland herself (though many contemporaries assumed she had).[35]

Nevertheless, von Arnim used Grunholzer's reports, reworking them only slightly. In *This Book Belongs to the King*, those reports emerged as sparse stories of aging but proud soldiers, underemployed spinners and weavers, widows and widowers desperately trying to feed their children, and workers whose injuries and illnesses kept them from attaining a livelihood.[36] The most re-markable thing about the poor as portrayed here was their basic stance—their *Haltung*. Loyal to their regent, ashamed of their own poverty, they were hum-ble people, and they made only modest appeals for help. Indeed, the book adduces many examples of how the denizens of the Vogtland helped each other, sparing a bit of coffee here, lending a Schilling there, taking care of the elderly among them, and giving every last measure to allow their children to attend school. Utterly absent from von Arnim's pages are the pietistic dia-tribes against the general degeneracy of the poor or the lurid descriptions of filth that had filled Thümmel's depictions of the tenements in 1827. Instead, von Arnim thought the poor's comradeship with each other impressive, and

---

35    Wolfgang Bunzel/Ulrike Landfester/Walter Schmitz/Sibylle von Steinsdorff (eds.), *Bet-tine von Arnim – Werke*, vol. 3: *Politische Schriften*, Frankfurt am Main 1995, 843.

36    Bunzel et al., *Arnim*, 331–368.

asked her readers to see the impoverished with a measure of understanding and empathy.

Despite modest sales—less than a thousand copies in the first year—the book was reviewed widely and discussed across the spectrum of opinions, with the arc of its reception ranging from the emerging circles of Communists around Karl Marx on the left to strict conservative Lutherans on the right.[37] Meanwhile, the inexperienced king vacillated in his opinions, and the ever-scheming courtiers turned a deaf ear to von Arnim's appeals to empathy.

To appreciate the audacity of von Arnim's depiction of the Vogtland, it helps to recall the novelty of sociologically precise depictions of the poor. The earliest ones—such as James Whitelaw's *An Essay on the Population of Dublin* (1805) and James Phillips Kay's *The Moral and Physical Condition of the Working Class Employed in the Cotton Manufacture in Manchester* (1832)—had been written by statisticians.[38] Fueled by moral outrage, these authors heaped dry facts upon forbidding statistics, creating a sense of dismal certainty. Official publications constituted a second tradition. Edwin Chadwick's grimly detailed *Report on the Sanitary Conditions of the Labouring Population of Great Britain* (1842), which appeared just a year before von Arnim's book, was no doubt the most famous.[39] Informative, policy-oriented, the official reports tended to lay bare the structural ills that kept people in poverty. Yet like the analyses of the statisticians, these accounts paid scant attention to individuals, rarely even telling us their names. Friedrich Engels' subsequently famous *The Condition of the Working Class in England*, which appeared the year after von Arnim's book (to a much narrower contemporary reception), was no different in this regard. In his hurry to amass "facts, facts, facts," Engels barely allowed workers to speak.[40] In von Arnim's work, they did not actually speak either—as Grunholzer noted in a long letter he wrote to von Arnim after the book's publication. In that letter, he conceded that he "did not illuminate the interesting side of poverty ... what the poor think about their own condition."[41]

---

37    Bunzel et al., *Arnim*, 847.

38    Mike Davis, *A Planet of Slums*, London 2006, 20–21.

39    On Chadwick, see Himmelfarb, *Idea*, 356–360.

40    Tristram Hunt, *Marx's General: The Revolutionary Life of Friedrich Engels*, London 2010, 77, 109.

41    Grunholzer to von Arnim, November 21, 1843, reprinted in: Bunzel et al., *Arnim*, 1050–1060.

The possibilities of penetrating deeper into the world of the poor nevertheless transfixed Bettina von Arnim. In the early months of 1844, less than a year after the publication of *This Book Belongs to the King*, the misery of the weavers of Silesia set the pens in motion of would-be German ethnographers of the poor, and von Arnim was arguably the most prominent among them. Writing to doctors, medical statisticians, local officials, and factory owners, she implored friends, colleagues, and acquaintances to send her material. She also placed public calls for material in regional newspapers, like the *Breslauer Zeitung* and the *Magdeburger Zeitung*, using her celebrity status to encourage people to help her "erect a permanent monument to the German nation."[42]

Her informants sent her statistics, newspaper clips, and interviews. Some of her material was ordered like Grunholzer's notes on the Vogtland, as was the case of the "Poor Lists" of Leutmannsdorf. Some lists were sparser, like the register of the "poor, vulnerable wage earners in the community of Michelsdorf," which begins with a forty-six-year-old widower, August Haag, deep in debt, and needing to care for his own father as well as a four-year old child.[43] And some lists, like the one describing the "poorest and most vulnerable weavers in Altfriedland," were more parsimonious still, telling us only the barest information about name, age, number of family members, earnings, taxes and rent.[44] Taken together, the lists offered shocking evidence of squalor and struggle: they told of the ailments of old soldiers and widowed mothers, how many people slept in a room, what they ate ("mostly soup from dark flour, a bit of bread and small amounts of potatoes"), and what they wore ("mostly a cloak of rags" and "are in seldom cases in possession of a Sunday dress, which is why so many are hindered from participating in holy services").[45]

Von Arnim also began to conceptualize the Silesian material in a new way. In her drafts, she wrote about the spinners and weavers of Silesia not as an "other," and not as "a terrible counterweight" to existing society, but rather, and precisely, as "the people."[46] What is more, they were more authentically "the people" than the rich, who derived their virtue from luxury, are blind

---

42   Bunzel et al., *Arnim*, 1072.
43   Bunzel et al., *Arnim*, 375.
44   Bunzel et al., *Arnim*, 378.
45   Bunzel et al., *Arnim*, 411.
46   Bunzel et al., *Arnim*, 331.

to the poor, and have no real attachment to the fatherland. "When I talk to poverty I talk to the people, *das Volk*," she wrote.[47]

It is possible to dismiss this gesture as a quintessentially bourgeois tactic of artificial harmonization. Class, it might be said of von Arnim, was something she literally could not see, or admit to, especially if class is not understood as "structure" or "category," but instead, in E.P. Thompson's classic if agonistic formulation, as something that in fact happens.

> "And class happens when some men, as a result of common experiences (inherited or shared), feel and articulate the identity of their interests as between themselves, and as against other men whose interests are different from (and usually opposed to) theirs."[48]

By contrast, von Arnim smoothed solidarities based on class antagonism into a vision of how the poor helped each other, while eliding class conflict by focusing on individuals.

Yet it bears recalling that in the early nineteenth century, class conflict was not yet the obvious way forward, and equality, in the sense of obliterating differences between classes, was at this point a less urgent matter than alleviating extreme poverty. In this sense, too, Germany looked more like developing countries than historians, writing from the vantage of the late nineteenth-century and from the perspective of a remarkably successful socialist movement, have allowed. When we begin to see this, the perspective of von Arnim, emphasizing the horizontal kinship of nationhood, and consensual aspects of the relations between classes, comes more clearly to the fore. After all, if the history of populism teaches nothing else, it is surely that class conflict cannot simply be assumed to be the natural vocabulary for understanding the experience of the poor. What Bettina von Arnim did sense is that empathy is crucial, and that *das Volk* (the people) has the potential to be an inclusive category, at least within the bounds of the imagined community of the nation.

In June 1844, history turned out very differently, however. In the very towns whose poverty von Arnim hoped to describe, the weavers revolted, and the authorities blamed Bettina von Arnim for animating aspirations and raising false hopes. Despite von Arnim's status in polite society, the Prussian government promptly forbade publication of what was as yet an unfin-

---

47    Bunzel et al., *Arnim*, 528.

48    Edward P. Thompson, *The Making of the English Working Class*, Harmondsworth 1980, 8–9.

ished manuscript. Sharp-eyed and intelligent but no revolutionary, von Arnim stopped her work, and her so-called *Armenbuch* remained in a drawer.

Neither an early proletarian revolution nor the desperate scream of the hungry, the Silesian Weavers Revolt of 1844 was in essence a demand for better wages.[49] Directed at factory owners and their merchants who bought home woven cotton at depressed prices, the accompanying anger spilled from verbal tirades to revengeful destruction of property. But far from being revolutionary, the weaver's demands were local; protesters called for a just price for their homespun products and assumed the king had no knowledge of how the rich treated the poor. Not even the poorest of the poor, the rebellious cotton weavers still lived within four sturdy walls, wore untorn clothes on their backs, and hunger did not belong to their complaints. But rather than receive justice, or empathy, the protesters were fired on, killing eleven, wounding many more, with women and children among them. In the process, an old regime style protest alchemized into a dismal and dismaying tragedy.

## Germany as a Developing Nation

To place the German case in its wider context, it may help to consider two "facts" concerning the relationship between nations, states, and poverty. The first fact is that until very recently—circa 1950—nearly two-thirds of the population of the world lived in extreme poverty, with "extreme poverty" defined by a UN baseline of $1.90 per day.[50] If we factor in what development economists think of as multidimensional poverty (a way of defining and indexing poverty that includes data on health and education), this figure will be higher still—meaning more people will be seen as living in conditions of extreme poverty. The weight of this statistic for the German story becomes evident when we remember that the "Great Divergence" between the northwestern corner of Europe and Asia did not commence until the middle of the nineteenth century.[51] In terms of comparative development, this implies that

---

49  Christine von Hodenberg, *Aufstand der Weber: Die Revolte von 1844 und ihr Aufstieg zum Mythos*, Bonn 1997.

50  See the relation chart in "World Population in Extreme Poverty," in: Max Roser/Esteban Ortiz-Ospina, *Global Extreme Poverty* (2013), <https://ourworldindata.org/extreme-poverty> [last accessed: September 30, 2021].

51  The decisive text is, of course, Kenneth Pomeranz, *The Great Divergence. China, Europe, and the Making of the Modern World Economy*, Princeton 2000. For a recent assessment

until the 1860s, the German lands faced challenges akin to those of developing economies throughout the world.

To illustrate this admittedly abstract contention, consider how a crude measure (GDP per capita) of nineteenth-century German development for a single year aligns with the year in which that same GDP per capita is achieved in a series of developing countries. For Germany, the economist Jutta Boldt and Jan Luitan van Zeeden offer a general estimate for 1800 and the first non-interpolated data for 1850. In 1800, they estimate Germany's GDP per capita in international dollars (in 1990 prices) was $986.00 and $1428.00 in 1850. Let us round these figures to $1,000 and $1,500 respectively, and consider in which year other nations achieved these benchmarks.

*Table 1*

| German Benchmark | 1800 | 1850 |
|---|---|---|
| United Kingdom | <1660 | <1700 |
| Argentina | c. 1820 | 1870 |
| Chile | 1860 | 1879 |
| Mexico | 1895 | 1905 |
| Japan | 1892 | 1916 |
| Venezuela | 1917 | 1924 |
| El Salvador | 1939 | 1952 |
| Brazil | 1931 | 1956 |
| Congo | 1951* | 1959 |
| Egypt | 1961 | 1976 |
| India | 1983 | 1995 |
| Ghana | 1950* | 2004 |

< = already higher than the German mark;
c. = circa (interpolated value)
* already slightly above the German mark at the time of independence.
Source: Jutta Bolt/Jan Luiten van Zanden, "GDP per Capita". IISH Data Collection, V1. Data (2015), <https://hdl.handle.net/10622/8FCYOX> [last accessed: September 30, 2021].

of the wide-ranging debate, see Victor Court, A Reassessment of the Great Divergence Debate: Towards a Reconciliation of Apparently Distinct Determinants, in: *European Review of Economic History* 24 (4/2020), 633–674.

One must underscore the inexactitude of the data and recall that GDP per capita tells us nothing about the distribution of wealth, or about other markers of well-being, including access to education, health, and the availability of food in times of dearth. Nevertheless, the rough figures underscore a general point, and this is that in many ways the early nineteenth-century German case reflects structural parameters closer to any number of developing nations than to the contemporaneous case of the United Kingdom.

The second "fact" is that the populations of many newly independent nations lived close to or even below Germany's early nineteenth-century level of GDP per capita. In numerical terms, this will become obvious when we consider that in 1945, forty-five sovereign countries comprised the United Nations, whereas thirty years later, in 1975, that number had increased to 151 countries. Most of those countries were recently decolonized nations in Africa and Asia, and typically their GDP per capita were in the range of Germany's between 1800 and 1850. A few examples from Africa will suffice:

*Table 2*

|  | Year of independence | GDP/Capita in that year |
|---|---|---|
| Tunisia | 1956 | $1223.00 |
| Morocco | 1956 | $1451.00 |
| Cameroon | 1960 | $832.00 |
| Senegal | 1960 | $14445.00 |
| DR Congo | 1960 | $748.00 |
| Algeria | 1962 | $1433.00 |
| Kenya | 1963 | $726.00 |
| Mozambique | 1975 | $1404.00 |

Source: Jutta Bolt/Jan Luiten van Zanden, *"GDP per Capita". IISH Data Collection, V1. Data* (2015), <https://hdl.handle.net/10622/8FCYOX> [last accessed: September 30, 2021].

Note the proximity of GDP per capita of Tunisia, Morocco, Senegal, and Mozambique to Germany in 1850. Note too that Cameroon, the Democratic Republic of Congo, and Kenya began below Germany's interpolated 1800 mark. But there is a great difference, and it is not about the relation of pre-independence nationalist movements to poverty, but rather about the divergence between economic growth in Saharan Africa and post-independence economic stagnation and decline to the south. It would take us too far afield to explicate this divergence. Suffice that development economists, like Paul Collier, Abhijit V. Banerjee, and Esther Duflo have begun to shy away from single-explanation approaches, and tend to cite a range of factors—such as the persistence of armed conflict, an overconcentration on a single natural resource, an undeveloped infrastructure, and bad governance. These factors, they argue, turned the tables against "the bottom billion," and dragged down countries already adversely affected by skewed terms of trade with developed nations.[52]

For the argument advanced here, germane is simply the relative proximity of a range of developing countries to the German lands prior to the Revolution of 1848. It must be remembered, after all, that for those who lived through German history in this period, they had no reliable idea of what the future would bring. It was entirely possible that the violence of the Revolution of 1848 would unfold in altogether different dimensions, as occurred in France and then Europe following the Revolution of 1789. It was likewise possible that the Austro-Prussian War of 1866 would not have ended with a swift Prussian victory and an equally swift concession, but may have, as many feared, dragged out for a number of years, as did the American Civil War. Friedrich List's concern that Germany could not protect its infant industries was likewise not entirely off the mark either, even if it is hard to imagine the German lands enduring the full scale of damage that Great Britain inflicted on the economic development of nineteenth century India.

The point is simply to bring like histories together—both within and beyond Europe. Admittedly, this point is not new, and it was, in fact, a standard claim of economic history, labor history, and the history of everyday life. As E.P. Thompson famously put it in 1963:

> "... the greater part of the world today is still undergoing problems of industrialization, and of the formation of democratic institutions, analogous in many ways to our own experience during the Industrial Revolution. Causes which were lost in England might, in Asia or Africa, yet be won."[53]

Nearly sixty years later, a great deal has changed. Perhaps the single most important transformation is that when Thompson wrote these remarks, more

---

52    Abhijiy V. Banerjee/Esther Duflo, *Poor Economics. A Radical Rethinking of the Way to Fight Global Poverty*, New York 2011; Paul Collier, *The Bottom Billion. Why the Poorest Countries are Failing and What can be Done about it*, Oxford 2007.

53    Thompson, *The Making of the English Working Class*, 13.

than half the world lived in extreme poverty, as defined by the UN benchmark of less than $1.90 a day. Nearly sixty years later, less than ten percent of the people in the world endure this debilitating level of impoverishment.[54] What this also means is that a half century of development—sometimes spectacularly successful, sometimes a dismaying failure—has occurred, and the field of development economics, as well as historians of Asia, Africa, and Latin America, have been following it closely. They have comprehended how it is that not bad harvests but price mechanisms create famine, understood how gender interacts with growth, and unpacked the relation between capital and technological change. In the process, they have dissected debilitating dependencies and rewritten Ricardo's rules of comparative advantage. They have also redefined measures of poverty, and come to see its severe price as "capability deprivation," in Amartya Sens' evocative term: the cost to a society (of potentialities not developed) for denying the poor access to food, health support, education, infrastructure, and capital.[55] This interdisciplinary work has, in short, become rich, complex, and insightful.

This chapter has argued that how thinkers addressed the problem of poverty was more central to German nation thinking than is often admitted, and that some early nineteenth-century German intellectuals took seriously the "deep, horizontal comradeship" that Benedict Anderson argued was central to the "imagined community" of nationhood. This becomes more evident when we see Germany in the pre-1848 period as a "developing nation," in both senses of the term—as a country striving for sovereignty and as one struggling for economic development. Finally, there is a methodological point about altering our angle of vision and taking in the vast new scholarship on economic development. To reverse and slightly alter E.P. Thompson's words: this would mean to look to "Asia and Africa" to understand better what was once a cause in Europe.

---

54  See the relation chart in: Max Roser/Esteban Ortiz-Ospina, *Global Extreme Poverty* (2013), <https://ourworldindata.org/extreme-poverty> [last accessed: September 30, 2021].

55  Poverty as Capability Deprivation, in: Amartya Sen, *Development as Freedom*, New York 1999, 87–110.

## References

Allen, Richard, *Global Economic History. A Very Short Introduction*, Oxford 2011.

Alter, George/Clark, Gregory, The Demographic Transition and Human Capital, in: Broadberry, Stephen/O'Rourke, Kevin H. (eds.), *The Cambridge Economic History of Modern Europe*, vol. 1: 1700–1870, Cambridge 2010, 43–69.

Anderson, Benedict, *Imagined Communities: Reflections on the Origin and Spread of Nationalism*, 2nd rev. ed., London 1991.

Arndt, Ernst Moritz, *Versuch einer Geschichte der Leibeigenschaft in Pommern und Rügen – Nebst einer Einleitung in die alte teutsche Leibeigenschaft*, Berlin 1803.

Banerjee, Abhijiy V./Duflo, Esther, *Poor Economics. A Radical Rethinking of the Way to Fight Global Poverty*, New York 2011.

Baumgart, Winfried/Duchhardt, Heinz/Knipping, Franz (eds.), *Handbuch der Geschichte der internationalen Beziehungen*, vol. 6, Paderborn 2007.

Bolt, Jutta/Zanden, Jan Luiten van, "GDP per Capita." IISH Data Collection, V1. Data (2015), <https://hdl.handle.net/10622/8FCYOX> [September 30, 2021].

Brophy, James M., The End of the Economic Old Order: The Great Transition, 1750–1860, in: Smith, Helmut Walser (ed.), *The Oxford Handbook of Modern German History*, Oxford 2011, 169–194.

Bunzel, Wolfgang/Landfester, Ulrike/Schmitz, Walter/Steinsdorff, Sibylle von (eds.), *Bettine von Arnim – Werke*, vol. 3: *Politische Schriften*, Frankfurt am Main 1995.

Collier, Paul, *The Bottom Billion. Why the Poorest Countries are Failing and What can be Done about it*, Oxford 2007.

Court, Victor, A Reassessment of the Great Divergence Debate: Towards a Reconciliation of Apparently Distinct Determinants, in: *European Review of Economic History* 24 (4/2020), 633–674.

Dann, Otto, *Nation und Nationalismus in Deutschland*, München 1993.

Davis, Mike, *A Planet of Slums*, London 2006.

Echternkamp, Jörg, *Der Aufstieg des deutschen Nationalismus 1770–1840*, Frankfurt am Main 1998.

Fogel, Robert William, *The Escape from Hunger and Premature Death, 1700–2100*, Cambridge 2004.

Geist, Johan Friedrich/Kürvers, Klaus, *Das Berliner Mietshaus*, vol. 1: 1740–1862, München 1980.

Gellner, Ernest, *Nations and Nationalism*, London 1983.

Geremek, Bronislaw, *Poverty. A History*, Oxford 1994.

Guttormsson, Loftur, Parent-Child Relations, in: Kertzer, David I./Barbagli, Mario (eds.), *Family Life in the Long Nineteenth Century: 1789–1913*, New Haven 2002, 251–281.

Hardtwig, Wolfgang, *Hochkultur des bürgerlichen Zeitalters*, Göttingen 2005.

Himmelfarb, Gertrude, *The Idea of Poverty. England in the early Industrial Age*, New York 1984.

Hobsbawm, Eric, *Nations and Nationalism since 1780: Programme, Myth, Reality*, Cambridge 1983.

Hodenberg, Christine von, *Aufstand der Weber: Die Revolte von 1844 und ihr Aufstieg zum Mythos*, Bonn 1997.

Hunt, Tristram, *Marx's General: The Revolutionary Life of Friedrich Engels*, London 2010.

Kohn, Hans, *The Mind of Germany*, New York 1960.

Levinger, Matthew, *Enlightened Nationalism. The Transformation of Prussian Political Culture, 1806–1848*, New York 2000.

List, Friedrich, *Das deutsche National-Transport-System in volks- und staatswirthschaftlicher Beziehung*, Altona 1838.

List, Friedrich, *Schriften, Reden, Briefe*, vol. 4: *Das nationale System der politischen Ökonomie*, ed. by Edgar Salin, Berlin 1927.

List, Friedrich, *Schiften, Reden, Briefe*, vol. 8: *Tagebücher und Briefe, 1812–1846*, ed. by Edgar Salin, Berlin 1933.

Malthus, Thomas Robert, *An Essay on the Principle of Population*, London 1798.

Mieck, Ilja, Von der Reformzeit zur Revolution (1815–1848), in: Ribbe, Wolfgang (ed.), *Geschichte Berlins*, vol. 1: *Von der Frühgeschichte bis zur Industrialisierung*, München 1987, 407–602.

Mokyr, Joel/Voth, Hans-Joachim, Understanding Growth in Europe, 1700–1870: Theory and Evidence, in: Broadberry, Stephen/O'Rourke, Kevin H. (eds.), *The Cambridge Economic History of Modern Europe*, vol. 1, 1700–1870, Cambridge 2010, 7–42.

Moltmann, Günter/Schöberl, Ingrid (eds.), *Aufbruch nach Amerika: Friedrich List und die Auswanderung aus Baden u. Württemberg 1816/17: Dokumentation einer sozialen Bewegung*, Tübingen 1979.

Pamuk, Şevket/Zanden, Jan Luiten van, Standards of Living, in: Broadberry, Stephen/O'Rourke, Kevin H. (eds.), *The Cambridge Economic History of Modern Europe*, vol. 1: 1700–1870, Cambridge 2010, 217–234.

Pfister, Ulrich, Economic Growth in Germany, 1500–1850, paper presented to the Quantifying Long Run Economic Development Conference, University of Warwick in Venice, 22–24 March 2011.

Pomeranz, Kenneth, *The Great Divergence. China, Europe, and the Making of the Modern World Economy*, Princeton 2000.

Ricardo, David, *On the Principles of Political Economy and Taxation*, London 1817.

Roser, Max, Economic Growth (2013), <https://ourworldindata.org/economic-growth> [last accessed: September 30, 2021].

Roser, Max/Ortiz-Ospina, Esteban, Global Extreme Poverty (2013), <https://ourworldindata.org/extreme-poverty> [September 30, 2021].

Roser, Max/Ritchie, Hannah/Dadonaite, Bernadeta, Child and Infant Mortality (2013), <https://ourworldindata.org/child-mortality> [last accessed: September 30, 2021].

Sen, Amartya, *Development as Freedom*, New York 1999.

Shammas, Carole, Standard of Living, Consumption, and Political Economy over the Past 500 Years, in: Trentman, Frank (ed.), *The Oxford Handbook of the History of Consumption*, Oxford 2012, 211–228.

Smith, Helmut Walser, *Germany. A Nation in its Time. Before, During, and After Nationalism, 1500–2000*, New York 2020.

Smith, Helmut Walser, *The Continuities of German History: Nation, Religion, and Race across the Long Nineteenth Century*, Cambridge 2008.

Stedman Jones, Gareth, *An End to Poverty. A Historical Debate*, New York 2004.

Szporluk, Roman, *Communism and Nationalism: Karl Marx versus Friedrich List*, Oxford 1993.

Thompson, Edward P., *The Making of the English Working Class*, Harmondsworth 1980.

Walle, Etienne van de, Historical Demography, in: Poston, Dudley L./ Micklin, Michael (eds.), *Handbook of Population*, New York 2005, 577–600.

# Minority Protection under the League of Nations: Universal and Particular Equality[1]

Ulrike Davy

**Abstract**

*The chapter traces the notion of equality that evolved under the League of Nations' minority regime. The regime was introduced to appease populations that, after World War I, found themselves living among majorities who conceived of themselves as being different in language, religion, or race, and aspired to form unified nation states. Against the backdrop of the realities and based on the equality clause of the regime, the Permanent Court of International Justice developed a novel understanding of equality. The equality clause was understood to imply a duty of the state to guarantee the very existence of minorities, in particular in cultural terms, shifting the focus from formal equality to substantive equality and even to state duties to actively preserve minorities. Yet distrust and hatred, fanned by practices of comparing, prepared the ground for war and the end of equality thinking.*

## Introduction

The idea that human beings are equal and ought to be treated equally before the law became prominent during the Enlightenment. Yet, the idea took various shapes during the long nineteenth century. The American Revolution gen-

---

1    This contribution draws on research conducted in the context of Collaborative Research Center "Practices of Comparing. Ordering and Changing the World" (SFB 1288). Some of my findings have been published in German in: Ulrike Davy, Wenn Gleichheit in Gefahr ist. Staatliche Schutzpflichten und Schutzbedürftigkeit am Beispiel des Minderheitenschutzes vor rassischer Diskriminierung, in: *Zeitschrift für öffentliches Recht* 74 (4/2019), 773–844.

erated the first constitutional documents, the Declaration of Independence adopted in 1776,[2] the Bill of Rights of Virginia also adopted in 1776,[3] and the United States Constitution adopted in 1787,[4] as amended.

Both, the Declaration of Independence and the Virginia Bill of Rights proclaimed certain inalienable and inherent rights. The Declaration of Independence mentioned "Life, Liberty, and the pursuit of Happiness" (second recital). The Virginia Bill of Rights referred to "the enjoyment of life and liberty, [...] happiness and safety" (Section I). 'Equality' was missing from the list of rights. Yet, the notion of equality was not absent from the documents. Obviously, for the founding assemblies, 'equality' pertained to the realm of natural law or nature, in other words, equality was supposed to predate the society established through man-made law and was not made part of statutory law, unlike the rights explicitly enumerated. Section I of the Virginia Bill of Rights states:

> "That all men are by nature equally free and independent, and have certain inherent rights, of which [...] they cannot [...] deprive [...] their posteriority; namely, the enjoyment of life and liberty [...] and pursuing and obtaining happiness and safety."

The Virginia Bill of Rights conceived of 'equality' as being a characteristic of men, and we can take that term literally, the Virginia Bill of Rights does not speak about human beings, but of men, more precisely of wealthy white men.[5] And as men who were deemed equally free, they all had certain rights, certain "inherent rights" that must not and could never be taken away from them. In short, 'equality' inspired the idea that all (wealthy white) men have the same rights. Or, from the perspective of rights, rights were conceptualized as being universal, i.e. the same for all right-holders.

In France, the Déclaration des Droits de l'Homme et du Citoyen, adopted in 1789,[6] took a similar stance. Article 1 spoke about men being born free and

---

2    Howard W. Preston, *Documents Illustrative of American History 1660–1863 with Introductions and References*, New York & London 1886, 211.

3    Preston, *Documents Illustrative*, 206.

4    Preston, *Documents Illustrative*, 253.

5    On the implicit limitations of (seemingly) universal terms in early modern times see Antje Flüchter, Hierarchy as Order—Equality as Chaos? The Mughal Empire through the Eyes of Early Modern European Travelers, *in this volume*.

6    P.-A. Dufau/J.-B. Duvergier/J. Guadet, *Collection des Constitutions, Chartres et Lois Fondamentales des Peuples de L'Europe et des deux Amériques*, Tome I, Paris 1823, 97.

equal and about men remaining free and equal.[7] That is very much a rehearsal of the Virginia Bill of Rights of 1776. Also, the list of core rights—the so-called *droits naturels*—did not include equality. The list included "la liberté, la propriété, la sûreté, et la résistance à l'oppression" (Article 2). Still, there are two points where the French Déclaration moved beyond the American model. For one, the notion of the law (*la loi*) encapsulated the idea of universality and through universality the idea of equality. Article 6 of the French Déclaration stated:

> "La loi est l'expression de la volonté générale. [...] Elle doit être la même pour tous, soit qu'elle protège, soit qu'elle punisse. Tous les citoyens, étant égaux à ses yeux, sont également admissibles à toutes dignités, places et emplois publics [...]."

Because the law was conceived of as being universal, it was necessarily the same for all citizens. The universality of law secured equality, not the other way around. For another, the Déclaration was more outspoken as to what 'equality' was about. Article 1 alluded to rights being equal (*égaux en droits*) and then added: "Les distinctions sociale ne peuvent être fondées que sur l'utilité commune." All social distinctions were supposed to be abandoned, that was the rule. Where social distinctions persisted, they needed to be based on some aspect of the common good. In short, 'equality' negated the idea of estates. The post-revolutionary world was envisioned as a world without privileges, and the ground for conceptualizing 'equality' in such manner, was prepared by popular visualizations that were widely spread and shared among the people.[8]

Post-World War II human rights law moved beyond the gender divide, the color line and other racial divisions. The Universal Declaration of Human Rights, adopted in 1948,[9] talked again of equal rights, yet not of men, but of all human beings (Article 1). And against the backdrop of history (European as well as non-European), the Universal Declaration refrained from presupposing that the having equal rights was self-understood. Mindful of the contempt and the hatred promoted by various ideologies of superiority—laying

---

7    Article 1 of the Déclaration reads in French: "Les hommes naissent et demeurent libres et égaux en droits. Les distinctions sociales ne peuvent être fondées que sur l'utilité commune."

8    See Lynn Hunt, Envisioning Equality in the French Revolution, *in this volume.*

9    United Nations Documents (UN Doc.) A/RES/217 (III).

the groundwork for gruesome colonial exploitation in non-European territories and for war, mass murder and genocide in Europe—the having of equal rights needed to be reaffirmed. Article 2 of the Universal Declaration stated (and states):

> "Everyone is entitled to all the rights and freedoms set forth in this Declaration, without distinction of any kind, such as race, colour, sex, language, religion political or other opinion, national or social origin, property, birth or other status."

Like the French Déclaration, Article 2 of the Universal Declaration spoke of distinctions. However, Article 2 of the Universal Declaration was concerned with distinctions made in order to withhold rights (not with distinctions made in order to preserve certain privileges for the aristocracy). Article 2 was not about the suspension of privileges and the abolition of the estates, but about making sure that no-one was denied access to the rights defined by the Universal Declaration. In short, the post-World War II world was meant to be a world without anyone left to live in inferiority.

How did the law get from a concept of equality that was directed against privileges to a concept of equality that was directed against the denial of (equal) rights? My contention is that the regime of minority protection—established after World War I—was an important turning point in conceptualizing equality. More precisely, the minority regime was a turning point in the notion of equality as envisioned in Europe and for Europeans. The minority regime was a political response at the international level to the specific 'minority questions' that were created by the re-drawing of borders in Eastern Europe at the Paris Peace Conference in 1919 and, in addition, to the 'Jewish question' in Eastern Europe, time and again manifesting itself physically in violent pogroms.[10] The minority regime also challenged the idea that rights

---

10    On the historical background of the post-World War I minority regime see H.W.V. Temperley (ed.), *A History of the Peace Conference of Paris*, Vol. 5, London 1924, reprint 1969, 112–149. On the "Jewish question" see Carole Fink, *Defending the Rights of Others. The Great Powers, the Jews, and International Minority Protection, 1878–1938*, Cambridge 2004. For a contemporary perspective see Amitai, Zur polnischen Judenfrage, in: *Der Jude: Eine Monatsschrift* 1 (12/1916-1917), 785–791; S.M. Dubnow, *History of the Jews in Russia and Poland from the Earliest Times until the Present Day*, Vol. II, Philadelphia 1918; Max Rosenfeld, Die europäische Polenfrage und die polnische Judenfrage, in: *Der Jude: Eine Monatsschrift* 2 (10-11/1917-1918), 642–654.

should be the same, for all human beings. One could even contend the minority regime undermined the idea that 'equality' is formal and universal.

I shall proceed in three steps. The first step involves the international regime of minority protection. I shall elaborate on the problem that eventually led to what has been called "minority protection" and the regime established by the Principal Allied Powers (United States of America, British Empire, France, Italy, Japan) and other states at the Paris Peace Conference in 1919. In a second step, I shall talk about the disputes that were brought before the Council of the League of Nations, mainly by petitioners drawing on the mechanism established by the minority regime. The third step turns to the judicial realm and the approach of the Permanent International Court of Justice. I want to show that the minority regime was triggered by the fear (shared among powerful actors at the Paris Peace Conference) that certain groups of people might be ripped of their status as citizens with equal rights. I also want to show that the idea of securing equal rights (at the national level) through allowing disputes to be brought before an international forum was—eventually—undermined when practices of comparing became more and more hostile. 'Equality' was indeed under threat. Finally, I want to show that, against all odds, the idea of equality was fiercely defended by the Permanent International Court of Justice even in the 1930s. Interestingly, when the idea of equality went under, the concept was deepened, and quite innovatively so.

## "Minority Protection"

### The Problem: Co-Nationals, Secessionists, Jews

Under the nation-state thinking prevalent around 1900, the existence of minorities prompted, almost by necessity, tensions between majorities and minorities: Minorities were conceived of as groups of people who defined themselves (or were defined by the majority) along what has, at the relevant time, been called racial or national lines. The racial or national make-up of minorities was deemed different from the make-up defining the majority.[11] The po-

---

11    Generally Jacques Fouques Duparc, *La Protection des Minorités de Race, de Langue et de Religion*, Paris 1922; Helmer Rosting, Protection of Minorities by the League of Nations, in: *American Journal of International Law* 17 (4/1923), 641–660; André Mandelstam, La Protection Internationale des Minorités, in: *Annuaire de l'Institut de Droit International* 32

litical claim attached to the concept of the nation state of the time was "One state for one nation only."[12] The existence of minorities was an irritation from the perspective of the concept because minorities were not seen as part of the "one nation."[13] Also, States feared that minorities might question the legitimacy of the State they were residing in, some observers might even have said, were forced to reside in by the dictate of the Principle Allied Powers in Paris, but not willing to reside in. These fears were quite specific. Minorities residing in border regions were thought to (and often did) perceive themselves as "co-nationals" of a different nation, as brothers and sisters of a people living in a neighboring State (such as the Germans residing in what had become Poland or Poles residing in what had become Lithuania). Some minorities living in a defined part of the territory were believed to aspire to form a nation state of their own, such as some factions of the Ruthene peoples residing in what had become Czecho-Slovakia or some factions of the Montenegrins residing in what had become the Serb-Croat-Slovene State.

In cases like that, a number of principles that organize peaceful relations among individuals and among States, seem not to work. First, democracy and majority rule: Minorities can and might be ignored by the majority simply because they lack sufficient representation in decision-making processes. Secondly, self-determination: Racial or national minorities that were forced to live in a State that they deemed "foreign" might rightfully claim that their right to self-determination was still unfilled. Thirdly, trust: Trust may be absent on all sides. Racial or national minorities might rightfully fear that the majority expected them to de-nationalize and assimilate. And the majority might rightfully fear that the minority engaged in disloyal activities, in "irridentism," as contemporaries used to call it.

Clearly, the case of the Jews living in Eastern Europe at the end of World War I was different. Jews could not conceive of themselves as co-nationals. There was no Jewish state. Moreover, Jewish communities were dispersed, across Eastern European States eager to evolve into nation states, and within

---

(1925) 246–392; Arthur von Balogh, *Der internationale Schutz der Minderheiten*, München 1928.

12   Josef L. Kunz, Prolegomena zu einer allgemeinen Theorie des internationalen Rechts nationaler Minderheiten, in: *Zeitschrift für öffentliches Recht* 12 (2/1932), 221–272, see 237: "[Der] 'Nationalstaat' der Wirklichkeit ist [...] ausschließlich der Staat einer Nation, des Mehrheits-, des 'Staats'volkes."

13   Kunz, Prolegomena zu einer allgemeinen Theorie des internationalen Rechts nationaler Minderheiten, 237: "[Jede] Nation läßt eben nur die eigene Nation gelten."

States. Contemporary estimates spoke of 5 million Jews[14] or of 7 million Jews.[15] A claim to self-determination on European soil seemed unthinkable. Antisemitism—an important source when it came to defining the so-called Jewish question—focused on distrust.[16] Antisemitism, in particular Antisemitism in Poland, claimed that Jews were the ultimate other, the ones who would never integrate into the majority nation, the ones who would stay forever alien, a sort of an inner enemy.[17]

## The Stance of the Allied Powers: An Evident Necessity

### Tackling Oppression

When the (principle and other) Allied Powers assembled in Paris to negotiate the treaties ending World War I, some issues had been settled already. It had been settled that there would be new States at the expense of existing ones, in particular at the expense of Germany, Austria, the Ottoman Empire, and the Russian Empire.[18] Poland, Czechoslovakia, Hungary, the Kingdom of the Serbs, the Croats and the Slovenes, the Baltic States, Finland or Ukraine are cases in point. Some existing States would gain new territories, in particular in the Southeast of Europe, such as Romania or Greece. Hence, borders needed to be redrawn and, clearly, the principle of self-determination was

---

14  William E. Rappard, Minorities and the League, in: *International Conciliation* 11 (222/1926), 330–343, see 332.

15  American Jewish Congress (ed.), *Memorials Submitted to President Wilson Concerning the Status of the Jews of Eastern Europe, and in Palestine, by Representatives of the American Jewish Congress, on March 2, 1919*, New York 1919, 1.

16  On Antisemitism in Poland Theodore R. Weeks, *From Assimilation to Antisemitism. The "Jewish Question" in Poland, 1850–1914*, DeKalb 2006.

17  See Weeks, *From Assimilation to Antisemitism*, 90, 94, 115, 161; Alina Cała, Die Anfänge des Antisemitismus im Königreich Polen in der zweiten Hälfte des neunzehnten Jahrhunderts, in: *International Review of Social History* 30 (3/1980), 342–373 (Aus dem Polnischen von J. Rojahn). For a contemporary perspective see Roman Dmowski, Gedanken eines modernen Polen, in: François Guesnet (ed.), *Der Fremde als Nachbar. Polnische Positionen zur jüdischen Präsenz. Texte seit 1800*, Frankfurt am Main 2009, 276–282 (Aus dem Polnischen von Peter Oliver Loew).

18  Ifor L. Evans, The Protection of Minorities, in: *British Year Book of International Law* 4 (1923-24), 95–123, see 101; Temperley, *A History of the Peace Conference of Paris*, Vol. 5, 157.

sometimes sacrificed in order to satisfy strategic or economic interests.[19] Statistical information is obviously unreliable, and numbers given by contemporaries from law or history vary greatly. Raymond Leslie Buell speaks of 17 million people who became minorities in the wake of the treaties, among them 7.6 million Germans, and almost 3 million Magyars.[20] Others refer to 20 million people or 30 million people,[21] still others speak of 40 million people.[22] Whatever the real numbers were, a lot of people have been affected by the redrawing of borders.

One of the most prominent and explicit goals of the Allies and Associated Powers gathering in Paris was to secure a lasting peace in Europe, and the minority problem caused by the redrawing of borders seemed an obvious stumbling block. The rampant antisemitism was separate issue, even though some of the Jewish claims drew on the idea that Jews might be classified as a national minority.[23] Violent forms of antisemitism in Eastern Europe predated the redrawing of borders by far. In Paris, antisemitism was addressed with a humanitarian impetus, against the backdrop of recurring pogroms late in 1918, just as the war had come to an end.[24] Still, the minority problem created through redrawing borders and the dire straits of the Jewish communities in Eastern Europe had one common feature, namely the (actual or potential) oppression by the majority of a group that was smaller in terms of numbers and conceptualized as different in racial or national terms.

In 1919, the world was, because of precedents, well aware of how oppression could look like, in particular because of precedents in the territories of

---

19    E.g., Rappard, Minorities and the League, 330. Later Michla Pomerance, The United States and Self-Determination: Perspectives on the Wilsonian Conception, in: *American Journal of International Law* 70 (1/1976), 1–76, see 4 for the most obvious examples.

20    Raymond Leslie Buell, The Protection of Minorities, in: *International Conciliation* 11 (222/1926), 348–366, see 348.

21    Rappard, Minorities and the League, 332 (over twenty million); H. Wilson Harris, The League and Minorities, in: *International Conciliation* 11 (222/1926), 344–347, see 344 (30,000,000).

22    Kunz, Prolegomena zu einer allgemeinen Theorie des internationalen Rechts nationaler Minderheiten, 222.

23    American Jewish Congress (ed.), *Memorials Submitted to President Wilson Concerning the Status of the Jews of Eastern Europe*, 10.

24    S. Gewürz, *Lemberg. Eine kritische Beleuchtung des Judenpogroms vom 21. bis 23. November 1918*, Berlin 1919; L. Chasanowitsch, *Die polnischen Judenpogrome im November und Dezember 1918. Tatsachen und Dokumente*, Stockholm 1919; Israel Cohen, *A Report on the Pogroms in Poland*, London 1919.

Eastern Europe. Acts of oppression could take varying forms, ranging from acts of physical violence to the assigning of an inferior civil status, the denial of political rights, the denial of access to public services, limitations regarding access to certain professions, limitations regarding the choice of residence, subjection to particular taxes, restrictions regarding religious services or practices, or the use of language in public.[25] Whatever its shape and appearance, oppression regularly (also) took the form of legal disabilities, in other words, the form of the denial of equal rights. And some European Allied Powers had, beginning in the nineteenth century, sought to make sure that the (newly recognized) States in Eastern Europe would, in certain respects and vis à vis certain groups, refrain from imposing disabilities. To give but a few examples: As Greece gained additional territory from the Ottoman Empire in 1830 (and, with the territory, non-Christian inhabitants), Greece undertook to grant equal political rights without distinction according to religion.[26] The guaranties were a *quid pro quo* for Greece's admission to the European Concert. Or, when signing the Treaty of Berlin in 1878, Bulgaria, Montenegro, Serbia, Romania, and the Ottoman Empire promised that differences in religion would not hamper the enjoyment of civil and political rights.[27] These and similar rules were the forerunners of the minority regime introduced by the League of Nations. Jewish lobby groups epitomized these politics and, accordingly, their demands in a "watchword:" "Equal rights to all men in all lands."[28]

## Politics of Comparison

When deciding on the territorial reach of the minority regime and the beneficiaries, the making of comparisons was the most important argumentative tool relied on in the decision-making processes. The minority regime was intended to be unequal, with regard to territorial application as well as with regard to beneficiaries. In order to justify unequal treatment (of States, of individuals belonging to minorities), the Allied Powers sought to argue that

---

25    For ample testimony see American Jewish Congress (ed.), *Memorials Submitted to President Wilson Concerning the Status of the Jews of Eastern Europe*.

26    Duparc, *La Protection des Minorités de Race, de Langue et de Religion*, 90.

27    Duparc, *La Protection des Minorités de Race, de Langue et de Religion*, 93; von Balogh, *Der internationale Schutz der Minderheiten*, 9.

28    American Jewish Congress (ed.), *Memorials Submitted to President Wilson Concerning the Status of the Jews of Eastern Europe*, 4.

significant differences existed among those entities. The politics of re-mapping Europe mixed with politics of comparison.

Regarding territorial reach, the Allied Powers believed that some States, in particular the States in the East and Southeast of Europe, were—from the perspective of willingness and ability to accommodate the fears of minorities—less trustworthy than others.[29] One important yardstick for measuring and comparing trustworthiness was the degree of civilization.[30] And, when compared to Germany or Italy, the odds were against the Eastern European States. That is why the Allied Powers pressed for minority treaties to be signed by Poland, the Kingdom of Serbs, Croats and Slovenes, Czecho-Slovakia, Romania, and Greece, and why the peace treaties with Bulgaria, Hungary and Turkey contained sections on minority protection. The Baltic States and Albania were pressed to give reassurances in the form of "declarations" before being admitted to the League of Nations.[31] Germany and Italy went free.

When Poland protested, Poland and, in an indirect manner, other Eastern European countries were told in a letter signed by Georges Clemenceau that it was to the "endeavors and sacrifices of the [Great] Powers"—and not their own doing—that their sovereignty over certain territories was being reinstated.[32] Hence, so the argument ran, the Allied Powers had an obligation vis à vis the inhabitants of those territories who are being incorporated into the Polish nation:

> "There rests, therefore, upon these Powers an obligation [...] to secure in the most permanent and solemn form guarantees for certain essential rights which will afford to the inhabitants the necessary protection whatever changes may take place in the internal constitution of the Polish state."

In response to another argument, Eastern Europeans were told that, even though the minority regime under the League of Nations differed from earlier provisions, the new provisions were "necessary" because the current situation was different from the former one: The territories transferred to Poland

---

29    Temperley, *A History of the Peace Conference of Paris*, Vol. 5, 123–132.

30    Temperley, *A History of the Peace Conference of Paris*, Vol. 5, 116.

31    Evans, The Protection of Minorities, 114.

32    Letter addressed to M. Paderewski by the President of the Conference transmitting to him the Treaty to be signed by Poland under Article 93 of the Treaty of Peace with Germany, Paris, June 24, 1919, printed in: Temperley, *A History of the Peace Conference of Paris*, Vol. 5, 432; in: *Supplement to the American Journal of International Law* 13 (1919), 416; and in: *British Treaty Series*, No. 8 (1919).

and other Eastern European States would "include a large population speaking languages and belonging to races different from that of the people with whom they will be incorporated." And, to bring the comparison to a full circle, the letter continued: "[The] races have been estranged by long years of bitter hostility." These suppressed populations ought to know from the beginning of the new border regimes that they had "guarantees against any danger of unjust treatment or oppression."

Regarding the beneficiaries of the minority regime, Harold William Temperley, the chronicler of the Paris Peace Conference, acknowledged openly that the Allied Powers ranked minorities also according to sympathy, at least to a certain extent: Some belonged, so Temperley reasoned, to enemy states, some were basically unknown to the Allies, such as the Ruthenians, some had all the sympathies because of their particular plight.[33] When it came to sympathies, the Jews in Eastern Europe ranked high, and numerous comparisons stressed that their culture and their history of repression was unique and deserving attention. In Temperley's words:

> "[It] has been calculated that 14 per cent. of the inhabitants of Poland would be Jews [...] during recent years there had been evidence of strong animosity towards the Jews [...] Many of [the Poles] looked with suspicion and dislike upon the presence within their borders of an alien population [...] They lived an isolated life, they used their own language, Yiddish [...] By their religion, their dress, their customs, they were separated from the rest of the population. In Rumania it was represented with much force that the engagements which had been made to secure the equality of the Jewish population had not been kept [...] a large number were existing in a condition of civil and political inferiority [...] It was, therefore, clearly incumbent upon the Conference to give to the unfortunate members of this race securities, the necessity of which was evident."[34]

Variations in the scales of sympathies, manifested in and generated through acts of comparing alluding to differences, might explain why the minority treaty with Poland contained provisions providing for rights to be granted to Jews, while, for instance, the German minority in Italy was basically left to its own devices.

---

33    Temperley, *A History of the Peace Conference of Paris*, Vol. 5, 122.
34    Temperley, *A History of the Peace Conference of Paris*, Vol. 5, 122–123.

## The Minority Regime: Equal Rights in all Lands

The minority regime—basically confined to Eastern European States—was eventually fleshed out in a series of legal acts, some of them peace treaties (Austria, Bulgaria, Hungary, Turkey), some of them treaties focusing exclusively on the legal status of minorities (Poland; Kingdom of the Serbs, Croats and Slovenes; Czecho-Slovakia; Roumania; Greece), some of them declarations accepted by the League of Nations in the course of admission to the League (the Baltic States, Albania).[35] All these acts established a new legal category, namely, "nationals who belong to racial, religious or linguistic minorities." The word "minority" has never been used before in international law. And yet, the international lawmakers refrained from defining the term. All we know from the legal texts is that, according to the understanding of the lawmakers, the term "minorities" was meant to comprise racial, religious and linguistic minorities. The lack of guidance by the lawmakers left room in the 1920s and 1930s for scholarly articles trying to elaborate on the elements of the newly introduced category.[36] The outcomes of these efforts were rather inconclusive, though. In the language used in documents issued by the League of Nations, the term "racial minority" quickly gained prominence.[37] The other terms ("linguistic minority;" "religious minority") were barely used. Instead, minorities acting before the League as well as majorities were consistently addressed as "races." However, the term "race" was not reflected upon either.

From the perspective of the framing of the minority problem—oppression by the majority of a minority through the denial of rights—it is no wonder that the minority regime is nothing but a regime of (varying) equality rights. Put differently, the minority regime was nothing but a cascade of equality rights that Eastern European States promised to grant on the national level, ranging from thin equality rights to thick equality rights. The rights alluded to in the texts, were supposed to prevail even over national legislation: The Eastern

---

35    Ulrike Davy, Wenn Gleichheit in Gefahr ist. Staatliche Schutzpflichten und Schutzbedürftigkeit am Beispiel des Minderheitenschutzes und des Schutzes vor rassischer Diskriminierung, in: *Zeitschrift für öffentliches Recht* 74 (4/2019), 773–844, see 785 referencing relevant legal sources.

36    On the contemporary academic semantics see Stefan Dyroff, From Nationalities to Minorities? The Transnational Debate on the Minority Protection System of the League of Nations, and Its Predecessors, in: Xosé M. Núñez Seixas (ed.), *The First World War and the Nationality Question in Europe*, Leiden 2020, 245–265.

37    Davy, Gleichheit, 832.

European States promised, at the opening of the cascade, to recognize the international provisions as "fundamental laws" that could not be abrogated by national law. The Minority Treaty with Poland,[38] for instance, stated in Article 1:

> "Poland undertakes that the stipulations [...] shall be recognised as fundamental laws, and that no law, regulation or official action shall conflict or interfere with these stipulations, nor shall any law, regulation or official action prevail over them."

The minority treaties brokered by the Allied Powers and, later, by the League of Nations, defined three groups of beneficiaries: inhabitants, nationals, and nationals belonging to racial, religious or linguistic minorities. The first group was all-encompassing, it comprised all persons staying in the territory. The second group was smaller and comprised only inhabitants who were, under nationality law, nationals of the State concerned. The third group was the smallest. The third group comprised only nationals who also belonged to a minority. The following sketch relies on the minority treaty with Poland. That treaty was the first to be negotiated and a blueprint for the treaties and declarations to follow.

Thin equality rights were assigned to "all inhabitants." Under Article 2 of the minority treaty, Poland undertook to assure to all inhabitants the full and complete protection of life and liberty and the free exercise of religion. Life, liberty and religion were singled out as the core interests of human beings. Thicker equality rights were assigned to "nationals." Under Article 7, all "Polish nationals shall be equal before the law and shall enjoy the same civil and political rights." Hence, Article 7 stipulated that nationals must, by law, be treated the same, at least with respect to civil and political rights. The thickest equality rights were granted to "Polish nationals who belong to racial, religious or linguistic minorities" (Article 8). The promise given in Article 8 was neither conditioned nor specified with regard to rights. The promise simply said: Nationals belonging to a relevant minority "shall enjoy the same treatment and security in law and in fact as other Polish nationals." That promise clearly had no forerunner in prior treaty provisions. The promise did not only refer to the "same treatment," but also to "security," and the promise did not only refer to

---

38    Treaty of Peace between the United States of America, the British Empire, France, Italy and Japan and Poland, signed at Versailles, June 28, 1919, in: *British Treaty Series* no. 8 (1919) (hereafter Minority Treaty Poland).

treatment and security "in law," but also to treatment and security "in fact." I shall come back to that promise later.

The cascade of equality rights came with some additional rights (and corresponding State duties). The additional rights were innovative too. For one, Poland was, under the treaty, obliged to ensure that nationals belonging to a minority had an equal right to establish (at their own expense) charitable institutions or schools (Article 8 sentence 2). For another, Poland was, under defined conditions, obliged to provide for primary schools where instruction would be given in the language of the minority (so-called minority schools, Article 9 para 1). Finally, and that is the last general innovation I want to mention, minorities were promised to have an equitable share in public money dedicated to educational, religious or charitable purposes (Article 9 para. 2). In the case of Poland, there were even specific additional rights. Poland undertook to respect the Sabbath (Article 11) and to let educational committees appointed by the Jewish communities have a free hand in the management of public money dedicated to educational purposes (Article 10).

## Disputes before the Council of the League of Nations

### Procedure

The nineteenth century treaties protecting the interests of certain populations living in the Southeast of Europe, e.g., the Treaty of Berlin 1878, had unmistakably signaled that the Great Powers assembled in the European Concert (i.e. the British Empire, France, Germany, Austria-Hungary, Russia) were, collectively or individually, watching over the fulfilment of the promises given.[39] In 1919, that was no longer an option. Still, part of the minority regime established in 1919 or in the 1920s, was a clause stating that the stipulations given by the various States constituted "obligations of international concern" and that they would be "placed under the guarantee of the League of Nations."[40] Also, the States agreed that "any Member of the Council of the League of Nations" would have the right to "bring to the attention of the Council any infraction, or any danger of infraction" of any of these obligations.[41]

---

39    Duparc, *La Protection des Minorités de Race, de Langue et de Religion*, 93.
40    Minority Treaty Poland, Article 12(1).
41    Minority Treaty Poland, Article 12(2).

This clause was the procedural innovation of the 1919 Peace Conference. The minority treaties established an international venue—the Council of the League of Nations—for discussing and resolving minority issues. And as the Council was comprised of (high ranking) delegates representing their States, the focus of the debates was clearly on the political dimensions of the minority problems. In the early 1920s, the Council of the League of Nations consisted of the representatives of eight States.[42] Four were "born" members; they were explicitly mentioned in the Covenant of the League of Nations. Article 4 of the Versailles Treaty spoke of the "Principal Allied and Associated Powers," thus referring to the British Empire, France, Italy and Japan as the four permanent members. Four additional States were selected regularly to be represented in the Council. The four additional States were the non-permanent members of the Council. Belgium, Brazil, Greece and Spain took that position in 1920 until the first elections were held in the Assembly of the League of Nations.[43] Hence, when the members of the Council met, it was statesmen who gathered, not justices or experts. Those statesmen were not independent from their governments, and they were not necessarily legal experts. Decision-making required unanimity.

The procedural rules laid down in the early 1920s[44] were quickly under critique, and not only from scholars sympathizing with minorities. Procedures were criticized for not being open to the public, minorities had no (formal) standing, reasons were barely given.[45] But I do not want to go into the de-

---

42    See, e.g., Treaty of Peace between the Allied and Associated Powers and Germany and Protocol, signed at Versailles, June 28, 1919, reprinted in: *British Treaty Series*, no. 4 (1919) (hereafter Versailles Treaty), Part I, The Covenant of the League of Nations, Article 4.

43    The number of States represented in the Council of the League of Nations changed several times in the course of the 1920s and 1930s. In 1939, the Council comprised fifteen States.

44    See Report, presented by the Italian Representative, M. Tittoni, and adopted by the Council of the League, in: *League of Nations Official Journal*, November–December 1920, 8. See later the compilation in: League of Nations, Protection of Linguistic, Racial or Religious Minorities by the League of Nations, Document No. C.24.M.18 1929. For summaries see Rosting, Protection of Minorities by the League of Nations, 653; Rappard, Minorities and the League, 338; von Balogh, *Der internationale Schutz der Minderheiten*, 222.

45    Details are given in Benjamin Davy/Ulrike Davy, Haltung in finsteren Zeiten. Die Zeitschrift für öffentliches Recht zwischen 1933 und 1945, in: *Zeitschrift für öffentliches Recht* 69 (4/2014), 715–804, see 783.

tails of these allegations here. I just want to briefly outline the steps that were usually followed in minority matters.

Although minorities had no formal standing, procedures were usually triggered by petitions lodged by associations representing minority interests or, not as often, by individuals alleging to belong to a minority. If and when the petitions were considered admissible, they were passed on to the State concerned. Petitions and responses by the States concerned were then dealt with by a Committee comprising three members of the Council, the so-called (and *ad hoc* elected) Minorities Committee. The minorities committees would appoint a rapporteur, and finally the petition and the report of the committee would be discussed in the Council of the League of Nations. Under the terms of the Covenant, it was up to any Member of the Council to draw the attention of the Council to (potential) infractions in a formal manner. But formal proceedings were barely initiated. The Council and the minorities committees rather engaged in informal discussions, using all sorts of means for conflict resolution, in particular informal ones, such as mediation, involving the responding State, interested other States, appointed experts. The reports of the minorities committees and the ensuing resolutions of the Council were then published in the Official Journal of the League of Nations.

## Petitions and Claims: Minority Issues

It is impossible to count 'cases' or 'petitions' that have been dealt with by the minorities committees and the Council by studying the Official Journal of the League of Nations. The Official Journal does not provide case identifiers (numbers, names). But it is possible to count the documents that have been published in the Official Journal and that relate to minority issues. I have created a database that comprises all documents, identifiable through an entry, usually a heading consecutively numbered and, sometimes, a line at the beginning and the end; the database covers the years from 1920 through 1939.[46] During those years, about 700 documents have been published that relate to minority issues, i.e. issues raised under one of the minority treaties, under one of the minority clauses in peace treaties, or under one of the minority declarations. In addition, the database includes documents that relate to specific conflicts involving minorities, without explicitly being marked as involving minority issues, such as the Aaland Islands question, the conflicts involving the Free

---

46    See also Davy, Gleichheit, 795–798.

City of Danzig, or the documents relating to the Armenian question. From 1920 through 1935, the document count reaches 200 in every five-year period (1920–1924; 1925–1929; 1930–1934). The number of documents dropped sharply after Germany had left the League of Nations late in 1933[47] and Poland had declared that it considered itself no longer bound by the minority regime.[48]

From 1920 through 1925, the most prominent minority issues related to the Swedish minority residing on the Aaland Islands (the islands were claimed by Finland as their own), to issues originating in the population transfers sanctified by a treaty between Bulgaria and Greece,[49] to atrocities accompanying the population transfers between Greece and Turkey, sanctified by the Treaty of Lausanne of 1923,[50] and to issues pertaining to agrarian reforms that took place in various countries in Eastern Europe, in particular in Poland and Romania.

In the second half of the 1920s, the issue of minority schools was put on the table, in particular by the German minority residing in Polish Upper Silesia.[51] German minority associations (the *Deutsche Volksbund* was on the forefront) claimed that Polish school authorities would, in an improper manner,

---

47    Letter from the German Government to the Secretary-General of the League of Nations, dated October 19, 1933, printed in: *League of Nations Official Journal* 1934, 16. Germany also withdrew from the International Labour Organisation and the Permanent International Court of Justice. Under Article 1(3) Versailles Treaty, Germany was bound to keep a notification period of two years before actually withdrawing from the League of Nations. Yet, Adolf Hitler decided to hold a referendum on November 12, 1933. 95 per cent of the voters approved Germany's secession. Hence, Germany ceased to participate in the activities of the League of Nations after the referendum was held. See Konstantin D. Magliveras, The Withdrawal From the League of Nations Revisited, *Dickinson Journal of International Law* 10 (1/1991), 25–72, 32.

48    Oscar I. Janowsky, The Treatment of Minorities, in: *International Conciliation* 20 (369/1941), 286–294, see 292.

49    Convention between Greece and Bulgaria Respecting Reciprocal Emigration, signed at Neuilly-sur-Seine, November 27, 1919, printed in: *Supplement to the American Journal of International Law* 14 (1920), 356.

50    Convention concerning the Exchange of Greek and Turkish Populations, and Protocol, signed at Lausanne, January 30, 1923, printed in: *League of Nations Treaty Series* 32 (1925), 76. For the background see J. R., The Exchange of Minorities and Transfers of Population in Europe since 1919–I, in: *Bulletin of International News* 21 (15/1944), 579–588.

51    The first complaints lodged by the *Deutsche Volksbund* were dealt with by the Council of the League of Nations on March 8, 1927, in: *League of Nations Official Journal* 1927, 376.

turn away parents wishing to see their children being enrolled in a minority school, i.e. a German primary school. Allegedly, the numbers of children
whose requests for enrollment were rejected reached several thousands.[52]
Similar claims were made by Polish associations with regard to Polish minority schools in German Upper Silesia.[53] During the late 1920s, a second issue
remained quite dominant, namely problems evolving around the implementation of the Treaty of Lausanne 1923, this time in particular with respect to
Albanian Moslems living in Greece and the Greek community living in Con-
stantinople.[54]

   In the 1930s, problems relating to minority schools stayed on the agenda,
and now petitioners also targeted the policy of the Albanian government.[55]
Relations between Germany and Poland became more strained, for one over
the issue of minority schools, for another during the electoral campaign and
in the wake of the elections to the Warsaw Diet and the Silesian Diet in the fall
of 1930.[56] Eventually, after Germany had factually left the League of Nations by
the end of 1933 and Poland had declared itself free of obligations with regard
to the German minority residing on Poland's territory, there were basically no
more claims to be dealt with involving Poland or Germany and their respective

---

52    For details on the dispute see Manley O. Hudson, The Tenth Year of the Permanent
      Court of International Justice, in: *American Journal of International Law* 26 (1/1932), 1–30,
      see 6.

53    The first complaints were lodged in October 1928 by the Association of Poles in Ger-
      many and dealt with by the Council of the League of Nations on March 9, 1929, in: *League
      of Nations Official Journal* 1929, 554. Compared to the number of complaints tabled by
      German associations, the number of Polish complaints was very small.

54    The debates in the Council of the League of Nations relating to the issue of „Moslems
      of Albanian Origin in Greece" and the issue of "Greek Minority in Constantinople" were
      primarily initiated by the respective governments: Albania intervened on behalf of
      the Albanians living in Greece, and the Greek government intervened on behalf of the
      Greeks living in Constantinople.

55    The debates in the Council of the League of Nations were prompted by a letter signed
      by the United Kingdom, Mexico and Portugal asking that "petitions relating to the po-
      sition of minorities in Albania" be placed on the Council's agenda, in: *League of Nations
      Official Journal* 1935, 106.

56    Carole Kapiloff Fink, *The Weimar Republic as the Defender of Minorities, 1919–1933. A Study
      of Germany's Minorities Diplomacy and the League of Nations System for the International
      Protection of Minorities*, Dissertation, Yale University 1969; Carole Fink, Defender of Mi-
      norities: Germany in the League of Nations, 1926–1933, in: *Central European History* 5
      (4/1972), 330–357; Carole Fink, Germany and the Polish Elections of November 1930: A
      Study in League Diplomacy, in: *East European Quarterly* 15 (2/1981), 181–207.

minorities. Attention turned to the Middle East, the Assyrian minority in Iraq after the termination of the mandatory regime[57] and the Turkish minority in Alexandretta and Antioch, a region that had been ceded by Turkey under the terms of the Treaty of Lausanne 1923 and was—in the late 1930s—meant to become part of Syria.[58]

In numbers: Germans residing in Poland (primarily in Polish Upper Silesia) were clearly the most active minority under the minority regime established by the League of Nations. Almost 200 documents recorded in my database relate to petitions lodged by Germans, followed by 57 documents relating to Turkish minorities in the Southeast of Europe, by 48 documents relating to Hungarians (mostly the Hungarian minority residing in Romania), by 42 documents relating to the Polish minorities (residing in German Upper Silesia or Lithuania), by 41 documents relating to Albanian minorities (residing in Greece), and by 38 documents relating to Greeks expelled from Asia Minor. The respondent States rank accordingly. Poland is on top of the list, followed by Greece, Turkey, Germany and Romania.

## Practices of Comparing: Arguing Equality

Whatever minority turned to the Council of the League of Nations for help, the minority's right to equality was always at the center of the grievances, and the making of comparisons was always pivotal for the arguments brought forward. The popularity of making comparisons when raising claims echoes a doctrinal demand and standard: If someone wants to make a case under the right to equality, they need to show that they—in comparison to some significant other—have been or are being treated differently, and they need to show that this different treatment cannot be justified by some good and

---

57   The starting point was a series of communications from the Assyrian population that had been forwarded to the Council of the League of Nations by the Secretary-General, Doc. C.770.1932.VI. See also H. Müller-Sommerfeld, The League of Nations. A-Mandates and Minority Rights during the Mandate Period in Iraq (1920–1932), in: S.R. Goldstein-Sabbah/H.L. Murre-van den Berg (eds.), *Modernity, Minority, and the Public Sphere. Jews and Christians in the Middle East*, Leiden 2016, 258–310.

58   From a contemporary perspective see Majid Khadduri, The Alexandretta Dispute, in: *American Journal of International Law* 39 (3/1945), 406–425; Avedis K. Sanjian, The Sanjak of Alexandretta (Hatay): Its Impact on Turkish-Syrian Relations (1939–1956), in: *Middle East Journal* 10 (4/1956), 379–394.

valid reason.[59] In their petitions to the Council of the League of Nations, minorities simply adhered to that standard.

To give but a few examples: Minorities arguing that the agrarian reform introduced by the respondent State (e.g. Poland, Romania) would disregard their right to equality would emphasize that relevant laws affected them in a particular manner and they would also claim that the only reason for being treated differently was their belonging to a minority. To put it more concretely: German farmers residing in Poland would, in the early 1920s, claim that they, but no Polish farmers, had been expelled from their property, and that the expulsion had taken place for one reason only, that is, their being of German descent. In early November 1921, for instance, the Secretary-General of the League of Nations received a telegram from the Germanic League of Bydgoszcz (Bromberg) stating

> "that the agrarian law was passed in order to deprive the Germans of their landed property. In districts where there are a majority of landowners of Polish race, the cutting-up of the estates should not be applied to estates of less than 400 hectares, whereas, in districts where the German element predominates, subdivision may take place in respect of estates as small as 180 hectares."[60]

The statement of the Germanic League involves three strands of comparisons, one between Germans and Poles, one between that the size of the estates concerned, and one between localities inhabited by German majorities on the one hand and Polish majorities on the other. The discriminatory treatment (of the Germans) is marked by making a difference: German landowners are more affected by the measure, because they must leave their properties (already) if the size of their property exceeds 180 hectares whereas Polish farmers have to leave (only) if their landed property exceeds the size of 400 hectares. And it was well known at the time that German estates were, generally, much larger than the estates owned by Poles. Hence, many Germans were affected by the law, but only very few (if any) Poles.

In response to such (or similar) allegations, Poland would, for one, claim that up to the present, no landed property located in that part of Poland which

---

59    See, e.g., Permanent Court of International Justice, Advisory Opinion of September 10, 1923, on certain questions relating to settlers of German origin in the territory ceded by Germany to Poland, in: *Collection of Advisory Opinions* (1923), Serie B. No. 6, 23–25.

60    *League of Nations Official Journal* 1922, 703.

formerly had belonged to Prussia had been expropriated.[61] If that proved true, the petitioners would have no valid claim as they were not affected by the law. For another, Poland would claim that the law was aimed at German colonists only who had no legal title.[62] If that proved true, the German claim would not be legitimate. Thirdly, Poland would claim that the law would affect only the owners whose lands exceeded a certain amount of hectares, say 400 hectares. If that proved true, the petitioners would, face value, not be specifically targeted as Germans by the law.[63] Finally, Poland would claim that the law was a reaction to the unfair politics of Prussianization starting in the late nineteenth century.[64] If that was a legitimate argument, Poland might have a valid reason for enacting a law affecting mostly German farmers, at least in political arenas.

In petitions relating to minority schools, petitioners preferred to argue with numbers: The Polish minority living in Lithuania, for instance, complained that, in the early 1920, less than 2,800 children were attending Polish primary schools, although almost 64,000 people had voted for Polish lists in the national election.[65] Compared to the number of people voting for Polish candidates, the number of pupils enrolled seemed utterly small. And, so the petitioners continued, the number of pupils attending Polish schools was much smaller than the number of pupils attending Jewish schools, even though the Jewish population was approximately the same in size as the Polish population. The number of pupils attending Jewish schools would reach even 4,500.[66] Obviously, these acts of comparing were intended to signal that the Polish minority in Lithuania would not dare to show their preferences freely, when they enrolled their children, and that the Polish minority fared even worse than the Jewish minority. Engaging in the making of comparisons made things visible that were not visible for the innocent eye.

---

61    See response by the Polish government in: *League of Nations Official Journal* 1922, 1294.
62    See the response by the Polish government in: *League of Nations Official Journal* 1922, 703-704.
63    See the response by the Polish government in: *League of Nations Official Journal* 1922, 703.
64    See the response by the Polish government in: *League of Nations Official Journal* 1922, 704.
65    Situation of the Polish Minority in Lithuania, Summary of Documents, in: *League of Nations Official Journal* 1925, 582–587, see 584.
66    Situation of the Polish Minority in Lithuania, Summary of Documents, 584.

During the late 1920s, the making of comparisons, when addressing the Council of the League of Nations, changed its character, even significantly so. In the early 1920s, comparing primarily addressed the subject-matter of politics and often involved numbers, of German farmers or colonists affected or expelled, of property in land and its size, of schools closed down, teachers dismissed, or pupils enrolled. During the late 1920s, comparing went "racial," one could say there was something like an "racial" turn and, with that turn, comparing became more and more aggressive in tone. To remain in the context of minority schools: Around 1927, Voivodeships in Poland stepped up their scrutiny regarding the enrollment of children for the German minority schools. The entries of thousands of children were rejected, most of them because the Voivodships doubted that the children belonged to the German minority. That again enraged the German minority because the very existence of their schools depended on the number of children enrolled. In the battle that ensued Polish authorities called on the national conscience of the parents who were suspected to be Poles yet opted for their children to attend a German school, and they did so quite graphically. Polish pamphlets or newspapers, for example, published reminders such as these:

> "Mothers! The school entries are made between May 4th and 8th. See that your children are entered for the Polish schools. Remember, Mothers, that in this way you are fulfilling your duty to your own children. Only children from Polish schools will find easy employment in Poland and provide for your old age."[67]

> "A father or mother who sends a child to the Polish school declares openly, loyally and freely that he or she is a Pole and loves and respects Poland. Fathers or mothers or guardians who send children to the German school show that they are enemies of Poland and all that is Polish."[68]

This was a new kind of making comparisons: Poles were set against Germans, and good Poles against treasonous Poles. Mediation—facilitated by the Council of the League of Nations or courts—was no longer an option for resolving

---

67    Extract from a pamphlet distributed by the *Westmarken Verein*, In: *League of Nations Official Journal* 1929, 239.

68    Extract from the *Polska Zachodnia*, No. 138, May 19, 1928, in: *League of Nations Official Journal* 1929, 240.

tensions, on both sides of the aisle. These comparisons were meant to threaten and to fan tensions.

## Disputes before the Permanent Court of International Justice

### Procedure

The Council of the League of Nations was certainly the most important venue for minorities for putting their grievances on the political agenda. Yet, there were other venues, where experts dominated the scene. Some of the venues were informal and *ad hoc*, such as committees of jurists consisting of three legal experts who were, time and again, asked to give their legal opinion, in particular, when the Council faced intricate legal questions and wanted conciliation to have a firm basis in law. One of the venues was permanent. That venue was the Permanent International Court of Justice, based in The Hague. The court was briefly mentioned in the Covenant of the League of Nations as an important element of the post-war international order. Under Article 14 of the Covenant, the court was supposed to determine disputes of an international character and to give advisory opinions. The court was eventually established by a Protocol adopted on 16 December 1920 by the Members of the League of Nations, declaring that the Member States were willing to accept the jurisdiction of the court subject to the conditions laid down by a statute attached to the protocol.[69] The court became eventually operative in 1922. Yet, access to the court was narrowly defined. Regarding disputes, the court could be called upon only if there was a prior agreement by the States Parties involved, either a general agreement or an *ad hoc* agreement.[70] Regarding advisory opinions, the Council and the Assembly of the League of Nations only were given the power to refer a question to the court (Article 14 of the Covenant).

One of the keystones of the minority regime created in 1919 was a provision in the treaties ensuring that disputes among States Parties could eventually be resolved by the Permanent International Court of Justice. All the

---

69    Protocol of Signature, December 16, 1920; Statute for the Permanent Court of International Justice provided for by Article 14 of the Covenant of the League of Nations, both in: *League of Nations Official Journal* 1921, 14.

70    Statute for the Permanent Court of International Justice, Article 36.

treaties contained clauses whereby the States concerned consented that disputes arising out of these regimes were to be held to be disputes of an international character under Article 14 of the Covenant and that any such dispute could be referred to the Permanent International Court of Justice by any of the Allied Powers or other members of the League of Nations.[71] Apart from minority issues arising under the specific minority treaties, States could refer to the court based on minority clauses contained in several peace treaties. In the mid-1920s, sixteen European States were bound by such a clause.[72] States could also refer to the court based on clauses contained in the mandate regime, and, as the case might have been, under international or bilateral treaties sponsored by the League of Nations.[73] The advisory procedure was initiated by a request of the Council or at the instigation of a State or international organization.[74]

## Court Opinions and Judgments

Between 1922 (the year of the delivery of the first advisory opinion) and 1939 (the final year of the court's judicial activities), the court delivered twenty-eight advisory opinions and thirty-one judgments, an overall of 59 opinions and judgments.[75] Most of these opinions or judgments dealt with minorities issues proper, i.e. issues that related to treaties making up what has explicitly been termed the minority protection regime, or with issues relating to treaties brokered in Paris in 1919 or in the aftermath in another move to reorganize Eastern Europe, including the Balkan region, and Asia Minor or the Middle East (e.g. issues relating to the Memel Statute, questions relating to the Treaty of Neuilly signed by Bulgaria and Greece, the Treaty of Lausanne, or concessions in Palestine). The overall number of judgments and opinions deal-

---

71    For Poland, e.g., see Minority Treaty Poland, Article 12(3).

72    Second Annual Report of the Permanent Court of International Justice (June 15, 1925–June 15, 1926) in: *Publications of the Permanent Court of International Justice*, Series E. No. 2, 50, namely: Albania, Armenia, Austria, Bulgaria, Danzig, Estonia, Finland, Greece, Hungary, Latvia, Lithuania, Poland, Roumania, Serb-Croat-Slovene State, Czechoslovakia, Turkey.

73    Second Annual Report of the Permanent Court of International Justice, 52–61.

74    Second Annual Report of the Permanent Court of International Justice, 92.

75    Court orders are not included in the count.

ing with minority issues proper is 13.[76] Most of these judgments and opinions were prompted by Germany and dealt with the situation of the German minority residing in Poland. One judgment was prompted by an application of Czechoslovakia in the early 1930s seeking to overturn the judgment of a Mixed Arbitral Tribunal holding that Czechoslovakia was bound to restore to the righteous owner (a Hungarian university) immovable property situated in Czechoslovakia, free from restrictions such as compulsory administration (*Appeal from a Judgment of the Hungaro-Czechoslovak Mixed Arbitral Tribunal*). And one judgment answered to an application lodged by Hungary in the mid 1930s questioning the legality of certain measures under an agrarian reform enacted by the Kingdom of Yugoslavia that implicated the expropriation of Hungarian nationals residing in Yugoslavia (*The Pajzs, Csáky, Esterházy Case*). In its judgments and opinions, the court tended to take the side of the minorities. That is not to say that the court tended to bend the law in the favor of the minorities concerned. Rather, the court stood by the law that was supposed to protect minorities against hostile majority politics. And the court, more often than not, concluded that pertinent provisions of the minority regime had indeed been violated.

---

76    Judgments: Case concerning certain German interests in Polish Upper Silesia, August 25, 1925, in: *Collection of Judgments*, Series A. No. 6; Case Concerning Certain German Interests in Polish Upper Silesia (The Merits), May 25, 1926, in: *Collection of Judgments*, Series A. No. 7; Case Concerning the Factory of Chorzów (Claim for Indemnity) (Jurisdiction), July 26, 1927, in: *Collection of Judgments*, Series A. No. 9; Interpretation of Judgments Nos. 7 and 8 (The Chorzów Factory), in: *Collection of Judgments*, Series A. No. 13; Rights of Minorities in Upper Silesia (Minority Schools), April 26, 1928, in: *Collection of Judgments*, Series A. No. 12; Case Concerning the Factory of Chorzów (Claim for Indemnity) (Merits), September 13, 1928, in: *Collection of Judgments*, Series A. No. 13; Appeal from a Judgment of the Hungaro-Czechoslovak Mixed Arbitral Tribunal (The Peter Pázmány University v. the State of Czechoslovakia), December 15, 1933, in: *Judgments, Orders and Advisory Opinions*, Series A./B. No. 61; The Pajzs, Csáky, Esterházy Case, December 16, 1936, in: *Judgments, Orders and Advisory Opinions*, Series A./B. No. 68. Advisory Opinions: Certain Questions Relating to Settlers of German Origin in the Territory ceded by Germany to Poland, September 10, 1923, in: *Collection of Advisory Opinions*, Serie B. No. 6; Acquisition of Polish Nationality, September 15, 1923, in: *Collection of Advisory Opinions*, Serie B. No. 7; Access to German minority schools in Upper Silesia, May 15, 1931, in: *Judgments, Orders and Advisory Opinions*, Series A./B. No. 40; Treatment of Polish nationals and other persons of Polish origin or speech in the Danzig territory, February 4, 1932, in: *Judgments, Orders and Advisory Opinions*, Series A./B. No. 44; Minority Schools in Albania, April 6, 1935, in: *Judgments, Orders and Advisory Opinions*, Series A./B. No. 64.

## Approach to Equality

On three occasions, questions pertaining to equality came up and were dealt with not just in passing.[77] One advisory opinion of the court is of particular interest to us, the advisory opinion dealing with minority schools in Albania. The advisory opinion introduced a new aspect to the concept of equality, and it did so against the backdrop of a minority policy that threatened existing minorities, yet allegedly nonetheless honored the principle of equal treatment before the law. In order to declare that such a policy—non-discriminatory on its surface—was in violation of international law, the court needed to be inventive, and it was inventive indeed, even though it could draw to some extent on a former advisory opinion.[78]

When Albania was admitted to the League of Nations in 1920, the Assembly and the Council made Albania accept the main content of the League's minority regime.[79] The League worried because of the tensions that existed in relation to Greece and to Serbia. Albania was the home of a large Greek minority residing in the South of the country and a smaller Serbian minority in the North. Both minority groups were Eastern Orthodox, whereas the Albanian majority were Moslems and, politically, under the influence of (left leaning) Turkey. To calm down anxieties, Albania signed a declaration in 1921 that repeated standard minority norms, *inter alia*, the promise that Albanian nationals belonging to minorities would enjoy "the same treatment and security in law and in fact as other Albanian nationals." Albania also promised that minorities "shall have an equal right to maintain [...] or establish" their own schools.[80] In the late 1920s, the promise given at the international level

77    *Certain Questions Relating to Settlers of German Origin in the Territory ceded by Germany to Poland*, Advisory Opinion of September 10, 1923, 23; *Rights of Minorities in Upper Silesia (Minority Schools)*, Judgment of April 26, 1928, 43; *Minority Schools in Albania*, Advisory Opinion of April 6, 1935, 15.

78    *Certain Questions Relating to Settlers of German Origin in the Territory ceded by Germany to Poland*, Advisory Opinion of September 10, 1923, 23–24.

79    See Resolution of the Assembly of the League of Nations, adopted on December 15, 1920, in: *League of Nations Official Journal 1921*, 123, stating: "In the event of Albania [...] being admitted to the League, the Assembly requests that [Albania] should take the necessary measures to enforce the principles of the Minority Treaties [...]."

80    Text of the Declaration and the Resolution of the Council of the League of Nations taking note of the declaration in: *League of Nations Official Journal 1921*, 1162–1164.

was backed by a constitutional provision stating that all religions "shall be respected" and that Albanian subjects of any creed "may found private schools," provided that certain requirements were met.[81] And actually, at the beginning of the century, there were hundreds of Greek schools in the Southern part of Albania, some private, some subsidized by the State.

Politics changed in the early 1930s, when a suspicious Albanian majority government thought that minority schools were the breeding grounds for disloyal political movements. The government decided to abolish minority schools, however, to abolish minority schools in a manner that would not violate the League's minority regime. In 1933, a constitutional amendment asserted that education and instruction were reserved to the State and would, from now on, be given in State schools only. The amendment further provided that "[p]rivate schools of all categories at present in operation" were to be closed.[82] The measure affected almost 80 schools located in the minority areas. When the Council of the League of Nations debated Albania's move at the initiative of Greece, the Albanian government contended that the constitutional amendment was in keeping with the minority regime, in particular with the equality clause. The Albanian government emphasized: All private schools had been dissolved, Moslem, Catholic, and Orthodox alike. Hence, same treatment was guaranteed: "The constitutional law applied par excellence to the whole nation. If it did away with a right belonging to the majority, that right could not subsist for the minority."[83] Also, Albania wanted the Council to understand the political background of the measure. At stake was, so the government stressed, "the ideal of moral unity which had been shaken by the cultural diversity that had prevailed among the Albanians for centuries."[84] We can safely assume that Albania's move as well as the arguments exchanged before the court were accompanied by competing practices of comparing: on the one hand by comparisons tailored to demonstrate how the Greek minority and other minorities undermined the unity of Albania, on the other hand by comparisons aiming to proof that the Albanian government was wrong or to insist on the legitimacy and the harmlessness of cultural differences.

---

81    In: *League of Nations Treaty Series 1935*, 109.
82    In: *League of Nations Official Journal 1935*, 151.
83    In: *League of Nations Official Journal 1935*, 113.
84    In: *League of Nations Official Journal 1935*, 112.

The Council of the League of Nations, unable to resolve the issue, referred to the Permanent International Court of Justice seeking an advisory opinion on the question whether the Albanian government was justified in its plea that, as the abolition of the private schools in Albania constituted a general measure applicable to the majority as well as to the minority, the measure was in conformity with the League's minority regime.[85] The court's answer in *Minority Schools in Albania* was as innovative as it was clear. The court reflected, for the first time, on the relation between universal norms and the notion of equality. In the nineteenth century constitutions, equality clauses primarily aimed at guaranteeing the same treatment for everyone, targeting privileges preserved for the aristocracy and the clergy. In 1935, the court conceded that universal norms would and could not necessarily ensure equality. Equality was not only about same treatment (formal equality), but also about different treatment. Indeed, the court held that 'equality' might demand that lawmakers favor particularism over universalism.

The Permanent International Court of Justice took three steps to unfold its understanding of what 'equality' meant and implied in the context of the minority regime.

The court first compared the wording of Article 4 and Article 5 of the Albanian Declaration relating to the minority regime. Article 4 of the Declaration promised same treatment by the law; the beneficiaries were all "nationals." The Article 4 read "All Albanian nationals shall be equal before the law, and shall enjoy the same civil and political rights without distinction as to race, language or religion." Article 5 targeted minorities. The first sentence of Article 5 read "Albanian nationals who belong to racial, religious or linguistic minorities will enjoy the same treatment and security in law and in fact as other Albanian nationals." And a second sentence added: "In particular, they shall have an equal right to maintain, manage and control at their own expense, or to establish in the future, [...] schools [...], with the right to use their own language and to exercise their religion freely therein." Noting that equality before the law had already been stipulated in Article 4 and that the wording of Article 5 differed from the wording of Article 4, the court concluded that the notion of equality referred to in Article 5 could not be the same than the notion of equality underlying Article 4.[86] Equality under Article 5, the court asserted, was not about mere "formal equality," i.e. equality before the law. Because

---

85    In: *League of Nations Official Journal 1935*, 151.
86    *Minority Schools in Albania*, Advisory Opinion of April 6, 1935, 18.

that was the stipulation under Article 4. For the court, the equality concept underlying Article 5 rather presupposed that equality of treatment might result in inequality in fact, and that would run counter to the stipulation given in the first sentence of Article 5. 'Equality' in the sense of the first sentence of Article 5 was, so the court suggested, "effective" and "genuine equality."[87] In other words, inequality in fact had to be overcome or avoided.

In a second step the Permanent Court of International Justice turned to the second sentence of Article 5. Pointing to the words "in particular" the court held that the second sentence gave an "illustration" of what was meant to be a prerequisite for the minority for being able to then enjoy the same treatment (not only in law but also) in fact, and that is, having institutions that kept the minority alive, such as charitable institutions, religious institutions, schools and other educational establishments. For the court it was clear that the Albanian move—the abolition of all private schools—was (though indiscriminate on its surface) particularly harmful to the minorities residing in Albania. Comparing the effects of the measure for the majority on the one hand and the minorities on the other, the court contended: The effect of the Albanian measure would be to deprive the minority of the institutions they needed in order to maintain their identities and their cultures, whereas the majority would have their needs covered by the institutions created by the State.[88] The measure would, therefore, undermine effective and genuine equality. Under those circumstances, 'equality' demanded different treatment in order to accommodate minority needs. In short, minorities must not be deprived of their right to run, at their own expense, private schools.

In the third step, the Permanent Court of International Justice rejected the argument of the Albanian government that the keeping of private minority schools only would (unduly) privilege the minorities over the majority. From the point of view of effects, so the court held, the minorities' right to have their schools left operating involved no privileges. Quite to the contrary, keeping and maintaining minority schools would ensure that the majority would not be given a privileged situation as compared with the situation of the minority. Identities and cultures of the majority were not threatened by the abolition of private schools. The majority's needs were well protected and served by the

---

87  *Minority Schools in Albania*, Advisory Opinion of April 6, 1935, 19.

88  *Minority Schools in Albania*, Advisory Opinion of April 6, 1935, 20.

State schools.[89] The same could not be said for the minorities. Their private schools were indispensable.

The 1935 advisory opinion marked a high point in the minority protection regime that took shape under the League of Nations. In order to give effective protection to minorities, the Permanent Court of International Justice developed a new notion of equality. The notion had its basis in international law (the clauses in the minority treaties and the minority declarations), but also in the creative thinking of the court. The concept of "genuine equality"—open to paying attention to inequalities in fact—prevailed over the concept of "formal equality." Yet, even if the advisory opinion in *Minority Schools in Albania* marked a high point in the evolving minority regime, it marked at the same time the end of it. It was the penultimate advisory opinion given by the court, and the last judicial statement in minority matters. The activities of the court ceased when war commenced.[90]

## Conclusion

From the perspective of international law, 'equality' was one of the most important political issues of the interwar period. The interwar concept of equality was tightly linked to the minority problem as defined by the (principle and other) Allied Powers. One could even say that the minority regime constitutes an important link between late eighteenth-century constitutionalism and twentieth century human rights law. The idea of equality was not born in 1919. Clearly, 'equality' was a concept that gained strength through Enlightenment thinking and practices spreading the idea among common people. But the idea of equality occurred, for the first time, forcefully at the international level. And the idea took a specific turn after World War I. The Allied Powers were convinced that, at the national level, i.e. at the level of nation state politics, equality for all might be endangered by the aspirations of a majority that was strong enough to install and dominate the government and, at the

---

89   *Minority Schools in Albania*, Advisory Opinion of April 6, 1935, 20.

90   That is not to say that legal debates about conflicting equality concepts died with the court. Quite on the contrary. The tensions between 'formal equality' on the one hand and 'genuine equality,' equality 'in fact' or 'substantive equality' on the other hand remain on the agenda of the politics of equality, doctrinal efforts, and court rulings. See Gautam Bhatia, Equality under the Indian Constitution, and Malika Mansouri, Equality through the Lens of Racial Discrimination, *in this volume*.

same time, hostile toward a minority defined by certain characteristics, such as religion, language, or what has been termed race. The equality clauses enshrined in the post-World War II human rights regime very much look like the clauses that were part of the former minority regime. Both regimes generally promise equal treatment in a certain respect (before the law) and then add that the right is granted without distinctions relating to some personal characteristics, such as language, religion, race, sex, property, social origin. The specific add-on—the "without distinction"- or "without discrimination"-clauses—have their roots in the minority regime created in 1919.

Still, there is also a caveat in order. From the perspective of legal theory, the minority regime under the League of Nations drew on two different concepts of equality. One concept could be termed 'equality among imagined equals.' That concept picks up on the Enlightenment idea of all men being born free and equal (notwithstanding all kinds of differences), but also specifies the idea. The clauses define the context (for instance, civil and political rights), and they define the beneficiaries (inhabitants, nationals, persons belonging to a minority). The idea is, equals ought to be treated the same. The idea echoes the universality of the law. In *Minority Schools in Albania*, the Permanent Court of International Justice introduced a different concept. The concept could be termed 'equality among real unequals.' What the court called "genuine equality," is a concept that is sensitive to the power relations on the ground. Given the imbalance of power relations between majority and minority, treating majority and minority alike by and before the law might prove harmful to the minority, yet not to the majority. If that is the case, "genuine equality" demands unequal treatment, even preferential treatment. That is particular equality, i.e. group-specific equality, not universal equality; it is substantive equality, not formal equality. In the context of human rights law, "genuine equality" and—per implication—state duties to undo inequalities in fact is still contested ground.

Another caveat relates to identity politics involving (imagined) groups. In the aftermath of World War II, human rights law refrained from recognizing rights aimed at preserving the identity of groups that could be defined as distinct and identifiable communities (such as minorities) residing in a state that was not "their" state. Human rights were conceived of as rights of individuals only, even though some rights presupposed a community of right holders, such as the right to form associations or the right to freely manifest one's religion in teaching or worship, also in community with others. Minorities received some attention in 1992, and indigenous peoples in 2007.[91] But minority rights and the rights of indigenous people have—so far—been internationally recognized by way of United Nations General Assembly declarations only. These rights have not yet made it into a legally binding instrument. When it comes to rights implying "positive" state duties relating to ethnically defined groups, human rights law still lags behind the minority regime established by the League of Nations.

These caveats notwithstanding, the concepts underlying the equality clauses seem both fragile. Norms granting equality rights necessarily presuppose that the right holders (the ones who ought to be equal before the law) share certain features, such as being male, being wealthy, being nationals, being Germans, or being Poles. These narrowly or broadly conceived assumptions make, if shared, the having of equal rights self-understood. In the case of minorities that assumption proved very precarious. Under the minority regime, nationality was the main anchor of equality. Minorities were—like the majority—the nationals of a particular state. The minority regime was intended to make sure that equality among nationals was not being questioned by politics at state level. Still, the (relative) universality of the concept became elusive in the course of the 1930s. Practices of comparing were pivotal in the process. Comparing minorities and majorities in a manner that marked deep and irreconcilable differences dominated the scene and became routine. Nationality—the presumed commonality—turned into a mere formality and eventually lost its meaning altogether. Racially defined nationalities mattered, because nationalities were thought to have substance. Nationalities were equally grounded in practices of comparing, in this case practices emphasizing sameness. In post-World War II human rights law, 'humanity' and 'mankind' serve as the main foundation of an all-encompassing concept of equality. Yet, humanity and mankind are highly abstract notions, even more abstract than nationality. When under attack or ridiculed, the idea that we all participate in 'humanity' and, hence, ought to have the same rights might as quickly vanish as in the 1930s. Equality is not self-understood in a stable and reliable manner. Equality needs assertion.

---

91    Declaration on the Rights of Persons Belonging to National or Ethnic, Religious and Linguistic Minorities, adopted December 18, 1992, UN Doc. A/RES/47/135; United Nations Declaration of the Rights of Indigenous Peoples, adopted September 13, 2007, UN Doc. A/RES/61/295.

# References

American Jewish Congress (ed.), *Memorials Submitted to President Wilson Concerning the Status of the Jews of Eastern Europe, and in Palestine, by Representatives of the American Jewish Congress, on March 2, 1919*, New York 1919.

Amitai, Zur polnischen Judenfrage, in: *Der Jude: Eine Monatsschrift* 1 (12/1916-1917), 785–791.

Buell, Raymond Leslie, The Protection of Minorities, in: *International Conciliation* 11 (222/1926), 348–366.

Cała, Alina, Die Anfänge des Antisemitismus im Königreich Polen in der zweiten Hälfte des neunzehnten Jahrhunderts, in: *International Review of Social History* 30 (3/1980), 342–373 (Aus dem Polnischen von J. Rojahn).

Chasanowitsch, L., *Die polnischen Judenpogrome im November und Dezember 1918. Tatsachen und Dokumente*, Stockholm 1919.

Cohen, Israel, *A Report on the Pogroms in Poland*, London 1919.

Davy, Benjamin/Davy, Ulrike, Haltung in finsteren Zeiten. Die Zeitschrift für öffentliches Recht zwischen 1933 und 1945, in: *Zeitschrift für öffentliches Recht* 69 (4/2014), 715–804.

Davy, Ulrike, Wenn Gleichheit in Gefahr ist. Staatliche Schutzpflichten und Schutzbedürftigkeit am Beispiel des Minderheitenschutzes vor rassischer Diskriminierung, in: *Zeitschrift für öffentliches Recht* 74 (4/2019), 773–844.

Dmowski, Roman, Gedanken eines modernen Polen, in: François Guesnet (ed.), *Der Fremde als Nachbar. Polnische Positionen zur jüdischen Präsenz. Texte seit 1800*, Frankfurt am Main 2009, 276–282 (Aus dem Polnischen von Peter Oliver Loew).

Dubnow, S.M., *History of the Jews in Russia and Poland from the Earliest Times until the Present Day*, Vol. II, Philadelphia 1918.

Dufau, P.-A./ Duvergier, J.-B./Guadet, J., *Collection des Constitutions, Chartres et Lois Fondamentales des Peuples de L'Europe et des deux Amériques*, Tome I, Paris 1823.

Duparc, Jacques Fouques, *La Protection des Minorités de Race, de Langue et de Religion*, Paris 1922.

Dyroff, Stefan, From Nationalities to Minorities? The Transnational Debate on the Minority Protection System of the League of Nations, and Its Predecessors, in: Xosé M. Núñez Seixas (ed.), *The First World War and the Nationality Question in Europe*, Leiden 2020, 245–265.

Evans, Ifor L., The Protection of Minorities, in: *British Year Book of International Law* 4 (1923-24), 95–123.

Fink, Carole, Defender of Minorities: Germany in the League of Nations, 1926–1933, in: *Central European History* 5 (4/1972), 330–357.

Fink, Carole, Germany and the Polish Elections of November 1930: A Study in League Diplomacy, in: *East European Quarterly* 15 (2/1981), 181–207.

Fink, Carole, *Defending the Rights of Others. The Great Powers, the Jews, and International Minority Protection, 1878–1938*, Cambridge 2004.

Gewürz, S., *Lemberg. Eine kritische Beleuchtung des Judenpogroms vom 21. bis 23. November 1918*, Berlin 1919.

Harris, Wilson, The League and Minorities, in: *International Conciliation* 11 (222/1926), 344–347.

Hudson, Manley O., The Tenth Year of the Permanent Court of International Justice, in: *American Journal of International Law* 26 (1/1932), 1–30.

J. R., The Exchange of Minorities and Transfers of Population in Europe since 1919–I, in: *Bulletin of International News* 21 (15/1944), 579–588.

Janowsky, Oscar I., The Treatment of Minorities, in: *International Conciliation* 20 (369/1941), 286–294.

Kapiloff Fink, Carole, *The Weimar Republic as the Defender of Minorities, 1919–1933. A Study of Germany's Minorities Diplomacy and the League of Nations System for the International Protection of Minorities*, PhD, Yale University 1969.

Khadduri, Majid, The Alexandretta Dispute, in: *American Journal of International Law* 39 (3/1945), 406–425.

Kunz, Josef L., Prolegomena zu einer allgemeinen Theorie des internationalen Rechts nationaler Minderheiten, in: *Zeitschrift für öffentliches Recht* 12 (2/1932), 221–272.

Magliveras, Konstantin D., The Withdrawal From the League of Nations Revisited, *Dickinson Journal of International Law* 10 (1/1991), 25–72.

Mandelstam, André, La Protection Internationale des Minorités, in: *Annuaire de l'Institut de Droit International* 32 (1925) 246–392.

Müller-Sommerfeld, H., The League of Nations. A-Mandates and Minority Rights during the Mandate Period in Iraq (1920–1932), in: Goldstein-Sabbah, S.R./Murre-van den Berg, H.L. (eds.), *Modernity, Minority, and the Public Sphere. Jews and Christians in the Middle East*, Leiden 2016, 258–310.

Pomerance, Michla, The United States and Self-Determination: Perspectives on the Wilsonian Conception, in: *American Journal of International Law* 70 (1/1976), 1–76.

Preston, Howard W., *Documents Illustrative of American History 1660–1863 with Introductions and References*, New York & London 1886.

Rappard, William E., Minorities and the League, in: *International Conciliation* 11 (222/1926), 330–343.

Rosenfeld, Max, Die europäische Polenfrage und die polnische Judenfrage, in: *Der Jude: Eine Monatsschrift* 2 (10-11/1917-1918), 642–654.

Rosting, Helmer, Protection of Minorities by the League of Nations, in: *American Journal of International Law* 17 (4/1923), 641–660.

Sanjian, Avedis K., The Sanjak of Alexandretta (Hatay): Its Impact on Turkish-Syrian Relations (1939–1956), in: *Middle East Journal* 10 (4/1956), 379–394.

Temperley, H.W.V. (ed.), *A History of the Peace Conference of Paris*, Vol. 5, London 1924, reprint 1969.

von Balogh, Arthur, *Der internationale Schutz der Minderheiten*, München 1928.

Weeks, Theodore R., *From Assimilation to Antisemitism. The "Jewish Question" in Poland, 1850–1914*, DeKalb 2006.

# Equality through the Lens of Racial Discrimination[1]

Malika Mansouri

**Abstract**

*This chapter addresses concepts of equality in the context of racial discrimination and explores their nexus by analyzing the drafting history and the interpretation of the International Convention on the Elimination of All Forms of Racial Discrimination. Distinguishing different meanings of equality that operate in the negotiation and interpretation of ICERD, the chapter concludes that concepts of equality and the prohibition of racial discrimination both interact harmoniously and diverge at the same time. Most importantly, they are mutually dependent and influence each other: On the one hand, equality has been crucial in giving rise to and shaping the prohibition of racial discrimination. On the other hand, the prohibition of racial discrimination has produced diverse notions of equality. To make these (at least potentially) contradictory notions of equality useful for combating racial discrimination, both flexibility and further development as well as fixed constants of equality are needed.*

## Introduction

Equality and the prohibition of racial discrimination are two subjects that are supposed to fit together without difficulty; they are taken for granted as two sides of the same coin and are often referred to as twin principles. However, further analysis reveals complex relationships and ambivalent connections between them. Neither the discourses nor the attendant practices of

---

1    This contribution draws on research conducted in the context of the Collaborative Research Center "Practices of Comparing. Ordering and Changing the World" (SFB 1288).

equality and the prohibition of racial discrimination can be strictly separated from one another, for the two concepts are linked. Equality and the prohibition of racial discrimination can interact in ways that serve, stabilize, or counteract each other. Thinking in terms of racial categories is a much-theorized paradox that partially presupposes equality, since people can be categorized into different racial groups only if and because they are considered equal with regard to their humanity. Equality therefore allows racialization on the one hand, but on the other hand is also the source of the prohibition of racial discrimination. This paper investigates the latter: Whether and to what extent the concept of equality is entangled with the elimination of racial discrimination, and how closely the two are related to each other. These questions can be usefully approached through the International Convention on the Elimination of All Forms of Racial Discrimination (hereafter ICERD) to show the ambiguously linked struggle for equality and against racial discrimination.

As early as 1965 the UN adopted ICERD, which remains the most important instrument against racial discrimination in international law to date. ICERD is the first human rights treaty of the United Nations and as such influenced the subsequent UN human rights treaties in many ways. In addition, ICERD has many member states, with 181 states—almost all states of the world—having by now signed the treaty. ICERD contains a comprehensive set of provisions for the elimination of racial discrimination. In systematic terms, the convention can be divided into three parts. Part I (Article 1 to Article 7) contains substantive legal provisions. Part II (Article 8 to Article 16) contains provisions of a procedural nature. Part 3 (Article 17 to Article 25) contains the final provisions. The Convention prohibits all forms of racial discrimination. Racial discrimination is defined in Article 1 (1) as

> "any distinction, exclusion, restriction or preference based on race, color, descent, or national or ethnic origin which has the purpose or effect of nullifying or impairing the recognition, enjoyment or exercise, on an equal footing, of human rights and fundamental freedoms in the political, economic, social, cultural or any other field of public life."[2]

Article 2 lists the states parties' obligations, which are further elaborated in Articles 3 to 7. Article 3 prescribes the condemnation of segregation and

---

2    For a more detailed discussion on discrimination on account of descent, see David Keane, India, the UN and Caste as a Form of Racial Discrimination: Resolving the Dispute, *in this volume*.

apartheid and the undertaking to prevent, prohibit, and eradicate all practices of this nature. Article 4 deals with the dissemination of ideas of racial
superiority and organizations that justify racial discrimination or that are
based on the idea of racial supremacy; alongside Article 1, Article 4 might be
called one of the core articles of ICERD. Article 5 requires that any political,
civil, economic, social, and cultural rights granted by states—for example
with regard to property, freedom of movement, or nationality—must be
granted without discrimination as defined by the Convention. In addition,
Article 6 of the Convention obliges states to ensure effective legal protection
against discrimination and to provide compensation for victims of racial
discrimination. Furthermore, according to Article 7, educational and cultural measures must be taken to combat prejudices that may lead to racial
discrimination. A body of independent experts—the Committee on the
Elimination of Racial Discrimination (CERD)—is established under Articles
8 and 10 to ensure that the Convention is observed and implemented. CERD
fulfills this function based on the procedures provided by the Convention:
the state reporting procedure (Article 9), procedure on communications from
individuals (Article 14), procedure on interstate communications (Article 11 to
Article 13), and early warning measures. Of these, the first two are relevant
for the present chapter. In accordance with the state reporting procedure
(Article 9), CERD receives state reports and adopts concluding observations
on the manifestation of racial discrimination in the member states, and it
submits recommendations to solve the problems identified. The framework
of the individual communication procedure (Article 14) provides the citizens
of states parties with the right to petition the Committee. In addition, the
Committee shares its interpretation of the Convention in general recommendations. The analysis in this chapter is based on the text of the treaty,
the *travaux préparatoires*, a selection of concluding observations adopted by
the Committee within the framework of the state reporting procedure, the
Committee's opinions responding to individual communications, and the
general recommendations of the Committee.

    This chapter is divided into three parts. It begins by briefly outlining the
notions of equality that were operative in the adoption of the convention by
summarizing the genesis of the convention. Secondly, the chapter then elaborates on the CERD's approach towards equality and the elimination of racial
discrimination. More specifically, it analyzes whether and how concepts of
equality have been developed, consolidated, and shifted in the practice of the
CERD. Finally, the chapter sums up and concludes how equality and the pro-

hibition of racial discrimination both interact harmoniously and diverge at the same time.

## The Birth of the Convention

### Historical Background

Equality has been described as "without doubt one of the central principles of human rights law"[3] and a basic idea of modern law,[4] and its beginnings have been traced back to ancient Greece.[5] By contrast, the consensus on the rejection of racial discrimination has a more recent history. Early calls for the recognition of racial equality under international law such as those made at the Paris Peace Conference in 1919 and at the founding of the League of Nations "rarely became a subject of diplomacy after World War I."[6] In the history of the League of Nations Covenant the focus was on minority rights,[7] whereas efforts to include provisions on racial and religious equality remained unsuccessful.[8] Lauren has argued that the reason was fear that such provisions would delegitimize colonial rule or race-based immigration policies.[9]

The few efforts against racial discrimination before World War II thus did not come to fruition. But World War II and its crimes against humanity, first and foremost the Shoah, created a new awareness. As the constitution of the United Nations Educational, Scientific and Cultural Organization (UNESCO), adopted in 1945, put it: "The great and terrible war which has now ended was a war made possible by the denial of the democratic principles [...] and by the propagation, in their place, through ignorance and prejudice, of the doctrine

---

3    Wouter Vandenhole, *Non-Discrimination and Equality in the View of the UN Human Rights Treaty Bodies*, Antwerp 2005, 1.

4    Christoph Menke, *Spiegelungen der Gleichheit*, Berlin 2000, 24.

5    Jarlath Clifford, Equality, in: Dinah Shelton (ed.), *The Oxford Handbook of International Human Rights Law*, Oxford 2013, 420–445.

6    Paul Gordon Lauren, First Principles of Racial Equality: History and Politics and Diplomacy of the Human Rights Provisions in the United Nations Charter, in: *Human Rights Quarterly* 5 (1/1983), 1–26, see 2.

7    For a detailed and differentiated view, see Ulrike Davy, Minority Protection under the League of Nations: Universal and Particular Equality, *in this volume*.

8    Warwich MacKean, *Equality and Discrimination under International Law*, Oxford, 1983, 14.

9    Lauren, First Principles of Racial Equality, 14.

of the inequality of men and races."[10] In the wake of this agreement, international efforts to link the prohibition of racial discrimination and equality acquired support and were rooted in the objective of the United Nations to combat discrimination in the world.

Equality is thus not only "one of the major themes of most UN core human rights treaties"[11] and "one of the most frequently declared norms of international human rights law."[12] From the founding of the United Nations, references to equality were linked with the elimination of discrimination[13] in ways that became increasingly concrete over time. One of the earliest bodies established by the United Nations in 1947 was the Sub-Commission on Prevention of Discrimination and Protection of Minorities (hereafter Sub-Commission), composed of independent experts, not state representatives. The early establishment of such a body "was a crucial reflection of the need for parallel work on the causes and extent of discrimination, as well as the need for new international instruments and standards to combat discrimination."[14] Studies followed that explored the meaning and content of the principles of equality and non-discrimination and established several general principles. The Charter of the United Nations enshrined the prohibition of discrimination as a binding principle of international law alongside the principle of equality.[15] Article 1(3), Article 13(1)(b), Article 55(c), and Article 76(c) of the Charter speak of respect for all without distinction among others as to race. This was followed by the UDHR, which devotes attention to the prevention of discrimination. Even

10    UN Doc. ECO/CONF./29, UNESCO, UNESCO Preparatory Commission (1946).

11    Bertrand G. Ramcharan, Equality and Nondiscrimination, in: Louis Henkin (ed.), *The International Bill of Rights: The Covenant on Civil and Political Rights*, New York 1981, 246–269, see 246.

12    Anne Bayefski, The Principle of Equality or Non-Discrimination in International Law, in: *Human Rights Law Journal* 11 (1990), 1–34, see 2.

13    Dinah Shelton, Prohibited Discrimination in International Law, in: Aristotle Constantinides/Nikos Zaiko (eds.), *The Diversity of International Law: Essays in Honour of Professor Kalliopi K. Koufa*, Leiden and Boston 2009, 261–292, see 265.

14    For details, see Kevin Boyle/Anneliese Baldaccini, A Critical Evaluation of International Human Rights Approaches to Racism, in: Sandra Fredman (ed.), *Discrimination and Human Rights: The Case of Racism*, Oxford and New York 2001, 135–191, see 139.

15    The International Court of Justice has stated that "to establish [...] and to enforce distinctions, exclusions, restrictions and limitations exclusively based on grounds of race; colour, decent or national or ethnic origin which constitute a denial of fundamental human rights is a flagrant violation of the purposes and principles of the Charter" (Opinion on the presence of South Africa in Namibia, ICJ Reports 1971, para. 131).

in the drafting of the UDHR, equality and discrimination were intertwined as two sides of the same coin.[16] Beyond the positive recognition of equality, which starts with the expression "born equal" as a denial of a supposedly "natural" racial hierarchy, the prohibition of discrimination is the reverse of the principle of equality: It serves to combat any denial of equality, first and foremost on racial grounds.[17] Article 2 of the UDHR provides a right to non-discrimination, stating that every human being is entitled to all rights and freedoms "without distinction of any kind, such as race, colour, sex, language, religion, political or other opinion, national or social origin, property, birth or other status." Therefore, the elimination of discrimination was set as a goal in order to ensure equality among all human beings. In 1949, the UN General Secretariat wrote a memorandum on the main types and causes of discrimination. This memorandum treated nondiscrimination and the protection of minorities in particular as two conflicting but related interests that need to be distinguished but are both inspired by the principle of equality.[18] It outlined different types of equality, differentiating moral and juridical equality from material equality.

> "The ambiguity of the term "equality" is eliminated if we consider it to refer only to moral and juridical equality as proclaimed in the Universal Declaration of Human Rights; that is to say, it is equality in dignity, formal equality in rights, and equality of opportunity, but not necessarily material equality as to the extent and content of the rights of all individuals."[19]

As early as in the 1950s, the Sub-Commission devoted several studies to the subject of discrimination.[20] Thus, the UN Charter, together with the Human

---

16    Johannes Morsink, World War Two and the Universal Declaration, in: *Human Rights Quarterly* 15 (2/1993), 357–405.

17    See Shelton, Prohibited Discrimination in International Law, 288.

18    See UN Doc. E/CN.4/Sub.2/40/Rev.1, para. 3, General Secretary, Memorandum (1949): "1. Prevention of discrimination is the prevention of any action which denies to individuals or groups of people equality of treatment which they may wish. 2. Protection of minorities is the protection of non-dominant groups which, while wishing in general for equality of treatment with the majority, wish for a measure of differential treatment in order to preserve basic characteristics which they possess, and which distinguish them from the majority of the population. The protection applies equally to an individual belonging to such groups and wishing the same protection."

19    UN Doc. E/CN.4/Sub.2/40/Rev.1, para. 30, General Secretary, Memorandum (1949).

20    See *The Yearbook of the United Nations* 1956, 224; 1958, 224; 1959, 202.

Rights Bills,[21] presents nondiscrimination as "the most fundamental of the rights of man [and] the starting point of all other liberties" and as an "indispensable element of the very notion of the rule of law."[22] Meanwhile equality and nondiscrimination are considered to constitute *jus cogens*.[23] ICERD was thus born at a time when this development had begun—by the adoption of the Charter and the UDHR and the ongoing force of the Covenant—but had not yet been consolidated. An understanding of equality that linked equality to the prohibition of discrimination had found its way into international law but had not yet taken firm form. "The distinctions identified in the Charter—race, sex, language, and religion—were at the time seen as the main categories of discrimination or exclusion believed in, practiced, and justified throughout the world."[24] Although the principles of equality and non-discrimination had been normatively formulated, the explanation, concretization, and implementation of their content fell to later specific international instruments and UN organs, of which ICERD was the first.

## Towards the Convention

The issue became particularly urgent when, between December 1959 and March 1960, hundreds of National Socialist symbols (swastikas) and anti-Semitic slogans appeared on houses, cemeteries, schools, and churches in Europe and the United States.[25] In light of these events, the prohibition of racial discrimination was brought up at the United Nations,[26] and a resolution was adopted.[27] However, there was disagreement about what legal form the response of the General Assembly should take. The idea of a convention

---

21    The Human Rights Bill consists of the Universal Declaration of Human Rights (adopted in 1948), the International Covenant on Civil and Political Rights (ICCPR, 1966) with its two Optional Protocols, and the International Covenant on Economic, Social and Cultural Rights (ICESCR, 1966).

22    Hersch Lauterpacht, *An International Bill of the Rights of Man*, New York 1945, 115–116.

23    MacKean, *Equality and Discrimination under International Law*, 283.

24    Boyle/Baldaccini, A Critical Evaluation of International Human Rights Approaches to Racism, 153.

25    Ehrlich reports 637 incidents in Europe and 236 in the United States; see Howard J. Ehrlich, The Swastika Epidemic of 1959–60: Anti-Semitism and Community Characteristics, in: *Social Problems* 9 (3/1962), 264–272, see 265.

26    See UN Doc. E/CN.4/815, pp. 149–189, Sub-Commission, Report (1961); UN Doc. E/CN.4/81, pp. 99–139, Human Rights Commission, Report (1961).

27    UN Doc. A/Res/1779(XVII), General Assembly, Resolution (1962).

was raised for the first time, but it was regarded as a "pioneer step" and not taken any further.[28] Instead, educational measures on the one hand and legislative obligations on the other gained support. A further step was taken in October 1962, when a group of African states[29] introduced a draft resolution in the Third Committee—a sub-organ of the General Assembly—to prepare a convention affirming "the principle of the equality of all men and all peoples without distinction as to race, color, or religion stated in the Charter of the United Nations."[30] With this renewed push for a convention, the issue took on a new legal form. In addition, there was a shift in the content of the discourse. Following a focus on discrimination in general in the 1950s, anti-Semitism in Europe rose to the forefront of the discussion between 1959 and 1961. In the following years, the link between colonialism and racism became a central theme. This shift reflected changing power relations within the United Nations. In 1960, in the so-called Year of Africa and at the height of decolonization, eighteen colonies on the African continent had gained their independence. A total of seventeen new member states acceded to the United Nations, all of them former colonies.[31] With Resolution 1780 (XVII), the General Assembly agreed on the preparation of a draft declaration and a draft convention on the elimination of all forms of racial discrimination[32] and on the preparation of a draft declaration and a draft convention on the elimination of all forms of religious intolerance.[33] Both resolutions referred to "the principle of the equality of all men and all peoples without distinction as to race, color or religion." The resolutions led first to the Declaration on the Elimination of All Forms of Racial Discrimination (hereafter Declaration), adopted by the General Assembly on November 20, 1963,[34] and then, two

---

28    UN Doc. E/CN.4/Sub.2/SR.330, p. 9 (Sapozhnikov), Sub-Commission, Summary Record (1961).

29    Central African Republic, Chad, Dahomey, Guinea, the Ivory Coast, Mali, Mauritania, Niger, and Upper Volta.

30    UN Doc. A/C.3/L.1006, Third Committee, Summary Record (1962).

31    The new states were Cameroon, the Central African Republic, Chad, Congo (Brazzaville), Congo (Kinshasa), Cyprus, Dahomey, Gabon, Côte d'Ivoire, the Malagasy Republic, Mali, Niger, Nigeria, Senegal, Somalia, Togo, and Upper Volta.

32    UN Doc. A/Res/1780(XVII), General Assembly, Resolution (1962).

33    UN Doc. A/Res/1779(XVII), General Assembly, Resolution (1962).

34    UN Doc. A/Res/1904(XVIII), General Assembly, Resolution (1963).

years later, to the adoption of ICERD on December 21, 1965.[35] The Convention entered into force on January 4, 1969, in accordance with the provisions of Article 19. It was hailed as a milestone in the efforts to combat racial discrimination and was praised as such by one of the state members:

> "We leave this rostrum convinced that, because of what you have done today when the story of the twentieth session of the General Assembly comes to be told, it can well be said, as it was once said by a great war leader: This was its finest hour."[36]

Thornberry comments on this narrative: "It was not a particularly difficult birth, nor was the gestation prolonged: Its emergence from drafting into the light of day was swift by UN standards, propelled forwards by an extraordinary political momentum."[37]

Although the negotiations culminated in agreement, it must be noted that they took place in a tense and ambivalent atmosphere and were at times in danger of failure.[38] The foremost problem was the confrontation between Western states and new states, especially those in Africa, over former colonial powers' disputed territorial possessions overseas, an issue entangled with racism since some felt that "to speak of colonialism in all its forms amounted to implicitly including racism, which was a manifestation of colonialism."[39] Also, a highly sensitive tension existed between the domestic and foreign policies of the states parties. Some states parties thought that racial discrimination was a matter of other countries and that national racial politics were not an issue. According to Banton, "most states saw accession to the Convention as a matter of foreign policy" and as a "way of demonstrating their anti-apartheid credentials, with but few implications for their internal affairs."[40]

---

35    UN Doc. A/Res/2106(XX), General Assembly, Resolution (1965); UN Doc. A/PV.1406, para. 60, General Assembly, Summary Record (1965). Mexico first abstained, but later changed its abstention to a vote in favor; UN Doc. A/PV.1408, para. 1, General Assembly, Summary Record (1965).

36    UN Doc. A/PV.1406, para. 96 (Ghana), General Assembly, Summary Record (1965).

37    Patrick Thornberry, *The International Convention on the Elimination of all Forms of Racial Discrimination: A Commentary*, Oxford 2016, 1.

38    UN Doc. A/C.3/SR.1310, para. 11 (Chairman), General Assembly, Summary Record (1965).

39    UN Doc. A/ CN.4/SR.764, para. 11, Commission on Human Rights, Summary Record (1963).

40    Michael Banton, *International Action against Racial Discrimination*, Oxford 1996, 111.

The Cold War and the Middle East conflict led to a growing focus on domestic race relations, especially those in Eastern Europe and the U.S.S.R., the United States, Great Britain, and Israel. Thus, accession to the Convention could be a double-edged sword: On the one hand, joining the ICERD allowed states to express a nonracist position, but on the other hand, joining also provided a means for states to justify disapproval of each other's policies. This tension had a catalyzing effect, and it can be seen as a curse and a blessing at the same time: The tension certainly contributed to reaching a consensus against racial discrimination, but this consensus remained fragile at essential points. The precise definition of what constituted racial discrimination was controversial and in need of negotiation, and in this process different notions of equality became virulent.

## The Drafting of the Convention

During the drafting of the Convention and its provisions, the elimination of racial discrimination was inextricably associated with concepts of equality. Schwelb comments that the Convention "represents the most comprehensive and unambiguous codification in treaty form of the idea of equality of races."[41] Equality is explicitly mentioned fifteen times in the treaty text, although the wording differs. In the Preamble, significant references are made to the principle of equality of all persons, as stated in Article 3 and reaffirmed in Article 55 of the UN Charter (paragraph 1 of the Preamble). Further reference is made to the UDHR. Paragraph 2 of the Preamble solemnly echoes the wording of Article 7 UDHR, stating that all human beings are "born free and equal in dignity and rights." Paragraph 3 of the Preamble refers to equality before the law and to equal protection of the law. Equality is further evoked in the guarantees of the "full and equal" enjoyment of human rights (Article 1(4), Article 2(2)), of equality before the law (Article 5), of "universal and equal suffrage" and "equal access to public service" (Article 5(c)), of "equal pay for equal work" (Article 5(e)(i)), and of "equal participation in cultural activities (Article 5(e)(vi)), to mention just some of the various provisions of the convention. To understand the ideas of equality that underpinned the Convention's wording, I reconstruct some of the discussions involved in its drafting from the *travaux*

---

41    Egon Schwelb, The International Convention on the Elimination of all Forms of Racial Discrimination, in: *The International and Comparative Law Quarterly* 15 (4/1966), 996–1068, see 1057.

*préparatoires* of 1963 and 1965. The discourse on equality encompassed two different angles: equality as equal treatment and equality despite differences.

## Equality Through Equal Rights

The clearest and most significant reference to equality in the operative text of the Convention is found in Article 1, which speaks of equal footing, and in Article 5, with its multiple references to equality, notably equality before the law. "The claim to equality before the law is in a substantial sense the most fundamental of the rights of man," Lauterpacht wrote. "It is the starting point of all other liberties."[42]

An initial discussion unfolded over the reference to equal footing in Article 1(1). Interestingly, many early drafts of this paragraph, which might be called the core of the convention, did not make any reference to equality; equality was incorporated into the text after a verbal proposal without much discussion.[43] It is revealing that the inclusion of equality was not questioned. Equality was taken for granted and therefore explicit mention was not considered necessary, thus it was stated: "All the experts agreed on the concept of equality of rights."[44] Indeed, explicit reference was thought unnecessary since "discrimination implied the idea of inequality of rights … (and) since the condemnation of discrimination necessarily included inequality."[45] Similarly, during further stages of the drafting process in the Human Rights Commission and the Third Committee, neither the wording nor the meaning of the reference to equality was questioned. This shows that equality was seen as a fixed, unquestionable, and pre-existing normative value.

Article 5 has a special position in the Convention. In contrast to the other substantive articles which contain general formulations, Article 5 spells out concise and concrete provisions which are not exhaustive, as indicated by the word "notably."[46] The notions of nondiscrimination and equality before the

---

42    Lauterpacht, *An International Bill of the Rights of Man*, 115.

43    See UN Doc. E/CN.4/Sub.2/SR.414, pp. 7–8 (Ingles), Sub-Commission, Summary Record (1964).

44    UN Doc. E/CN.4/Sub.2/SR.414, p. 9 (Capatorti), Sub-Commission, Summary Record (1964).

45    UN Doc. E/CN.4/Sub.2/SR.414, p. 9 (Chairman), Sub-Commission, Summary Record (1964).

46    Article 5(1): "In compliance with the fundamental obligations laid down in article 2 of this Convention, States Parties undertake to prohibit and to eliminate racial discrim-

law were addressed in several drafts prepared by the Sub-Commission.[47] The drafting regarding this point proceeded without significant discussions in the Sub-Commission and concluded in Article 5's references to equality before the law and to equal justice under the law. In the Commission on Human Rights (a sub-organ of the Economic and Social Council)[48] the provision took on a new form. A revised Polish amendment[49] that reflected suggestions made by the representatives of France and Lebanon and proposed that in the introductory paragraph of Article 5, after the words "States Parties undertake to prohibit and to eliminate racial discrimination in all its forms," the following additional phrase should be inserted: "and to guarantee the right of every person to equality before the law, without distinction as to race, colour or ethnic origin." The argument was that "that right was a general principle which the others merely served to illustrate."[50] This argument found general support,[51] and it was thus decided to state the general principle followed by the other rights. Further discussion concerned the phrase "equal justice before the law," which was included in the Sub-commission's draft as well as in the Polish amendment. The phrase seemed too vague to many representatives,[52] and it was finally replaced by the phrase "the right to equal treatment before the courts."[53] At that time, the two International Covenants on Human Rights were still only in draft form, and only the UDHR offered a secure textual basis in its Article 7 that guaranteed equality before the law and equal protection of the law. Nevertheless, at no time did "equal protection of the law" appear as

---

ination in all its forms and to guarantee the right of everyone, without distinction as to race, colour, or national or ethnic origin, to equality before the law, notably in the enjoyment of the following rights."

47    See UN Doc. E/CN.4/873, para. 85, Sub-Commission, Report (1964).

48    The Commission on Human Rights was replaced by the Human Rights Council in 2006.

49    UN Doc. E/CN.4/L.699/Rev.1, Commission on Human Rights, Draft, (1964).

50    UN Doc. E/CN.4/SR.796, para. 6 (Poland), Commission on Human Rights, Summary Record (1964).

51    UN Doc. E/CN.4/SR.796, para. 13 (Ukrainian Soviet Socialist Republic), Commission on Human Rights, Summary Record (1964); see also UN Doc. E/CN.4/SR.796, para. 7 (Austria), Commission on Human Rights, Summary Record (1964).

52    UN Doc. E/CN.4/SR.796, para. 7 (Austria), Commission on Human Rights, Summary Record (1964); UN Doc. E/CN.4/SR.796, para. 10 (Ecuador), Commission on Human Rights, Summary Record (1964).

53    The position of Poland is summarized in UN Doc. E/CN.4/SR.796, pp. 6–7, Commission on Human Rights, Summary Record (1964).

such in the drafts of the operative text,[54] in contrast to the Preamble which contained both concepts already in the sub-commission's draft.[55] Although there were no significant points of disagreement regarding the principle in the Commission on Human Rights, the topic became relevant again in the Third Committee. There, some felt that "equality before the law" was restrictive, and reference was again made to the phrase "equal before the law and entitled to equal protection under the law." In these debates, equality rights are an essential element of equality concepts. Equality rights did not, however, imply equality in fact, as the next section shows.

## Equality despite Differences

The second angle on equality that can be identified in the Convention's preparation, equality despite differences, is illustrated by the discussions that took place regarding paragraph 6 of the Preamble and paragraph 2 of Article 2. Paragraph 6 of the Preamble states: "any doctrine of superiority based on racial differentiation is scientifically false, morally condemnable, socially unjust and dangerous, and [...] there is no justification for racial discrimination, in theory or in practice, anywhere." This is mainly an adoption from the Declaration on the Elimination of All Forms of Racial Discrimination, but with an important shift in wording: Whereas the Declaration speaks of "racial differences or racial superiority," ICERD narrows the concept to "any doctrine of superiority based on racial differentiation." This shift in wording moves the focus from a general acknowledgment of races to assumptions of inferiority and superiority associated with them.[56] The deliberateness of the change is

---

54   Italy did not submit a formal proposal but suggested guaranteeing "equal protection of the law" and hence adopting the language of Art. 7 of the UDHR; UN Doc. E/CN.4/SR.796, p. 11 (Italy), Commission on Human Rights, Summary Record (1964). The suggestion was rejected, since it was the law itself that was responsible for protecting the individual. UN Doc. E/CN.4/SR.796, p. 14 (USSR), Commission on Human Rights, Summary Record (1964).

55   UN Doc. E/CN.4/Sub.2/241, p. 3, Sub-Commission, Report (1964).

56   Keane sees not only a reference but also a parallel development: "[the] departure from the position expressed by the signatories to the Declaration is similar to the difference between the first and second UNESCO statements on race, the second of which refused to deny the existence of [...] race in line with its predecessor, [...] condemning only the notion of racial superiority." David Keane, *Caste-Based Discrimination in International Human Rights Law*, Aldershot and Burlington 2007, 176.

made clear by the arguments made for and against abandoning the wording of Declaration.[57] Several proposals brought to the Sub-Commission endorsed the language of Declaration[58] on the grounds that "there were doctrines used to justify discrimination which did not assert the superiority of one race over another, but still insisted on separation of the races."[59] Statements of the UNESCO were cited by the experts of the Sub-commission to argue that there was no such thing as race.[60] The opponents of the Declaration formulation also referred to the UNESCO statements and concluded that the UNESCO had "stressed the purely physical nature of differences between races and had added that racial differences implied neither superiority nor inferiority."[61] Therefore, they maintained that the Sub-Commission should "stress the falsity and repugnance of ideas of racial superiority since it was difficult to deny the existence of racial differentiation" and that

> "it was inaccurate to maintain that doctrines of racial differentiation were scientifically false. On the contrary, the whole purpose of the effort to eliminate racial discrimination was to protect the differences between races apparent to any observer; those differences were indeed among the beauties and glories of the human race."[62]

This argument initially found supporters, but it was subjected to a second ballot and was rejected in the end.[63] However, the topic was brought up again in the Commission on Human Rights, where a proposal to condemn doctrines of "superiority based on racial differentiation"[64] was adopted unanimously.[65] This time, there was little controversy, although a UNESCO representative

---

57    UN Doc. E/CN.4/Sub.2/L.314, Sub-Commission, Draft (1964).

58    UN Doc. E/CN.4/Sub.2/L.313, Sub-Commission, Draft (1964); UN Doc. E/CN.4/Sub.2/L.314, Sub-Commission, Draft (1964).

59    UN Doc. E/CN.4/Sub.2/SR.413, p. 6 (Capotorti), Sub-Commission, Summary Record (1964).

60    UN Doc. E/CN.4/Sub.2/SR.410, p. 6 (Saario), Sub-Commission, Summary Record (1964).

61    UN Doc. E/CN.4/Sub.2/SR.413, p. 7 (Bouquin), Sub-Commission, Summary Record (1964).

62    UN Doc. E/CN.4/Sub.2/SR.410, p. 7 (Abram), Sub-Commission, Summary Record (1964).

63    UN Doc. E/CN.4/Sub.2/SR.414, p. 3 (Chairman), Sub-Commission, Summary Record (1964).

64    UN Doc. E/CN.4/L.682, para. 3, Commission on Human Rights, Draft (1964).

65    UN Doc. E/CN.4/874, para. 65, Commission on Human Rights, Report (1964).

concluded that "even if it could be said that different treatment for different racial groups was unjust that was no scientific matter."[66]

Another notion of equality became apparent in the drafting of the special measures described in Article 1(4) and Article 2(2). Both articles are interrelated. Article 1(4) states: "special measures taken for the sole purpose of securing adequate advancement of certain racial or ethnic groups or individuals [...] shall not be deemed racial discrimination." Such special measures are thus excluded from the legal definition of racial discrimination under Article 1(1).[67] Article 2(2) builds on this Article 1(1) and imposes on states parties an obligation to take special measures to safeguard "the adequate development and protection of certain racial groups or individuals belonging to them, for the purpose of guaranteeing them the full and equal enjoyment of human rights and fundamental freedoms." Special measures are not, however, to lead to "the maintenance of unequal or separate rights" after their goal has been achieved. The terms "special measures" in Article 1(4) and "special and concrete measures" in Article 2(2) are used synonymously. Beyond such differences in the wording of the two Articles, both clearly address the same question, and both insist on the temporary character of the special measures, which are to remain in force only as long as necessary to secure the goal of "adequate advancement" (Article 1) or "adequate development and protection" (Article 2).[68] Even the first drafts of both Articles dealt with these measures, shifting from the earlier terminology of simple "measures" to the subsequent "special measures." Various opinions on special measures and their legitimacy were expressed and several amendments were tabled in the drafting process. In general, there were two conflicting positions. Some felt that the different living conditions of certain groups could be remedied only through special measures.[69] The aim of these special measures should not be to emphasize the distinctions between

---

66    UN Doc. E/CN.4/SR.775, p. 9 (UNESCO), Commission on Human Rights, Report (1964). India supported this statement; see UN Doc. E/CN.4/SR.778, p. 4 (India), Commission on Human Rights, Summary Record (1964).

67    See Thornberry, *The International Convention on the Elimination of all Forms of Racial Discrimination*, 139; Natan Lerner, The U.N. Convention on the Elimination of All Forms of Racial Discrimination, Reprint Revised by Natan Lerner, in: *Nijhoff Classics in international Law*, Vol. 3, Leiden and Boston 2015, 37.

68    Lerner, The U.N. Convention on the Elimination of all Forms of Racial Discrimination, 38.

69    UN Doc. E/CN.4/Sub.2/SR.416, p. 12 (Krishnaswami), Sub-Commission, Summary Record (1964).

different racial groups, but rather to ensure that persons belonging to less-favored groups be integrated into the community. Others feared that such measures would serve only to maintain divisions within the population.[70] The discussion focused mainly on two points: First, how to circumscribe these measures in a clear manner and second, how to name the groups that should benefit from the measures.[71] Regarding the first, the circumscription, it was pointed out that the aim "to place such groups on an equal footing"[72] and to attain the objective of equal development for all citizens was tied to specific temporal conditions.[73] As for the second, the naming of the groups, the terms suggested at the drafting stage included "certain racial groups,"[74] "under-privileged,"[75] "backward,"[76] and "under-developed racial groups."[77] The last term—"under-developed racial groups"—was adopted without much discussion by the Sub-Commission and was initially used in Article 2. Although the term "under-developed racial groups" was criticized in the Commission on Human Rights,[78] the term was retained after a separate vote[79] and also included in Article 1 on the basis of an amendment put forward by Lebanon.[80] Finally, the Third Committee adopted the phrasing "adequate advancement of certain racial or ethnic groups or individuals"[81] in Article 1 and the expression "the adequate development and protection of certain racial groups or

---

70    UN Doc. E/CN.4/Sub.2/SR.416, p. 13 (Cruz), Sub-Commission, Summary Record (1964).

71    Another topic was the protection of groups as well as individuals; see the summary in: UN Doc. E/CN.4/874, para. 87, Commission on Human Rights, Report (1964).

72    UN Doc. E/CN.4/Sub.2/SR.411, p. 8 (Ivanov), Sub-Commission, Summary Record (1964).

73    UN Doc. E/CN.4/Sub.2/SR.414, p. 8 (Krishnawi), Sub-Commission, Summary Record (1964); UN Doc. E/3873, para. 88, Commission on Human Rights, Report (1964).

74    UN Doc. E/CN.4/Sub.2/L.308, Sub-Commission, Draft (1964); UN Doc. E/CN.4/Sub.2/ L.319, Sub-Commission, Draft (1964); UN Doc. E/CN.4/Sub.2/L.323, (Ketrzynski), Sub-Commission, Draft (1964); UN Doc. E/CN.4/Sub.2/L.326, Sub-Commission, Draft (1964).

75    UN Doc. A/C.3/SR.1305, para. 10 (Cameroon), Summary Record (1965).

76    UN Doc. E/CN.4/Sub.2/SR.416, p. 13 (Chairman), Sub-Commission, Summary Record (1964).

77    UN Doc. E/CN.4/Sub.2/L.328, Sub-Commission, Draft (1964); UN Doc. E/CN.4/Sub.2/ L.324/Rev.1, Sub-Commission, Draft (1964).

78    UN Doc. E/CN.4/SR.786, p. 7 (Philippines), Sub-Commission, Summary Record (1964).

79    UN Doc. E/3873, para. 134, Commission on Human Rights, Report (1964).

80    UN Doc. E/CN.4/L.691, Commission on Human Rights, Draft (1964).

81    UN Doc. A/C.3/SR.1306, para. 27 (India), Third Committee, Summary Record (1965); UN Doc. A/C.3/SR.1307, para. 22 (Chairman), Third Committee, Summary Record (1965).

individuals belonging to them" [82] in Article 2, thus harmonizing the parts of the Convention. From the perspective of the notion of equality, criticism was leveled at the label "underdeveloped" as being an inappropriate description of a human individual or a group.[83] The term's critics argued that "those who discriminated against others often chose to call them under-developed, in order to justify their own attitudes and actions. [...] There was no question that the term 'under-developed', which could be legitimately applied to countries in an economic context, was not valid in connection with human beings."[84] The proponents of the term, meanwhile, contended that it was not "considered a reflection on anyone's inherent qualities; it merely described those who through deprivation had been unable to develop their innate potentialities."[85] People could be regarded as "victims of under-development,"[86] "not because of any lack within themselves, but because they had for centuries been denied those advantages."[87] The proponents thus emphasized that it was not the individuals or groups but their condition that was underdeveloped.[88] This position had already been adopted by the Commission on Human Rights, which made it clear that certain groups "were economically and socially—and not racially—under-developed."[89]

At the level of law, in short, notions of equality led to the consensus that the right to equality before the law was not to be tied to racial ascriptions. On the level of facts, notions of equality did not have the effect of negating differences. But these differences were not regarded as naturalized or biological characteristics of people. The meanings of equality as "sameness" and "differences" were discussed as social constructions with legal implications—not, that is, as ontological features inherent to people as such, but as a result of

---

82    UN Doc. A/C.3/L.1226, Third Committee, Draft (1965); UN Doc. A/C.3/SR.1308, para. 29 (Costa Rica), Third Committee, Summary Record (1965).

83    UN Doc. A/C.3/SR.1306, para. 30 (Nigeria), Third Committee, Summary Record (1965).

84    UN Doc. A/C.3/SR.1304, para. 27 (United Republic of Tanzania), Third Committee, Summary Record (1965).

85    UN Doc. A/C.3/SR.1306, para. 24 (India), Third Committee, Summary Record (1965).

86    UN Doc. A/C.3/SR.1304, para. 26 (Guinea), Third Committee, Summary Record (1965).

87    UN Doc. A/C.3/SR.1306, para. 25 (India), Third Committee, Summary Record (1965).

88    UN Doc. A/C.3/SR.1304, para. 26 (Guinea), Third Committee, Summary Record (1965).

89    UN Doc. E/CN.4/SR.786, p. 7 (Costa Rica), Commission on Human Rights (1964); UN Doc. A/C.3/SR.1305, para. 32 (Democratic Republic of the Congo), Third Committee, Summary Record (1965); UN Doc. E/CN.3/SR.1306, para. 23 (Ivory Coast), Third Committee, Summary Record (1965).

living conditions, which in turn are often conditioned by structures of disadvantage.

## The Implementation of the Convention by CERD

CERD's work unfolded alongside an ongoing negotiation over equality issues in the context of racial discrimination through the examination of state reports and by adopting concluding observations, individual opinions as well as general recommendations. In practice, the issue that drove CERD's activities at all levels was no longer exclusively discrimination de jure but also discrimination de facto; not only de jure equality but also de facto equality. De jure refers to the legal situation that *should* exist, de facto to the situation that actually *does* exist. Whereas de jure equality focuses on equal treatment in law, by law, and through law, the discussion of de facto equality assumes that equal treatment in law does not automatically lead to equal treatment in fact. Thornberry points out that the distinction between "equality/discrimination" in fact and "equality/discrimination" in law was introduced into the discussion through the opinions of the Permanent Court of International Justice.[90]

Since ICERD includes purposive or intentional discrimination as well as discrimination in effect, CERD concluded that the Convention is concerned with goals and outcomes as well as processes and thus requires the elimination of not only de jure discrimination but also de facto discrimination. As Thornberry puts it, "In CERD practice, the essence of *de facto discrimination* (discrimination in fact) is the existence of discrimination in practice; analogously, *de facto* equality refers to equality in the enjoyment of human rights in practice."[91] This terminology was CERD's response to a changed reality: Although racial discrimination has been delegitimized in large parts of the world, it persists without necessarily being ordained, supported, or mandated by laws—as in the case of colonial law, apartheid laws, and the Jim Crow laws. One reason for the persistence of racial discrimination is that not all manifestations, actors, and victims of racial discrimination are covered by exist-

---

90    Thornberry, *The International Convention on the Elimination of all Forms of Racial Discrimination*, 17. For details, see: Davy, Minority Protection under the League of Nations, *in this volume*, 156.

91    Thornberry, The International Convention on the Elimination of all Forms of Racial Discrimination, 114.

ing protections. CERD's discussions reflect mainly three questions: What is meant by equality? Who is addressed by the concepts of equality? What are the consequences of the concepts of equality?

## From Formal Equality to Effective Equality

As in the drafting process, the central question in CERD's work has concerned the meaning of equality. Ideas of substantive equality are expressed in CERD's documentation in various terms—partly complementary, partly synonymous—including "effective equality,"[92] "equal access,"[93] and "equality of result."[94] With regard to the definition of equality, three overlapping key elements can be identified: going beyond purely formal equality, equal access, and individual equality.

### Beyond Formal Equality

Since its early days, the Committee has sought to address de facto discrimination to achieve not only formal but substantive equality. For this purpose, CERD scrutinizes the actual impact of legal norms. Whereas formal equality refers to the equal treatment of similarly situated individuals,[95] "substantive equality refers to the idea that equality provisions should be sensitive to the informal arrangements and barriers that cause inequality for some, and account for them by requiring different treatment for persons who are disadvantaged in society."[96] The basic idea behind this approach is that formal equality in the sense of equal treatment can perpetuate existing disadvantages[97] by failing to take differing circumstances into account. Accordingly, CERD requires the states parties to provide legal provisions to ensure equality before the law that go beyond formal equality. As CERD concluded, "It was not enough to provide merely for formal equality but [...] it was also necessary

---

92    UN Doc. CERD/C/GC/32, para. 11, CERD, General Recommendation 32 (2009).

93    UN Doc. CERD/C/IND/CO/19, para. 13, CERD, Concluding Observations on India (2007).

94    UN Doc. CERD/C/GC/32, paras. 10–11, CERD, General Recommendation 32 (2009).

95    Vandenhole, *Non-Discrimination and Equality in the View of the UN Human Rights Treaty Bodies*, 33.

96    Clifford, Equality, 21.

97    Daniel Moeckli, Equality and Non-Discrimination, in: Daniel Moeckli/Sangeeta Shah/ Sandesh Sivakumaran/David Harris (eds.), *International Human Rights Law*, Oxford 2017, 157-173, see 159.

to adopt specific measures to afford ethnic groups every possible opportunity for their development."[98]

Over time, formal equality has become less important—though not unimportant[99]—since most states have in general enshrined principles of equality in their constitutions. However, drawing on empirical data making de facto inequality visible,[100] the CERD has observed that despite constitutional and legal guarantees, racial discrimination continues to exist. CERD has thus adopted a holistic and comprehensive approach to equality, combining formal equality with substantive equality and de facto equality.[101] As CERD sums it up,

> "The principle of equality underpinned by the Convention combines formal equality before the law with equal protection of the law, with substantive or *de facto* equality in the enjoyment and exercise of human rights as the aim to be achieved by the faithful implementation of its principles."[102]

For dogmatic justification, CERD refers to Article 1, which guarantees not only the recognition, but "the enjoyment or exercise" of human rights, thus requiring equality in practice.

From this perspective, the prohibition of indirect discrimination is crucial. Indirect discrimination arises from the recognition that a practice might be formally "neutral" (on the surface) while not being neutral in fact because these rules affect a particular group exclusively or disproportionately.[103] According to CERD,

---

98  UN Doc. A/33/18, para. 306, CERD, Concluding Observations on Czechoslovakia (1978).

99  UN Doc. CERD/C/IND/CO/18, para. 13, CERD, Concluding Observations on India (2007); UN Doc. CERD/C/SVN/CO/8–11, para. 12, CERD, Concluding Observations on Slovenia (2015).

100  UN Doc. CERD/C/GC/32, para. 22, CERD, General Recommendation 32 (2009); UN Doc. CERD/C/ALB/CO/9–12, para. 20, CERD, Concluding Observations on Albania (2019); UN Doc. CERD/C/ZAF/CO/4–8, para. 14, CERD, Concluding Observations on South Africa (2016); UN Doc. CERD/C/MNG/CO/23–24, para. 20, CERD, Concluding Observations on Mongolia (2019).

101  UN Doc. CERD/C/DZA/CO/15–19, para. 16, CERD, Concluding Observations on Algeria (2013); UN Doc. CERD/C/FIN/CO/19, para. 19, CERD, Concluding Observations on Finland (2009); UN Doc. CERD/C/UKR/CO/19–21, para. 5, CERD, Concluding Observations on Ukraine (2011).

102  UN Doc. CERD/C/GC/32, para. 22, CERD, General Recommendation 32 (2009).

103  Moeckli, Equality and Non-Discrimination, 165.

"indirect, or de facto, discrimination occurs where an apparently neutral provision, criterion or practice would put persons of a particular racial, ethnic or national origin at a disadvantage compared with other persons, unless that provision, criterion or practice is objectively justified by a legitimate aim and the means of achieving that aim are appropriate and necessary (Article 1 (1))."[104]

Bearing in mind that a formally neutral rule can have a different impact on different groups, CERD criticizes general provisions such as language skill prerequisites[105] that can lead to de facto discrimination against a particular group. Given its nature, "by definition indirect discrimination can only be demonstrated circumstantially."[106]

## Beyond Equal Access

In the context of discrimination in fact, CERD observes and discusses the lack of access in general,[107] and in particular the lack of access to the justice system,[108] to education,[109] to healthcare services,[110] and to employment.[111]

---

104    UN Doc. CERD/C/USA/CO/6, para. 10, CERD, Concluding Observations on the USA (2014).

105    UN Doc. CERD/C/CZE/CO/7, para. 16, CERD, Concluding Observations on the Czech Republic (2007).

106    L.R. v Slovakia, UN Doc. CERD/C/66/D/31/2003, para. 10.4, CERD, Communication No. 31/2003 (2005).

107    UN Doc. CERD/C/THA/CO/1–3, para. 17, CERD, Concluding Observations on Thailand (2012).

108    UN Doc. CERD/C/ARG/CO/21–23, para. 21, CERD, Concluding Observations on Argentina (2017); UN Doc. CERD/C/GBR/CO/21–23, para. 21, CERD, Concluding Observations on United Kingdom of Great Britain and Northern Ireland (2016); UN Doc. CERD/C/HUN/CO/18–25, para. 23, CERD, Concluding Observations on Hungary (2019).

109    UN Doc. CERD/C/ARM/CO/5–6, para. 15, CERD, Concluding Observations on Armenia (2011); UN Doc. CERD/C/SVN/CO/8–11, para. 7, CERD, Concluding Observations on Slovenia (2016); UN Doc. CERD/C/JPN/CO/10–11, para. 30, CERD, Concluding Observations on Japan (2018).

110    UN Doc. CERD/C/USA/CO/7–9, para. 15, CERD, Concluding Observations on USA (2014); UN Doc. CERD/C/RWA/CO/18–20, para. 15, CERD, Concluding Observations on Rwanda (2016); UN Doc. CERD/C/KAZ/CO/4–5, para. 16, CERD, Concluding Observations on Kazakhstan (2010).

111    UN Doc. CERD/C/JPN/CO/10–11, para. 30, CERD, Concluding Observations on Japan (2018); UN Doc. CERD/C/DEU/CO/19–22, para. 17, CERD, Concluding Observations on

CERD takes a broad view of the meaning of access, stating that "living in a proper environment is an essential prerequisite for access [...] on an equal footing."[112] CERD thus again stresses "the exercise on an equal footing of human rights" (Article 1) and thus the necessity of "effective access."[113] Part of CERD's approach is to consider the wider context of discrimination in access—not only a single measure or the most recent action, but the whole environment as well as the entirety and history of measures, circumstances, and actions. According to CERD,

> "it would be inconsistent with the purpose of the Convention and elevate formalism over substance, to consider that the final step in the actual implementation of a particular human right or fundamental freedom must occur in a non-discriminatory manner, while the necessary preliminary decision-making elements directly connected to that implementation were to be severed and be free from scrutiny."[114]

In order to counter discrimination in access, CERD advocates measures that can be subsumed under the concepts of *equality of opportunity* and *equality of results.*

Equality of opportunity requires that chances are distributed not only with consideration to formal equality but equally with regard to different starting positions. Therefore, the disadvantages suffered by some groups must be considered and eliminated in order to equalize starting positions. Moeckli uses the metaphor of a race to explain this concept: "Like competitors in a race, everyone should be able to start from the same starting position. Once the race has begun, everyone is treated equally. Once the race has started, everyone is treated the same."[115] Equality of outcomes goes beyond equality of opportunity and recognizes that removing barriers does not guarantee

Germany (2015); UN Doc. CERD/C/RUS/CO/19, para. 14, CERD, Concluding Observations on Russia (2008).

112   UN Doc. CERD/C/LTU/CO/3, para. 21, CERD, Concluding Observations on Lithuania (2020).

113   UN Doc. CERD/C/TJK/CO/9–11, para. 18, CERD, Concluding Observations on Tajikistan (2017); UN Doc. CERD/C/RWA/CO/18–20, para. 21, CERD, Concluding Observations on Rwanda (2016); UN Doc. CERD/C/ISL/CO/21–23, para. 7, CERD, Concluding Observations on Iceland (2019); UN Doc. CERD/C/FRA/CO/16/Add. 1, para. 98, CERD, Concluding Observations on France (2007).

114   UN Doc. CERD/C/66/D/31/2003, CERD, Communication No. 31/2003 (2005).

115   Moeckli, Equality and Non-Discrimination, 55.

that disadvantaged groups will be able to take advantage of available opportunities. Equality of outcomes thus aims at achieving equal distribution, in Moeckli's metaphor, even after the race has started. Both notions of equality are reflected in CERD's work. CERD explicitly refers to equality of opportunity.[116] Within the scope of equality of opportunity, CERD has also addressed poverty,[117] recommended adding language as a ground for protection under national laws,[118] urged the elimination of illiteracy,[119] and, last but not least, required training for professionals—such as teachers, legal professionals, and public service personnel[120]—as well as victims of racism.[121]

Even though equality of outcome is not referred to explicitly, it is nonetheless present. Measures which can be subsumed under the concept of equality of outcomes are in particular the imposition of educational quotas[122] and the requirement of adequate representation in political bodies and public ser-

---

116   UN Doc. CERD/C/GTM/CO/16, para. 30, CERD, Concluding Observations on Guatemala (2019); UN Doc. CERD/C/KAZ/CO/6–7, para. 16, CERD, Concluding Observations on Kazakhstan (2014); UN Doc. CERD/C/NZL/CO/21–22, para. 30, CERD, Concluding Observations on New Zealand (2017).

117   UN Doc. CERD/C/ZAF/CO/3, para. 20, CERD, Concluding Observations on South Africa (2006); UN Doc. CERD/C/IND/CO/19, para. 25, CERD, Concluding Observations on India (2007).

118   UN Doc. CERD/C/MUS/CO/15–19, para. 10, CERD, Concluding Observations on Mauritius (2013).

119   UN Doc. CERD/C/COL/CO/14, para. 23, CERD, Concluding Observations on Colombia (2009); UN Doc. CERD/C/PRY/CO/4–6, para. 37, CERD, Concluding Observations on Paraguay (2016); UN Doc. CERD/C/CO/CHN/13, para. 23, CERD, Concluding Observations on China (2009).

120   UN Doc. CERD/C/KOR/CO/17–19, para. 16, CERD, Concluding Observations on the Republic Korea (2019); UN Doc. CERD/C/LTU/CO/9–10, para. 18, CERD, Concluding Observations on Lithuania (2019); UN Doc. CERD/C/ZMB/CO/17–19, para. 10, CERD, Concluding Observations on Zambia (2011).

121   UN Doc. CERD/C/304/Add.93, para. 120, CERD, Concluding Observations on Denmark (2000); UN Doc. CERD/C/BGR/CO/20–22, para. 23, CERD, Concluding Observations on Bulgaria (2017); UN Doc. CERD/C/UKR/CO/22–23, para. 26, CERD, Concluding Observations on Ukraine (2016).

122   UN Doc. CERD/C/MNG/CO/23–24, para. 20, CERD, Concluding Observations on Mongolia (2019); UN Doc. CERD/C/RUS/CO/19, para. 20, CERD, Concluding Observations on Russia (2010); UN Doc. CERD/C/FJI/CO/17, para. 17, CERD, Concluding Observations on Fiji (2008).

vices.[123] CERD points to statistical evidence of the lack of representation as the basis of demands to increase representation, but it does not stipulate a particular numerically equal distribution of goods, services, or benefits. Finally, CERD emphasizes that the provision of equality—both of opportunity and of results—may not lead to forced assimilation:[124]

> "The convention did not in any way require the elimination of the distinctive characteristics of any race or group, and indeed the Committee had over the years laid special emphasis on the protection of minorities and respect for their identity. At the same time, Governments had an obligation to ensure that diversity did not lead to racial discrimination."[125]

CERD thus stresses the imperative of allowing each group the enjoyment of its own culture while providing access in accordance with its way of living.[126]

## Beyond Equality of Individuals

The emphasis on the states parties' obligation to achieve equality in effect has prompted the Committee also to consider structural discrimination. The focus on structures shifts the view from individuals to groups, and thus this concept goes hand in hand with notions of equality focused not only on individuals but also on vulnerable groups. The Committee uses the terms structural and institutional discrimination and, interestingly, sometimes equates these with de facto discrimination.[127] From CERD's perspective, structural discrimination is a global phenomenon. Its manifestations range from liv-

---

123    UN Doc. CERD/C/ARM/CO/7–11, para. 21, CERD, Concluding Observations on Armenia (2017); UN Doc. CERD/C/PAK/CO/21–23, para. 4, CERD, Concluding Observations on Pakistan (2016).

124    UN Doc. CERD/C/FIN/CO/23, para. 15, CERD, Concluding Observations on Finland (2017); UN Doc. CERD/C/HND/CO/6–8, para. 33, CERD, Concluding Observations on Honduras (2019); UN Doc. CERD/C/DEU/CO/19–22, para. 4, CERD, Concluding Observations on Germany (2015).

125    CERD/106/Add.10, p. 8, CERD, Concluding Observations on New Zealand (1984).

126    UN Doc. CERD/C/NOR/CO/19–20, para. 20, CERD, Concluding Observations on Norway (2011); UN Doc. CERD/C/THA/CO/1–3, para. 16, CERD, Concluding Observations on Thailand (2012).

127    UN Doc. CERD/C/FJI/CO/18–20, para. 10, CERD, Concluding Observations on Fiji (2012).

ing conditions in general,[128] such as poverty,[129] to socioeconomic rights,[130] such as the access to and the amount of retirement pensions,[131] to the judicial system.[132] A particular concern, reflecting the experience of the apartheid system, is de facto segregation in housing and the "de facto ghettoization of some geographical area"[133] as well as de facto segregation in education and employment.[134] The Committee's understanding of structural discrimination is visible in its general recommendations and concluding observations on vulnerable groups, notably indigenous peoples, Roma, and people of African descent.

The Committee's General Recommendation 23 (1997) on the rights of indigenous people and General Recommendations 27 (2000) on discrimination against Roma does not use the term structural discrimination. However, the recommendation addresses elements of structural discrimination implicitly without using the term. With its General Recommendation 34 (2011) on racial discrimination against people of African descent, however, CERD uses and specifies its view in explicit terms:

> "Racism and structural discrimination against people of African descent, rooted in the infamous regime of slavery, are evident in the situations of inequality affecting them and reflected, inter alia, in the following domains: their grouping, together with indigenous peoples, among the poorest of the poor; their low rate of participation and representation in political

---

128 UN Doc. CERD/C/CUB/CO/19, para. 18 a, CERD, Concluding Observations on Cuba (2018); UN Doc. CERD/C/BEL/CO/16–19, para. 15, CERD, Concluding Observations on Belgium (2013).

129 UN Doc. CERD/C/HND/CO/6–8, para. 16, CERD, Concluding Observations on Honduras (2019).

130 UN Doc. CERD/C/COL/CO/14, para. 18, CERD, Concluding Observations on Colombia (2009).

131 UN Doc. CERD/C/VEN/CO/19–21, para. 20, CERD, Concluding Observations on Venezuela (2013).

132 UN Doc. CERD/C/COL/CO/14, para. 21, CERD, Concluding Observations on Colombia (2009); UN Doc. CERD/C/MEX/CO/16–17, para. 14, CERD, Concluding Observations on Mexico (2012).

133 UN Doc. CERD/C/DEU/CO/19–22, para. 12, CERD, Concluding Observations on Germany (2015).

134 UN Doc. CERD/C/DEU/CO/19–22, para. 13(c), CERD, Concluding Observations on Germany (2015); UN Doc. CERD/C/IND/CO/19, para. 13, CERD, Concluding Observations on India (2007); UN Doc. CERD/C/RUS/CO/20–22, para. 17(a), CERD, Concluding Observations on Russia (2013).

and institutional decision-making processes; additional difficulties they face in access to and completion and quality of education, which results in the transmission of poverty from generation to generation; inequality in access to the labor market; limited social recognition and valuation of their ethnic and cultural diversity; and a disproportionate presence in prison populations."[135]

Here, structural discrimination is represented not as the actions of individual actors ascribed to singular causes but as the interplay of multiple factors—especially social, economic, and political causes[136] and historical legacies[137]—that interact to distribute benefits to or withhold them from certain groups. Hence, structural discrimination can be regarded as the product of multiple inequalities affecting a particular group that needs to be addressed not individually but structurally.

Acting on this understanding, CERD urged Mexico, for example, to take steps to eliminate historical and structural discrimination by adopting social inclusion policies to reduce inequality.[138]

## From State Obligations to Private Obligations

In addition to the question of what is meant by equality, CERD addressed who is obliged by the equality clause. From the beginning of its efforts to combat discrimination, CERD has confronted the question of discrimination by private parties. Already at the drafting stage, there was controversy over whether the contracting states parties could be obligated to sanction discrimination by private parties. This possibility was and still is rejected by some states, and it has thus become a central and contentious issue of interpretation in the state party reporting procedure. The issue arose, in particular, in connection with private actors dealing with South Africa[139] as well as with "privatization

---

135    UN Doc. CERD/C/GC/34, CERD, General Recommendation 34 (2011).

136    UN Doc. CERD/C/COL/CO/15–16, para. 13, CERD, Concluding Observations on Colombia (2016).

137    UN Doc. CERD/C/CUB/CO/19–21, para. 17, CERD, Concluding Observations on Cuba (2018).

138    UN Doc. CERD/C/MEX/CO/16–17, para. 18, CERD, Concluding Observations on Mexico (2012).

139    UN Doc. A/39/18, para. 562, CERD, Concluding Observations on the Netherlands (1984); UN Doc. A/35/18, para. 199, CERD, Concluding Observations on Italy (1980); UN Doc. CERD/C/NZL/CO/18–20, para. 19, CERD, Concluding Observations on New Zealand

of apartheid"[140] and the exclusion of the private sector from anti-discrimination legislation.[141] Nevertheless, CERD has developed and conveyed a firm interpretive stance, according to which the Convention is not limited to public life, particularly with respect to Article 5. From the beginning, CERD has complained that "measures taken in the sphere of private law were unsatisfactory."[142] CERD has argued that measures should be binding on individuals and private companies[143] and urged states to withdraw or narrow reservations that granted leeway to private actors,[144] reminding states parties that unequal living conditions "might arise as an unintended by-product of the actions of a private person."[145] CERD has progressively concretized and deepened measures by, for example, demanding investigations of private individuals[146] and the imposition of controls on their hiring practices.[147] In view of this established practice, the fact that CERD's inclusion of private-sector discrimination was not written into its General Recommendation 14 indicates that such an explicit statement was no longer deemed necessary—and not that there was no consensus on the matter within CERD.[148] This interpretation is confirmed by repeated references to the private sector in the Committee's General Recommendations 19.[149] Its practice shows that CERD takes a holistic and comprehensive approach to equality, calling on states parties

---

(2013); UN Doc. CERD/C/PRY/CO/4–6, para. 24, CERD, Concluding Observations on Paraguay (2016).

140   UN Doc. A/50/18, para. 533, CERD, Concluding Observations on Germany (1994); UN Doc. A/46/18, para. 119, CERD, Concluding Observations on Portugal (1991).

141   UN Doc. CERD/C/SR.1420, para. 52 (Ukraine), CERD, Summary Record (2000).

142   UN Doc. CERD/C/SR.1196, para. 17 (Country Rapporteur on Germany), CERD, Summary Record (1997).

143   UN Doc. A/42/18, para. 557, CERD, Concluding Observations on Brazil (1987); UN Doc. A/48/18, para. 434, CERD, Concluding Observations on Germany (1993).

144   UN Doc. CERD/C/USA/CO/7–9, para. 5(b), CERD, Concluding Observations on USA (2014).

145   UN Doc. CERD/C/SR.1196, para. 20 (Country Rapporteur on Germany), CERD, Summary Record (1997); see also UN Doc. CERD/C/RUS/CO/20–22, para. 21 d, CERD, Concluding Observations on Russia (2013).

146   UN Doc. A/46/18, para. 119, CERD, Concluding Observations on Portugal (1991).

147   UN Doc. CERD/C/DEU/CO/19–22, paras. 23 and 14 c, CERD, Concluding Observations on Germany (2015).

148   Thornberry, *The International Convention on the Elimination of all Forms of Racial Discrimination*, 131.

149   UN Doc. A/50/18 at 140, para. 1, CERD, General Recommendation 19 (1995).

"to accelerate the adoption of a comprehensive anti-discrimination act to stipulate, inter alia, the definition of direct and indirect as well as de facto and de jure discrimination, together with structural discrimination, liability for natural and legal persons *extending to both public authorities and private persons*, remedies to victims of racial discrimination and the institutional mechanisms necessary to guarantee the implementation of the provisions of the Act in a holistic manner."[150] (emphasis mine)

## From Equal Treatment to Unequal Treatment

Finally, what are the consequences of equality clauses according to CERD? In the practice of CERD, notions of equality entail equal as well as unequal treatment, depending on the situation: "To treat in an equal manner persons or groups whose situations are objectively different will constitute discrimination in effect, as will the unequal treatment of persons whose situations are objectively the same."[151] To the same extent that those who are equal must be treated equally, differences in the treatment of those who are unequal in accordance with their inequality are not only permitted but under certain circumstances even required. Accordingly, unequal treatment in an unequal context is in itself an aspect of the concept of equality.[152] This standpoint differentiation is particularly evident in the call for special measures, that is, interventions under the provisions of the second paragraph of Article 2 that provide special assistance to disadvantaged groups or individuals on the condition that "such measures do not lead to the maintenance of separate rights for different groups and that they shall cease after the objectives for which they were taken have been achieved" (Article 1(4)). CERD's preferred term, "special measures," has certain substantive advantages over the largely synonymous terms "positive action," "affirmative action," and "positive discrimination," since it is necessary to distinguish legitimate special measures from prohibited "unjustifiable preferences,"[153] which can result from the perpetuation of special measures beyond the achievement of their stated goals.

---

150    UN Doc. CERD/C/UKR/CO/19–21, para. 5, CERD, Concluding Observations on Ukraine (2011).

151    UN Doc. CERD/C/GC/32, para. 8, CERD, General Recommendation 32 (2009).

152    Again, this practice is also not entirely new, see Davy referring to the practice under the League of Nations as "genuine" equality, Davy, Minority Protection under the League of Nations, *in this volume*, 159.

153    UN Doc. CERD/C/GC/32, para. 7, CERD, General Recommendation 32 (2009).

The difference between the two is that the "unjustifiable preferences" has an unjustifiable disparate impact on a group distinguished by race, color, descent, or national or ethnic origin and thus is considered discriminatory.

CERD urges the states parties to "raise awareness that special measures are necessary for achieving substantive equality,"[154] not only formal equality.[155] The obligation to implement special measures is applicable to a wide range of domains,[156] including

> "legislative, executive, administrative, budgetary and regulatory instruments, at every level in the State apparatus, as well as plans, policies, programmes and preferential regimes in areas such as employment, housing, education, culture, and participation in public life for disfavoured groups, devised and implemented on the basis of such instruments."[157]

CERD has occasionally concretized its call for special measures by endorsing specific policies, such as quotas,[158] especially in the areas of education,[159] parliamentary representation,[160] and public services,[161] or the adoption of other

---

154  UN Doc. CERD/C/MUS/CO/15–19, para. 14, CERD, Concluding Observations on Mauritius (2013).

155  UN Doc. CERD/C/ZAF/CO/3, para. 13, CERD, Concluding Observations on South Africa (2006); UN Doc. CERD/C/ARM/CO/5–6, para. 13, CERD, Concluding Observations on Armenia (2011); UN Doc. CERD/C/KEN/CO/5–7, para. 3, CERD, Concluding Observations on Kenya (2017); UN Doc. CERD/C/MUS/CO/15–19, para. 13, CERD, Concluding Observations on Mauritius (2013).

156  UN Doc. CERD/C/GTM/CO/16–17, para. 14, CERD, Concluding Observations on Guatemala (2019); UN Doc. CERD/C/HUN/CO/18–25, para. 21 c, CERD, Concluding Observations on Hungary (2019); UN Doc. CERD/C/MUS/CO/20–23, para. 11, CERD, Concluding Observations on Mauritius (2018).

157  UN Doc. CERD/C/GC/32, para. 13, CERD, General Recommendation 32 (2009).

158  UN Doc. CERD/C/CMR/CO/19–21, para. 11, CERD, Concluding Observations on Cameroon (2014).

159  UN Doc. CERD/C/MNG/CO/23–24, para. 20, CERD, Concluding Observations on Mongolia (2019); UN Doc. CERD/C/MDA/CO/15, para. 19, CERD, Concluding Observations on Moldova (2017).

160  UN Doc. CERD/C/CZE/CO/12–13, para. 1, CERD, Concluding Observations on Czechia (2019); UN Doc. CERD/C/SDN/CO/12–16, para. 18, CERD, Concluding Observations on Sudan (2015); UN Doc. CERD/C/IND/CO/19, para. 17, CERD, Concluding Observations on India (2007).

161  UN Doc. CERD/C/RUS/CO/19, para. 20, CERD, Concluding Observations on Russia (2008).

"positive legislative, judicial, administrative and other measures."[162] CERD sees special measures as a means of addressing structural discrimination against vulnerable groups, such as indigenous people, Roma, and people of African descent[163] through changing social and institutional structures.

In addition, the Committee has drawn attention to the distinction between special and temporary measures for the advancement of ethnic groups, on the one hand, and the permanent rights of indigenous peoples and other groups, on the other. Permanent rights include

> "the rights of persons belonging to minorities to profess and practice their own religion and use their own language; the rights of indigenous peoples; or rights of women to non-identical treatment with men on account of biological differences from men, e.g. maternity leave, while these groups are also entitled to benefit from special measures."[164]

CERD thus not only recognizes differences but also urges their maintenance. The Convention does not require the elimination of the distinctive characteristics of any race or group, and indeed the Committee has laid special emphasis on the protection of minorities and respect for their identities over the years. At the same time, however, governments have an obligation to ensure that diversity does not lead to racial discrimination.[165] In this respect, it is important that CERD assumes that the population is diverse and vehemently rejects claims of ethnic homogeneity, and it thus makes clear that it perceives equality in line with diversity and difference.

## Conclusions

The lens of the prohibition of racial discrimination has made visible several facets of equality. First and foremost, only because the idea of equality was already normatively anchored prohibitions of racial discrimination could be established.

---

162   UN Doc. CERD/C/SLV/CO/13, para. 9, CERD, Concluding Observations on El Salvador (2006).

163   UN Doc. CERD/C/SWE/CO/22–23, para. 15, CERD, Concluding Observations on Sweden (2018).

164   UN Doc. CERD/C/GC/32, para. 15, CERD, General Recommendation 32 (2009).

165   UN Doc. CERD/C/NAM/CO/12, para. 24, CERD, Concluding Observations on Namibia (2008).

The drafting of ICERD showed that equality rights were not questioned—at least not explicitly. At the same time, equality was not understood as the negation of differences but as equality despite differences. This simultaneity of sameness and difference continues in CERD's practice. The central issues in CERD's practice are not so many theories of equality but practical arguments guided by discrimination in fact. CERD realized the need to contextualize concepts of equality, rather than relying on a theoretical construct that is not grounded on the impact of reality. This leads to focus on questions of formal versus substantive equality, structural and institutional inequality, and perspectives on determining when differential treatment is permissible or impermissible under international law. The Committee opens the door for a broader understanding of equality, first, by making clear that formal commitment by states is not enough. Legislation and practice are put to the test. The Committee raises important discussions and critical questions that governments must address: Particularly, it raises extraordinary awareness of substantive manifestations of equality. In this context, CERD further makes clear that equal treatment does not produce equality per se. In a nutshell: equality through unequal treatment.

The examination of the drafting of the Convention as well as in CERD practice has revealed that equality—viewed through the lens of racial discrimination—is an interplay of several complementary and at points conflicting conceptions of equality. In both drafting and practice, the guiding principle was not that there are no differences, but that equality is assured despite those differences or even precisely because of them—since those who differ the most need equality rights the most. In the sense of a 'living instrument', CERD approached concepts of equality by confirming some, readjusting and contesting others to fit particular circumstances and challenges. These concepts are not separated strictly but merge into each other in discussions of who is obliged and to whom equality refers.

Through this lens, equality as a value requires a holistic view that is not fixed in static concepts in which concepts of de jure equality, legal equality, or formal equality stand in fixed opposition to de facto, substantive equality or sameness. Instead, they can merge cumulatively as well as fluidly. To be precise, neither equality and difference nor equality and inequality contradict each other. Thus, broadly speaking, equality has produced the prohibition of racial discrimination, but racial discrimination in turn has also shaped concepts of equality.

## References

Banton, Michael, *International Action against Racial Discrimination*, Oxford 1996.

Bayefski, Anne, The Principle of Equality or Non-Discrimination in International Law, in: *Human Rights Law Journal* 11 (1990), 1–34.

Boyle, Kevin/Baldaccini, Anneliese, A Critical Evaluation of International Human Rights Approaches to Racism, in: Fredman, Sandra (ed.), *Discrimination and Human Rights: The Case of Racism*, Oxford and New York 2001, 135–191.

Clifford, Jarlath, Equality, in: Shelton, Dinah (ed.), *The Oxford Handbook of International Human Rights Law*, Oxford 2013, 420–425.

Ehrlich, Howard J., The Swastika Epidemic of 1959–60: Anti-Semitism and Community Characteristics, in: *Social Problems* 9 (3/1962), 264–272.

Keane, David, *Caste-Based Discrimination in International Human Rights Law*, Aldershot and Burlington 2007.

Lauren, Paul Gordon, First Principles of Racial Equality: History and Politics and Diplomacy of the Human Rights Provisions in the United Nations Charter, in: *Human Rights Quarterly* 5 (1/1983), 1–26.

Lauterpacht, Hersch, *An International Bill of the Rights of Man*, New York 1945.

Lerner, Natan, The U.N. Convention on the Elimination of All Forms of Racial Discrimination, Reprint Revised by Lerner, Natan, in: *Nijhoff Classics in International Law*, Vol. 3, Leiden 2015.

MacKean, Warwick, *Equality and Discrimination under International Law*, Oxford, 1983.

Menke, Christoph, *Spiegelungen der Gleichheit*, Berlin 2000.

Moeckli, Daniel, Equality and Non-Discrimination, in: Moeckli, Daniel/Shah, Sangeeta/Sivakumaran, Sandesh/Harris, David (eds.), *International Human Rights Law*, Oxford 2017.

Morsink, Johannes, World War Two and the Universal Declaration, in: *Human Rights Quarterly* 15 (2/1993), 357–405.

Morsink, Johannes, The Universal Declaration of Human Rights: Origins, Drafting, and Intent, Philadelphia 1999.

Ramcharan, Bertrand G., Equality and Nondiscrimination, in: Henkin, Louis (ed.), The International Bill of Rights: *The Covenant on Civil and Political Rights*, New York 1981, 246–269.

Schwelb, Egon, The International Convention on the Elimination of all Forms of Racial Discrimination, in: *The International and Comparative Law Quarterly* 15 (4/1966), 996–1068.

Shelton, Dinah, Prohibited Discrimination in International Law, in: Constantinides, Aristotle/Zaiko, Nikos (eds.), *The Diversity of International Law: Essays in Honour of Professor Kalliopi K. Koufa*, Leiden and Boston 2009, 261–292.

Thornberry, Patrick, *The International Convention on the Elimination of all Forms of Racial Discrimination: A Commentary*, Oxford 2016.

Vandenhole, Wouter, *Non-Discrimination and Equality in the View of the UN Human Rights Treaty Bodies*, Antwerp 2005.

# India, the UN and Caste as a Form of Racial Discrimination: Resolving the Dispute

*David Keane*

"It was then that he started narrating.
A shower of moonlight.
The movement of quiet waves
in the lake.
The untouchable spring."
*G. Kalyan Rao*[1]


"A Dalit spring is on the horizon."
*Kancha Ilaiah*[2]

## Abstract

*It has been twenty-five years since India and the Committee on the Elimination of Racial Discrimination (CERD) disagreed on the interpretation of caste as a form of racial discrimination under the International Convention on the Elimination of Racial Discrimination (ICERD). In that time, India has reported just once to CERD. This disengagement is in marked contrast to India's contribution to the internationalization of racial discrimination in the early years of the United Nations (UN). The chapter examines that contribution and the raising of caste-based discrimination in response. It then looks at the dispute on caste as a form of racial discrimination under ICERD in the 1990s-2000s. Finally, it reflects on solutions to the dispute. The chapter argues strongly that India's opposition is*

---

1     G. Kalyan Rao,*Antarani Vasantam [The Untouchable Spring]*, New Delhi 2000. Translation Uma Sridhar, 2010.

2     Kancha Ilaiah Shepherd, A 'Dalit Spring' is on the Horizon, *Al Jazeera*, 8 April 2018, <https://www.aljazeera.com/indepth/opinion/dalit-spring-horizon-180407132053 298.html> [last accessed: October 30, 2021].

*misguided and has led to a troubling loss of the Indian voice in the international fight against racial discrimination.*

## Introduction

The International Convention on the Elimination of All Forms of Racial Discrimination (ICERD)[3] is the first of the core UN human rights treaties, with its adoption on 21 December 1965 by the General Assembly of the United Nations considered a "signal moment in international law and relations".[4] It has 182 states parties and in terms of ratifications, is nearing universal acceptance. In its early years it was perceived largely as an internationalist statement against apartheid and colonialism, and the initial and at times continuing task of the UN Committee on the Elimination of Racial Discrimination (CERD), which monitors the treaty, would be to convince states parties that the treaty applied equally to all states in their internal affairs, and to forms of racial discrimination beyond paradigmatic skin color prejudices.[5] In the more than 50 years since, CERD has seen its mandate evolve, so that today the treaty engages a range of groups such as national, ethnic and linguistic minorities; indigenous peoples; migrants, refugees and asylum-seekers; Roma; Afro-descendants; and others, on the basis of "race, colour, descent, or national or ethnic origin", the five grounds of its definition of racial discrimination in Article 1(1).[6]

In this context, in 1996, CERD interpreted the word "descent" in Article 1(1) as including caste, meaning caste-based discrimination was considered a form of racial discrimination and therefore within the scope of the treaty.

---

3   International Convention on the Elimination of All Forms of Racial Discrimination, G.A. Res. 2106 (XX), Annex, 20 UN GAOR Supp. (No. 14), 47, UN Doc. A/6014 (1966), 660 U.N.T.S. 195, entered into force 4 January 1969.

4   Patrick Thornberry, *The International Convention on the Elimination of All Forms of Racial Discrimination: A Commentary*, Oxford 2016, 1.

5   Michael Banton, *International Action against Racial Discrimination*, Oxford 1996, 106. Banton writes that in the early years of the treaty many states parties simply emphatically denied that any form of racial discrimination existed in their territories.

6   See also Malika Mansouri, Equality through the Lens of Racial Discrimination, *in this volume.*

India had contended in its 1996 state report to CERD that "the policies of the Indian Government relating to Scheduled Castes and Scheduled Tribes do not come under the purview of Article 1 of the Convention."[7] CERD responded in its concluding observations that "the situation of the Scheduled Castes and Scheduled Tribes falls within the scope of the Convention."[8] In 2002, CERD issued General Recommendation 29 on Article 1(1) of the Convention (Descent) (GR 29).[9] It strongly reaffirmed that "discrimination based on descent includes discrimination against members of communities based on forms of social stratification such as caste and analogous systems of inherited status which nullify or impair their equal enjoyment of human rights". In its 2006 state report to CERD, India reiterated its position that caste cannot be equated with race, nor is it covered under descent under Article 1 of the Convention.[10] India has not reported to the Committee since. The issue of caste-based discrimination as a form of racial discrimination has involved India in an entrenched interpretive dispute with CERD that is nearly 25 years old.[11]

This chapter outlines how that dispute may be resolved. Section 1 discusses India's historic role in the global fight against racial discrimination. It highlights how India championed the understanding that racially discriminatory policies are of concern to the United Nations, but that this necessarily brought scrutiny of its own domestic issues, including caste-based discrimination. Section 2 examines CERD's interpretation of "descent" in Article 1(1) ICERD as including caste and how this has led to an entrenched interpretive dispute between the Committee and India. It considers also the wider UN bodies and the need to move away from the "work and descent" terminology to focus only on caste as a form of descent-based discrimination. Section 3 reflects on means by which the interpretive dispute could be resolved. It explores the potential for resolution from the Government of India itself; the Indian judicial system; other states parties to ICERD through an inter-state communication; or enhanced pressure from UN bodies. All of these rely on

---

7    CERD, State Report – India (1996), UN Doc. CERD/C/299/Add.3, para. 7.

8    CERD, Concluding Observations – India (1996), UN Doc. CERD/C/304/Add.13, para. 14.

9    CERD, General Recommendation 29 on Article 1(1) of the Convention (Descent) (2002), UN Doc. A/57/18, pp. 111–117.

10   CERD, State Report – India (2006), UN Doc. CERD/C/IND/19, para. 16.

11   For an Indian perspective on caste and equality see Gautam Bhatia, Equality under the Indian Constitution, *in this volume*.

the role of Dalit Non-Governmental Organizations (NGOs) and civil society who drive change at the national and international level. The chapter concludes on how India's opposition to caste as a form of racial discrimination is an important legal and symbolic block on the realization of equality, and requires renewed action.

## India, the UN and Racial Discrimination

On 22 June 1946, India requested that the issue of the treatment of persons of Indian origin in the Union of South Africa be placed on the agenda of the first session of the United Nations (UN) General Assembly.[12] Its action was prompted by the passing in South Africa of the Asiatic Land Tenure and Indian Representation Act, with its discriminatory measures that confined Asian ownership and occupation of land to defined areas.[13] It was the first issue that India ever took to the UN.[14] South Africa strongly objected on the basis of Article 2(7) of the UN Charter, that "Nothing contained in the present Charter shall authorize the United Nations to intervene in matters which are essentially within the domestic jurisdiction of any state". It pointed out that it was not fighting the Article 2(7) "jurisdictional battle" only for itself, because other nations had "racial and minority problems".[15] The United States was concerned that the Indian complaint might result in the UN's investigatory powers applied against it, confessing great difficulty discerning the difference between "Indians in South Africa and negroes in Alabama".[16] The United Kingdom also argued that the issue was primarily one of domestic

---

12    Thornberry, *The International Convention on the Elimination of All Forms of Racial Discrimination*, 240.

13    Thornberry, *The International Convention on the Elimination of All Forms of Racial Discrimination*, 240.

14    Vineet Thakur, The "Hardy Annual": A History of India's First UN Resolution, in: *India Review* 16 (4/2017), 401–429, see 402.

15    Carol Anderson, From Hope to Disillusion: African Americans, the United Nations, and the Struggle for Human Rights, 1944–1947, in: *Diplomatic History* 20 (4/1996), 531–563, see 549.

16    Anderson, From Hope to Disillusion, 549, quoting UN Ambassador Warren Austin and Senator Vandenberg. Anderson also quotes Eleanor Roosevelt, who was worried that an "oppressed" minority "could get its case before the United Nations in spite of its own government".

jurisdiction and barred by virtue of Article 2(7).[17] It felt that if the UN admitted India's complaint it might have "enormous repercussions", because once such interventions began, it would be difficult to set limits. It thought India unlikely to benefit in the long-term from opening this Pandora's box.[18] In November 1946, Hartley Shawcross, who had been the lead British prosecutor at the International Military Tribunal at Nuremberg, was tasked with providing counter-arguments before the General Assembly. What would happen, Shawcross asked, if the UN should enquire into the denial of privileges "to those of negro blood"? And—"what if the UN should enquire into the caste system in India?"[19] It is possible that this is the very first mention of caste before a UN body.

On 8 December 1946, the General Assembly adopted resolution 44 (I) on the "Treatment of Indians in South Africa", stating that the General Assembly "is of the opinion that the treatment of Indians in the Union should be in conformity with the international obligations under the agreements concluded between the two Governments and the relevant Provisions of the Charter."[20] The resolution was "a moment of anti-colonial internationalism which established India as one of the leaders of the Afro-Asian bloc".[21] Lloyd notes that while India's complaint may not have brought relief for South African Indians, it "brilliantly succeeded in another aim, that of throwing the international spotlight on South Africa. As a result, India inscribed racial discrimination onto the international agenda".[22] India pursued annual UN resolutions on the racial treatment of Indians and apartheid, consistently seeking to make racism an international issue.[23] As Davis and Thakur investigate, India

---

17    Lorna Lloyd, 'A Most Auspicious Beginning': The 1946 United Nations General Assembly and the Question of the Treatment of Indians in South Africa, in: *Review of International Studies* 16 (2/1990), 131–153, see 132. Indeed Article 2(7) had been included in the Charter at the behest of Commonwealth countries who were anxious to prevent the UN discussing their racially discriminatory policies (see 131).

18    Lloyd, 'A Most Auspicious Beginning', 132.

19    Lloyd, 'A Most Auspicious Beginning', 142.

20    UN General Assembly resolution 44 (I), 8 December 1946, UN Doc. A/RES/44 (I), para. 2.

21    Alanna O'Malley, India, Apartheid and the New World Order at the UN, 1946–1962, in: *Journal of World History* 31 (1/2020), 195–223, see 196.

22    Lloyd, 'A Most Auspicious Beginning', 132.

23    Alexander E. Davis/Vineet Thakur, 'An Act of Faith' or a 'New Brown Empire'? The Dismissal of India's International Anti-Racism, 1945–1961, in: *Commonwealth & Comparative Politics* 56 (1/2018), 22–39, see 23.

framed its "anti-racism" discourse in numerous forms, loud and aggressive, or as a quiet emotion, or even as a quasi-religious struggle.[24] The responses to India's anti-racism were equally varied, but included a strand whereby India was accused of hypocrisy:

> "South Africa's response to India's tirades at the UN was to constantly em-phasise the latter's hypocrisy, but in a more aggressive fashion. South African diplomats pointed to India's stances on Kashmir and Hyderabad and the continuing practice of casteism as evidences of India's hypocrisy on human rights. Casteism was defined as 'Apartheid in India', despite India disman-tling its caste system in law while South Africa was doing the opposite on race."[25]

Thus in 1951, Mr. Donges (Union of South Africa) described to the General As-sembly how South Africa has "unfortunately been the first victim of arbitrary action beyond the terms of the Charter".[26] He continued: "But if South Africa was the first victim of such an arbitrary interpretation, it is gradually begin-ning to dawn on other Member States that South Africa may not be the last victim"; others may be forced "to visualize the possibility of their being hanged on the gallows designed by some countries for South Africa".[27] In 1955, Mr. du Plessis complained how for nine successive years, South Africa had been "attacked at the United Nations on the Indian question".[28] He countered that "many of our detractors fall far short of the principles of fundamental human rights and freedoms to which they so often pay lip service, and are guilty of racial and other forms of discrimination."[29] In 1961, Mr. Louw proceeded "to give some evidence about our attackers", beginning with India.[30] He docu-mented police violence at riots in India, oppression and violence against the Naga people and the Sikh minority, and the treatment of African students at Indian universities.[31] He described how "the cruel caste system is still being maintained on a large scale", quoting from official Indian reports "to show the

---

24    Davis/Thakur, 'An Act of Faith', 25.

25    Davis/Thakur, 'An Act of Faith', 31.

26    UN Doc. A/PV.344, 14 November 1951, para. 64.

27    UN Doc. A/PV.344, 14 November 1951, para. 64.

28    UN Doc. A/PV.528, 29 September 1955, para. 132.

29    UN Doc. A/PV.528, 29 September 1955, para. 133.

30    UN Doc. A/PV.905, 14 October 1960, para. 38.

31    UN Doc. A/PV.905, 14 October 1960, paras. 40–49.

shocking conditions under which the Scheduled Castes and Scheduled Tribes live".[32] He quoted the following statement from an Indian author:

"Our case at the United Nations would have been stronger, if the high moral standards of human rights that Pandit Nehru demands for our people elsewhere, were available to them at home. The maxim which says that whoever comes to equity, must come with clean hands, operates adversely on us, in view of some of the shocking manifestations of caste which are still to be seen in our 'deep south' [...]".[33]

Concurrent to the complaint brought by India against South Africa, civil society also began to petition the United Nations on racial discrimination. On 6 June 1946, the National Negro Congress submitted a petition to the UN Secretary-General, who it considered represented the "highest court of mankind".[34] Dr B. R. Ambedkar took note of the petition, and considered its relevance to caste. Ambedkar wrote to W. E. B. Du Bois, then leader of the National Association for the Advancement of Colored People (NAACP) in the United States: "I was very interested to read that the Negroes of America have filed a petition to the U.N.O. The Untouchables of India are also thinking of following suit."[35] Du Bois wrote back, saying: "I have your letter concerning the case of the Negroes in America and the Untouchables in India before the United Nations." Du Bois enclosed a copy of the petition, with the sentiment that he had "often heard of your name and work and have every sympathy with the Untouchables of India".[36] The NAACP would submit its own more detailed petition, *An Appeal to the World*, to the Commission on Human Rights

---

32    UN Doc. A/PV.905, 14 October 1960, paras. 46–47.

33    UN Doc. A/PV.905, 14 October 1960, para. 47, quoting an unnamed Indian official reproduced in Sir Alan Burns, *In Defence of Colonies*, London 1957, 155.

34    Anderson, From Hope to Disillusion, 545.

35    Manan Desai, What B.R. Ambedkar Wrote to W.E.B. Du Bois, in: *South Asian American Digital Archive* (SAADA), 22 April 2014, <https://www.saada.org/tides/article/20140422-3553> [last accessed: October 30, 2021].

36    Desai, What B.R. Ambedkar Wrote to W.E.B. Du Bois, <https://www.saada.org/tides/article/20140422-3553> [last accessed: October 30, 2021]. The NAACP would submit a petition to investigate racial discrimination in the United States to the Commission on Human Rights in 1947. See further: American Foreign Relations, African Americas: The United Nations Petition, <https://www.americanforeignrelations.com/A-D/African-Americans-The-united-nations-petition.html> [last accessed: October 30, 2021].

on 23 October 1947.[37] The petition would ultimately not go further than the Sub-Commission, on the basis that the UN "simply did not have in place the machinery to receive and investigate petitions alleging human rights abuses".[38] Later, in his 1951 resignation letter, Ambedkar wrote of that period:

> "I had prepared a report on the condition of the Scheduled Castes for submission to the United Nations. But I did not submit it. I felt that it would be better to wait until the Constituent Assembly and the future Parliament was given a chance to deal with the matter."[39]

It is unlikely that Ambedkar's report, had it been sent, would have met with more success than the NAACP petition. For its first 20 years the Commission on Human Rights largely concentrated its efforts on standard-setting, asserting that it had "no competence to deal with any complaint about violations of human rights".[40] It would require the realization of the UN international human rights treaties to provide a legal space akin to a "court", in which violations of human rights, including racial discrimination, could be raised by states, individuals and groups of individuals (including civil society). On 21 December 1965, ICERD was adopted, the first of the core UN human rights treaties. CERD, the first UN treaty body, was to monitor the treaty through state reports (Article 9); inter-state communications (Articles 11-13); and individual communications (Article 14). India participated in the drafting of ICERD and upon its adoption, Mr. Saksena (India) referenced its history of anti-racism:

> "the Indian people were partisans of racial and religious harmony and India itself had traditionally been a melting pot of human beings of almost every race. After achieving independence, his country had consistently pursued,

---

37    W.E.B. Du Bois (ed.), *An Appeal to the World: A Statement on the Denial of Human Rights to Minorities in the Case of Citizens of Negro Descent in the United States of America and an Appeal to the United Nations for Redress*, New York 1947.

38    Anderson, From Hope to Disillusion, 562.

39    Dr. Amberdkar's Resignation Speech, 10 October 1951, republished in *Ambedkarism*, <https://ambedkarism.wordpress.com/2011/03/10/dr-ambedkars-resignation-speech/> [last accessed: October 30, 2021].

40    UN Human Rights Council, *Background Information* and *Brief Historic Overview of the Commission*, <https://www.ohchr.org/EN/HRBodies/CHR/Pages/Background.aspx> [last accessed: October 30, 2021].

both nationally and internationally, a policy of racial harmony and its Constitution already included the basic principles of the Convention, as well as provisions for judicial remedy of violations. One of the first attempts to combat racial discrimination had been made by the Indian leader, Mahatma Gandhi, from 1907 to 1914 in South Africa, that citadel of racial discrimination. He was glad that Gandhi's vision was now embodied in a legal document adopted unanimously by the United Nations."[41]

The complaints of racial discrimination before the United Nations in 1946 could all have been addressed under the ICERD framework. It provides under Article 11 a mechanism for one state party to complain to CERD that another state party is not giving effect to the provisions of the treaty, as India sought to do before the General Assembly in relation to South Africa. ICERD provides under Article 14 a mechanism for an individual, or groups of individuals, to petition CERD alleging violations of the treaty by a state party, as Du Bois and Ambedkar sought to do before the Commission on Human Rights in relation to the treatment of African Americans and Dalits. Such cases never arose after the entry into force of ICERD. South Africa did not ratify ICERD when it was under apartheid rule, eventually ratifying it in 1998. Moreover, the Article 11 inter-state communications procedure remained unused by any ICERD state party until 2008.[42] Article 14 requires a declaration from a state party accepting the competence of the Committee to receive individual communications. Only around one-third of states parties to ICERD have made this declaration to date, which does not include India (or the United States). Hence an individual communication to CERD in relation to India and caste-based discrimination has never been possible. As a result, it is under the Article 9 reporting procedure only that caste has been addressed.

India ratified ICERD on 3 December 1968. Its first state reports provided information on the Scheduled Castes, detailing its constitutional affirmative action measures, with neither India nor the Committee commenting on whether the Scheduled Castes fell within the definition of racial discrimi-

---

41    UN Doc. A/C.3/SR.1374, 15 December 1965, para. 23.
42    See further David Keane, CERD Reaches Historic Decisions in Inter-State Communications, *Ejil: Talk!* 6 September 2019, <https://www.ejiltalk.org/cerd-reaches-historic-decisions-in-inter-state-communications/> [last accessed: October 30, 2021].

nation in Article 1(1) ICERD.[43] That changed in 1996, in which India's state report read: "The term 'caste' denotes a 'social' and 'class' distinction and is not based on race. It has its origins in the functional division of Indian society during ancient times."[44] The Committee responded in its concluding observations that it "affirms that the situation of the Scheduled Castes and Scheduled Tribes falls within the scope of the Convention."[45] This exchange comes 50 years after India's intervention in 1946. It marks the moment, as predicted by Hartley Shawcross, when the UN would come to investigate the caste system in India as a form of racial discrimination. It is an argument that India had heard previously in defense of apartheid South Africa, which may partly explain its hostility. As Thakur writes, "Ironically, year after year, it was apartheid South Africa that highlighted, at the UN, India's hypocrisy on racial issues by deeming casteism as a form of racism."[46] However the late 1940s-50s was a period in which Dalit voices could not be heard at the UN. By 1996 the UN treaty bodies, including CERD, had developed means for civil society to participate in the state reporting process. CERD's intervention was hardly a defensive strategy for a racist regime. It was based on substantial evidence of caste-based discrimination from Dalit organizations.

## India, the UN and Caste-Based Discrimination

Article 1(1) ICERD defines "racial discrimination" on the basis of five grounds, "race, colour, descent, or national or ethnic origin". It is a closed group lacking an indicative phrase (for example "such as"), meaning that in principle, any group that comes under the Convention has to fit within one or more of the

---

43    Annapurna Waughray/David Keane, CERD and Caste-Based Discrimination, in: David Keane/Annapurna Waughray (eds.), 50 Years of the ICERD: A Living Instrument, Manchester 2017, 121–149, see 132.

44    CERD, State Report – India (1996), UN Doc. CERD/C/299/Add.3, para. 6. The report acknowledged that "India's previous reports to the Committee have in response to queries from members incorporated information with regard to constitutional protection enjoyed in India by 'Scheduled Castes and Tribes' and the specific measures adopted by the Government for their economic and social improvement."

45    CERD, Concluding Observations – India (1996), UN Doc. CERD/C/304/Add.13, para. 14.

46    Vineet Thakur, When India Proposed a Casteist Solution to South Africa's Racist Problem, in: The Wire, 4 April 2016, <https://thewire.in/diplomacy/exploring-casteism-in-indias-foreign-policy> [last accessed: October 30, 2021].

five grounds. In practice, CERD adopts a living instrument approach to the treaty that may see it affirm or interpret certain groups as coming within its scope.[47] As an example, CERD has consistently viewed "indigenous peoples" as within its mandate, although the word "indigenous" does not appear in the five grounds of the definition of Article 1(1). In its General Recommendation 23 (GR 23), CERD stated that "discrimination against indigenous peoples falls under the scope of the Convention".[48] GR 23 does not specify where this group fits in the definition and does not name a particular ground or grounds, referencing only "the practice of the Committee" in which "the situation of indigenous peoples has always been a matter of close attention and concern."[49] States parties have not contested CERD's understanding of indigenous peoples as within the scope of the treaty. In general, while definitional differences between states parties and the Committee do arise, they are rare.[50]

Likewise the word "caste" is not found in Article 1(1) ICERD. As noted, in its 1996 state report, India argued that caste-based discrimination did not fall within the definition of racial discrimination in Article 1(1) and consequently fell outside the scope of the Convention. The Indian Government contended that the term caste is not based on race, denoting instead a social and class distinction.[51] It also disagreed that caste may come under "descent", the third ground in the Article 1(1) definition:

> "Article 1 of the Convention includes in the definition of racial discrimination the term 'descent'. Both castes and tribes are systems based on 'descent' since people are normally born into a particular caste or a particular tribe. It is obvious, however, that the use of the term 'descent' in the Convention clearly refers to 'race'. Communities which fall under the definition of Scheduled Castes and Scheduled Tribes are unique to Indian society and its histori-

---

47    See further David Keane, Mapping the International Convention on the Elimination of Racial Discrimination as a Living Instrument, in: *Human Rights Law Review* 20 (2/2020), 236–268.

48    CERD, General Recommendation 23 on the Rights of Indigenous Peoples (1997), UN Doc. A/52/18, 122–123, para. 1.

49    CERD, General Recommendation 23, UN Doc. A/52/18, 122–123, para. 1.

50    A further example would be Ireland's refusal to recognize Irish Travellers as an ethnic group for the purposes of ICERD. See Robbie McVeigh, 'Ethnicity Denial' and Racism: The Case of the Government of Ireland against Irish Travellers, in: *Translocations* 2 (1/2007), 90–133. Ireland eventually changed its position, issuing a Government statement recognizing Irish Travellers as an ethnic group.

51    CERD, State Report – India (1996), UN Doc. CERD/C/299/Add.3, para. 6.

cal process. As conveyed to the Committee during the presentation of India's last periodic report, it is, therefore, submitted that the policies of the Indian Government relating to Scheduled Castes and Scheduled Tribes do not come under the purview of Article 1 of the Convention."[52]

In its consideration of this state report, one CERD member, Van Boven, noted that India's previous report had provided information on the Scheduled Castes and had therefore clearly recognized that the Convention was applicable to the situation in India. He pointed out that "[t]here seemed to be some discrepancy between that historical contribution and the attitude that was being taken in the report."[53] CERD member Chigovera added: "the fact that castes and tribes were based on descent [...] brought them strictly within the Convention, under the terms of article 1."[54] There are two strands evident here – the first, the fact that India raised the issue of the Scheduled Castes before the Committee in the past means they come under the scope of the treaty, with no specification as to where precisely they fit in the definition; the second, that they specifically come under the term "descent". In its concluding observations, CERD emphasized the second strand. CERD regretted that the report and the delegation claimed that the situation of the Scheduled Castes did not fall within the scope of the Convention. CERD found: "the term 'descent' mentioned in article 1 of the Convention does not solely refer to race. The Committee affirms that the situation of the Scheduled Castes and Scheduled Tribes falls within the scope of the Convention."[55]

The term "descent" had in fact been introduced by India into the Convention in 1964, at the drafting stage.[56] This may have led to the later linking of descent with caste, although there is no direct evidence for this. Whether India meant caste when it introduced the term "descent" will never be known, as

---

52    CERD, State Report – India (1996), UN Doc. CERD/C/299/Add.3, para. 7.

53    CERD, Summary Records – India (1996), UN Doc. CERD/C/SR.1162, para. 15.

54    CERD, Summary Records – India (1996), UN Doc. CERD/C/SR.1162, para. 22. In reply, Singh (India) stated: "Constitutionally, the concept of race was distinct from caste. Engaged as it was in the task of eliminating all vestiges of caste discrimination, India could not accept another distinction. To confer a racial character on the caste system would create considerable political problems" (para. 35).

55    CERD, Concluding Observations – India (1996), UN Doc. CERD/C/304/Add.13, para. 14.

56    See further David Keane, *Caste-based Discrimination in International Human Rights Law*, New York 2007, 213–237.

the drafting history reveals no particular explanation for the term.[57] The formulation of descent as including caste was first articulated by Egon Schwelb
in a 1966 commentary on ICERD: "It is reasonable to assume that the term
'descent' includes the notion of 'caste'".[58] CERD would articulate an understanding of descent as including caste from 1996. It was prompted by Dalit
human rights organizations who had turned towards the UN in an attempt
to "internationalize" their situation as a human rights issue.[59] The Committee's concern reflected information provided by non-State sources including
human rights NGOs, urging CERD to raise the issue of caste-based discrimination with India.[60] These prompted CERD into taking a juridical position
on whether caste fell within the remit of the Committee.[61] In doing so, CERD
situated caste within a wider, international movement against descent-based
discrimination, of which caste was an example. CERD would not have wished
to focus on just one state, and in any case, understood that issues of caste and
descent were not confined to India or the South Asian region. Whatever the
original intention behind India's introduction of "descent", the Committee's
concerns were with a global pattern of discrimination that included, but was
not limited to, caste. Thus "descent" allowed CERD to articulate its jurisdiction over caste and analogous systems of discrimination globally.

In 2002, CERD issued General Recommendation 29 on "Descent" (GR 29).
The Preamble refers specifically to CERD's receipt of oral and written information from individuals and NGOs, who provided the Committee with evidence of the extent and persistence of descent-based discrimination around

---

57    Keane, *Caste-based Discrimination in International Human Rights Law*, 215. The conclusion
      reached however is that it is unlikely India meant "caste" when it introduced the term
      "descent".

58    Egon Schwelb, The International Convention on the Elimination of All Forms of Racial
      Discrimination, in: *International and Comparative Law Quarterly* 15 (4/1966), 996–1068,
      see 1003 note 43.

59    Clifford Bob, "Dalit Rights are Human Rights": Caste Discrimination, International Ac-
      tivism and the Construction of a New Human Rights Issue, in: *Human Rights Quarterly*
      29 (1/2007), 167–193, see 175.

60    Waughray/Keane, CERD and Caste-based Discrimination, 135.

61    Corinne Lennox, Norm-entrepreneurship on Caste-based Discrimination, in: David
      Mosse/Lisa Steur (eds.), *Caste Out of Development? The Cultural Politics of Identity and
      Economy in India and Beyond*, Abingdon, 2016, 177, cited in: Waughray/Keane, CERD and
      Caste-based Discrimination, 135.

the world.[62] It also stated the Committee's view that the term "descent" in Article 1(1) does not solely refer to race, and strongly reaffirmed that "discrimination based on descent includes discrimination against members of communities based on forms of social stratification such as caste and analogous systems of inherited status". The Recommendation does not provide a full definition of descent-based discrimination, but paragraph 1 provides a description, with caste as a specific example: "descent-based communities are those who suffer from discrimination, especially on the basis of caste and analogous systems of inherited status [...]". Former CERD member Patrick Thornberry writes on the motivation for GR 29:

> "The General Recommendation followed the debacle (for Dalits and others) at the Durban World Conference when the caste issue was talked out by vigorous diplomacy by India. The Committee had independent reasons to go ahead and explore the issue: to understand better a key term in the Convention; to understand better the contemporary scope of such discrimination; and, to respond to the victims who impressed the Committee so greatly. There are issues here: the target of the General Recommendation is not or should not be the caste system itself, but discrimination – although the distinction is a thin one. In the author's view, powerful victim perspectives greatly influenced the Committee."[63]

GR 29 marked an international understanding that would see CERD raise the issue of descent beyond India, Nepal and South Asia, to states parties such as Japan, Mali, Mauritania, Senegal, Suriname and Yemen. However, GR 29 did not alter India's position. In its subsequent 2006 state report to CERD, India reiterated that "caste cannot be equated with race, nor is it covered under descent under Article 1 of the Convention".[64] India emphasized this position when presenting its report to the Committee, insisting that it "had no doubt that the ordinary meaning of the term 'racial discrimination' did not include caste", and that caste discrimination was an issue outside the purview of racial

---

62    Patrick Thornberry, The Convention on the Elimination of Racial Discrimination, Indigenous Peoples, and Caste/Descent-Based Discrimination, in: Joshua Castellino/ Niamh Walsh (eds.), *International Law and Indigenous Peoples*, Leiden 2005, 17–53, see 42–3.

63    Patrick Thornberry, Confronting Racial Discrimination: A CERD Perspective, in: *Human Rights Law Review* 5 (2/2005), 239–269, see 264.

64    CERD, State Report – India (2006), UN Doc. CERD/C/IND/19, para. 16.

discrimination under Article 1(1).[65] As a result, "India was not in a position to accept reporting obligations [on caste] under the Convention."[66] In its concluding observations, CERD noted India's view that discrimination based on caste falls outside the scope of Article 1 of the Convention, but reaffirmed its position, as expressed in GR 29, that such discrimination is fully covered by Article 1 of the Convention. This was the last exchange between India and the Committee, as India has not reported to CERD since. In 2018, CERD wrote to the Permanent Representative of India to the UN Office in Geneva, recalling that "India has been in continuing breach of its obligation to submit its periodic report".[67]

Within South Asia, CERD has examined the issue of caste discrimination in Nepal, Pakistan, Bangladesh, and Sri Lanka. None of these states has objected to CERD's deployment of 'descent' to address caste-based discriminations. Even prior to GR 29, Nepal described its caste system in its state reports to CERD as constituting racial discrimination. Its 1997 state report accepted that "socially, the caste system, which has its origin in Hinduism, still operates in Nepal",[68] while its 1999 state report read: "racial discrimination in the society, especially in rural areas, is still in existence. So-called untouchables cannot even enter the houses of the people of so-called higher and middle-class castes."[69] Nepal's 2003 state report described how: "the Dalits of Nepal are the most marginalized and deprived group of Nepal, which has been subjected to caste-based discrimination from ancient times."[70] Its most recent state report, from 2017, discussed "rights against untouchability and caste-based discrimination" from its first page, as well as "the rights of Dalits as fundamental rights".[71] The report emphasized that "Nepal is fully committed to the XXIX General Recommendation [GR 29] of the CERD Committee."[72]

Japan by contrast, like India, has also opposed the Committee's interpretation of "descent". In March 2001, in its concluding observations on Japan, CERD noted that contrary to the state party's contentions, discrimination

---

65    CERD, Summary Records – India (2007), UN Doc. CERD/C/SR.1796, paras. 3 and 7.
66    CERD, Summary Records – India (2007), UN Doc. CERD/C/SR.1796, para. 3.
67    UN Doc. CERD/EWUAP/MJA/India/2018, 30 August 2018. The letter was issued under CERD's Early Warning Measures and Urgent Procedures.
68    CERD, State Report – Nepal (1997), UN Doc. CERD/C/298/Add.1. para. 17.
69    CERD, State Report – Nepal (1999), UN Doc. CERD/C/337/Add.4, paras. 38–39.
70    CERD, State Report – Nepal (2003), UN Doc. CERD/C/452/Add.2, para. 75.
71    CERD, State Report – Nepal (2017), UN Doc. CERD/C/NPL/17-23, paras. 5 and 12.
72    CERD, State Report – Nepal (2017), UN Doc. CERD/C/NPL/17-23, para. 41.

based on descent contained in article 1 of the Convention "has its own meaning and is not to be confused with race or national origin."[73] The Committee recommended that the state party ensure that all groups, including the *Burakumin* community, are protected against discrimination.[74] Japan stated in response that it did not share the Committee's interpretation of "descent".[75] Japan returned before the Committee in 2010, again refuting the applicability of descent-based discrimination. This has to be inferred from its state report, which simply makes no mention of the *Buraku* or descent-based discrimination.[76] CERD's concluding observations read: "the Committee regrets the State party's interpretation of racial discrimination based on descent".[77] Japan's most recent 2013 state report adopted the same tactic, with no mention in the document of caste, descent, the *Buraku*, or CERD's two previous concluding observations regarding descent.[78] CERD responded in its 2014 concluding observations with an extensive paragraph entitled "Situation of the *Burakumin*":

> "The Committee regrets the position of the State party, which excludes the *Burakumin* from the application of the Convention on grounds of descent. It is concerned that the State party has not yet adopted a uniform definition of *Burakumin*, as raised by the Committee in its previous concluding observations [...] Bearing in mind its general recommendation No. 29 (2002) on descent, the Committee recalls that discrimination on grounds of descent is fully covered by the Convention."[79]

The CERD state reporting procedure leads to a number of groupings of states parties' positions on caste, descent and racial discrimination. Firstly, India and Japan have both contested CERD's interpretation of descent-based discrimination, twice in the case of India, three times in the case of Japan. India's opposition is more stated, arguing directly that CERD is incorrect in its

---

73   CERD, State Report – Japan (2001), UN Doc. CERD/C/58/Misc.17/Rev.3, para 8.

74   CERD, State Report – Japan (2001), UN Doc. CERD/C/58/Misc.17/Rev.3, para 8.

75   CERD, Comments of States Parties on the Concluding Observations of the Committee (2001), UN Doc. A/56/18, p. 158, para 2.

76   CERD, State Report – Japan (2009), UN Doc. CERD/C/JPN/3–6.

77   CERD, Concluding Observations – Japan (2010), UN Doc. CERD/C/JPN/CO/3–6, para. 8. That information would presumably have been provided as part of the examination at Geneva, and was not furnished in the State Report.

78   CERD, State Report – Japan (2013), UN Doc. CERD/C/JPN/7–9.

79   CERD, Concluding Observations – Japan (2014), UN Doc CERD/C/JPN/CO/7–9, para. 22.

interpretation. Japan's views are not as direct, instead refusing to report on descent-based discrimination despite repeated urgings from the Committee, rather than arguing particularly on CERD's interpretation. While not opposed to CERD's views, none of the West African states have reported on caste or descent-based groups on their territories. Several have not yet reported back following the first promptings from the Committee. In South Asia, Pakistan and Bangladesh appear to acknowledge the relevance of caste but have not provided any real detail to the Committee. Nepal reports fully on caste and descent. Its extensive documentation of untouchability and caste discrimination as a form of racial discrimination is a clear acceptance of the competence of CERD on caste and descent from the perspective of states parties.

From August 2000, a parallel advocacy track developed in the UN Charter bodies, challenging caste discrimination via the concept of discrimination based on "work and descent". In August 2000, the UN Sub-Commission on the Promotion and Protection of Human Rights passed resolution 2000/4 on Discrimination based on Work and Descent, which declared this a form of discrimination prohibited by international human rights law.[80] The Sub-Commission followed its resolution with a working paper and two expanded working papers. The initial "working paper on the topic of discrimination based on work and descent", written by Rajendra Goonesekere, was presented to the Sub-Commission in June 2001.[81] The paper's focus was limited to Asian countries; however, the concluding remarks noted: "the problem was not limited to Asia alone and that it existed in some parts of Africa and perhaps in South America."[82] The paper was followed by the first "expanded working paper on discrimination based on work and descent", written by Asbjorn Eide

---

80    UN Sub-Commission on the Promotion and Protection of Human Rights Resolution 2000/4 on Discrimination based on Work and Descent (2000), UN Doc. E/CN.4/SUB.2/ RES/2000/4.

81    UN Sub-Commission on the Promotion and Protection of Human Rights, Working Paper by Mr. Rajendra Kalidas Wimala Goonesekere on the Topic of Discrimination based on Work and Descent, submitted pursuant to Sub-Commission resolution 2000/4, 14 June 2001, UN Doc. E/CN.4/Sub.2/2001/16.

82    UN Sub-Commission on the Promotion and Protection of Human Rights, Working Paper by Mr. Rajendra Kalidas Wimala Goonesekere on the Topic of Discrimination based on Work and Descent, submitted pursuant to Sub-Commission resolution 2000/4, 14 June 2001, UN Doc. E/CN.4/Sub.2/2001/16, para. 49.

and Yozo Yokoto in 2003.[83] It examined the situation in West Africa, North-East Africa, Somalia, and Yemen, describing *inter alia* the metalworkers, potters, musicians (or *"griots"*), leatherworkers, weavers, barbers and others in West Africa; the case of the Dime people of South-West Ethiopia; and the *akhdam* of Yemen. Hence the main purpose of the first expanded working paper was to identify communities *other than* those traditionally referred to as castes in the South Asian context, who continue to experience discrimination based on work and descent. The expanded working paper concluded:

> "the prevalence of discrimination based on work and descent is more widespread than might have been envisaged at the outset of this process [...] This form of discrimination is distinct, in its combination of causal factors and expressions, from other forms of discrimination examined in the history of the Sub-Commission."[84]

This led to a second "expanded working paper on discrimination based on work and descent", also written by Asbjorn Eide and Yozo Yokota, in 2004.[85] The second working paper engages the question of South Asian diaspora communities whose original culture and traditions include aspects of inherited social exclusion.[86] It describes how the "caste system has migrated with the South Asian diaspora", and is observed, to varying degrees, in the diaspora communities in East and South Africa, Mauritius, Fiji, Suriname, the Middle East (for example in Bahrain, Kuwait and the United Arab Emirates), Malaysia, the Caribbean, the UK, and North America.[87] The examination focused on the South-Asian diaspora in the United Kingdom and the United

---

83    UN Sub-Commission on Human Rights, Expanded working paper submitted by Mr. Asbjorn Eide and Mr. Yozo Yokota pursuant to Sub-Commission decision 2002/108 (2003), UN Doc. E/CN.4/Sub.2/2003/24.

84    UN Sub-Commission on Human Rights, Expanded Working Paper submitted by Mr. Asbjorn Eide and Mr. Yozo Yokota pursuant to Sub-Commission decision 2002/108 (2003), UN Doc. E/CN.4/Sub.2/2003/24, paras. 57–58.

85    UN Sub-Commission on Human Rights, [Second] Expanded Working Paper submitted by Mr. Asbjorn Eide and Mr. Yozo Yokota pursuant to Sub-Commission decision 2003/22 (2004), UN Doc. E/CN.4/Sub.2/2004/31.

86    UN Sub-Commission on Human Rights, [Second] Expanded Working Paper submitted by Mr. Asbjorn Eide and Mr. Yozo Yokota pursuant to Sub-Commission decision 2003/22 (2004), UN Doc. E/CN.4/Sub.2/2004/31, para. 35.

87    UN Sub-Commission on Human Rights, [Second] Expanded Working Paper submitted by Mr. Asbjorn Eide and Mr. Yozo Yokota pursuant to Sub-Commission decision 2003/22 (2004), UN Doc. E/CN.4/Sub.2/2004/31, para. 35.

States. In April 2005, the Commission on Human Rights appointed Yozo Yokota and Chin-Sung Chung as UN Special Rapporteurs with the task of preparing a comprehensive study on discrimination based on work and descent on the basis of the three working papers submitted on the issue. Their Final Report was submitted to the Human Rights Council in 2009.[88] It included "Draft Principles and Guidelines for the Effective Elimination of Discrimination based on Work and Descent". Importantly, these have never been adopted by the Human Rights Council, and remain as draft guidelines. The transnational advocacy network the *International Dalit Solidarity Network* (IDSN) continues to push for their implementation at UN level.[89]

More recently, in 2016 the UN Special Rapporteur on Minority Issues issued a thematic analysis on the topic of minorities and discrimination based on caste and analogous systems of inherited status.[90] The analysis affirmed: "at present, the term 'caste' has broadened in meaning, transcending religious affiliation. Caste and caste-like systems may be based on either a religious or a secular background and can be found within diverse religious and/or ethnic groups in all geographical regions, including within diaspora communities."[91] The report of the UN Special Rapporteur on Minority Issues is significant in bringing caste "within the minorities framework".[92] It underlines also that the elimination of caste-based discrimination is part of the work of the UN

---

88    Final report of Mr. Yozo Yokota and Ms. Chin-Sung Chung, Special Rapporteurs on the topic of discrimination based on work and descent (2009), UN Doc. A/HRC/11/CRP.3.

89    The *International Dalit Solidarity Network* (IDSN), based in Copenhagen, Denmark, was established in 2000. It has played an important role in further "internationalizing" caste discrimination by engaging with UN bodies, and other international and regional actors such as the European Union. See further IDSN, UN Principles and Guidelines, <https://idsn.org/un-2/un-principles-guidelines-on-caste/> [last accessed: October 30, 2021]. The site reads: "Although still a draft, IDSN promotes support for the framework among UN member states, experts and NGOs, and recommends the Human Rights Council to act in this regard."

90    Report of the Special Rapporteur on Minority Issues, Thematic Analysis on the Topic of Minorities and Discrimination based on Caste and Analogous Systems of Inherited Status (2016), UN Doc. A/HRC/31/56.

91    Report of the Special Rapporteur on Minority Issues, Thematic Analysis on the Topic of Minorities and Discrimination based on Caste and Analogous Systems of Inherited Status (2016), UN Doc. A/HRC/31/56, para. 27.

92    M. Bhimraj, The 'Caste' as 'Discrimination Based on Work and Descent' in International Law: Convincing or Compromising?, in: *International Journal on Minority and Groups Rights* 27 (4/2020), 796–825, see 798.

Special Procedures, despite the mandate of the UN Special Rapporteurs on work and descent not being continued.

In 2017, the UN issued a "Guidance Tool on Descent-Based Discrimination: Key Challenges and Strategic Approaches to Combat Caste-Based and Analogous Forms of Discrimination".[93] The title of this document is important, as the Guidance Tool presented an opportunity to clarify the terms involved. Since 2000, the two strands of international terminology appear to have been competing rather than complementary. One emanates from the UN treaty bodies, the other from the UN Charter bodies. Importantly, "descent-based discrimination" was used in the title, rather than the "discrimination based on work and descent" category. The sub-heading reference is then to caste as a form of descent-based discrimination, rather than a form of "work and descent". This is not to undermine the importance of the above Sub-Commission reports and Draft Principles or what has been achieved under the "work and descent" category. It underlines that if the Guidance Tool is to have traction, a primarily legal approach is required, focusing on descent-based discrimination as rooted in Article 1(1) ICERD. The term "work" has no specific reference in international human rights treaties. "Descent" has the stronger legal basis, being a term in ICERD with an authoritative interpretation that it includes caste.

Overall, 1996 marks the year that caste finds a juridical "home" in the UN human rights system. It also marks the formal opposition of India to the recognition of caste in international human rights law under Article 1(1) ICERD. India is not necessarily opposed to the inclusion of caste in the international human rights system. It may be inclined to contest the raising of caste in international bodies, but this is not necessarily formal or legal. By contrast, it is clearly formally opposed to the inclusion of caste in international human rights law via ICERD. The question is whether its objection is based on an international legal recognition of caste, which did not happen expressly in any international forum prior to 1996, or an international legal recognition of caste as a form of racial discrimination. India reports to other UN treaty bodies on caste, for example extensively discussing caste in its 2005

---

93    United Nations Network on Racial Discrimination and Protection of Minorities, Guidance Tool on Descent-Based Discrimination. Key Challenges and Strategic Approaches to Combat Caste-Based and Analogous Forms of Discrimination, Geneva 2017, <https://www.ohchr.org/Documents/Issues/Minorities/GuidanceToolDiscrimination.pdf> [last accessed: October 30, 2021].

state report to the Committee on the Elimination of Discrimination Against Women (CEDAW),[94] among others. Hence formal or legal Indian opposition is to the international legal understanding of caste as a form of racial discrimination, and not to the "internationalization" of caste per se, although it may oppose or contest this in other ways. This distinction has not been clearly enunciated by India, but that is what its state practice suggests.

## Resolving the Dispute

While serving as UN High Commissioner for Human Rights, Navi Pillay stated that "there may well have to be a new international convention written to apply directly to caste".[95] While there are on occasion similar calls from Dalit NGOs,[96] and academic commentators,[97] it appears to be a minority viewpoint. Given that India would be unlikely to support such a convention, it would suffer from the same problem, in that the state with the largest incidence of caste-based discrimination would fall outside the international protections. The focus has to be on ending India's opposition to CERD's interpretation of descent as including caste. There are four potential sources for this. Firstly, the Government of India itself; secondly, the Indian judicial system; thirdly, other states parties to ICERD; and fourthly, wider UN bodies.

---

94    CEDAW, State Report – India (2005), CEDAW/C/IND/2–3. Among the many references, there is a paragraph entitled "Caste- based discrimination, including violence, suffered by women of [the] dalit community" (para. 20).

95    Quoted in Barbara Crosette, Putting Caste on Notice, in: *The Nation*, 26 October 2009, <https://www.thenation.com/article/archive/putting-caste-notice/> [last accessed: October 30, 2021].

96    For example Manjula Pradeep, Executive Director of the Indian Dalit rights organization *Navsarjan*, stated following the UN Special Rapporteur on Minorities report: "We dream that this could be a step on the way to a UN Convention on the elimination of caste-based discrimination". Quoted in: *Minority Rights Group International*, News, UN Expert Calls on States to End Caste Discrimination, 17 March 2016, <https://minorityrights.org/2016/03/17/un-expert-calls-on-states-to-end-caste-discrimination/> [last accessed: October 30, 2021].

97    Bhimraj likewise believes that "Dalit activists should advocate a Convention specific to caste discrimination". M. Bhimraj, The 'Caste' as 'Discrimination Based on Work and Descent' in International Law, 799.

## Government of India

The impasse on caste has cost India in terms of its contribution to the global fight against racial discrimination. As highlighted, it has played in the past a remarkable leadership role against racism. India backed up its rhetoric in the UN General Assembly by becoming the first state to impose sanctions against apartheid South Africa and boycott it, mobilizing other states to boycott as well.[98] India's role in drafting ICERD is a matter of record, in which it contributed significantly to a number of provisions, in particular those on special measures. It is clear however that India viewed the treaty as an internationalist statement that did not have internal relevance, as many other states did at the time. As Lady Gaitskell (United Kingdom) commented: "to judge from the [Third] Committee's discussions, the world suffered greatly from racial discrimination, but no particular country seemed to have it."[99] This would continue into the early years of monitoring the treaty, with states parties emphatically denying that any form of racial discrimination existed in their territories. Michael Banton highlights that of the first 45 state party reports to CERD, only five states admitted there was any racial discrimination occurring, with some of these explaining it was being practiced by another state or part of their inheritance from the colonial era.[100]

Today, such a position is anachronistic. There are legitimate arguments around the respective meanings of "caste" and "race", and the differences between the terms. However the umbrella term for the Convention is "racial discrimination", which includes race but four other terms as well. CERD in viewing the treaty as a living instrument has applied it to a range of groups, many of whom would not easily satisfy an understanding of "race", to the extent that this is possible at all. In the absence of an international minority rights treaty, ICERD is a natural "home" in the UN treaty system for issues involving marginalized groups. That the Dalits fit within the scope of ICERD appears obvious when we step back from discussions around the meaning of caste and race. The object and purpose of ICERD when applied to India could not be realized without addressing caste-based discrimination. At the time of drafting, the Indian representative Mr. Saksena commented: "the Convention

---

98    M. Muslim Khan, India-South Africa Unique Relations, in: *The Indian Journal of Political Science* LXII (2/2019), 613–634, see Abstract and 619.

99    Lady Gaitskell (United Kingdom) (1965), UN Doc. A/C.3/SR.1374, para. 61.

100   Michael Banton, *International Action against Racial Discrimination*, 106.

was merely a document. If all States accepted it and implemented it, it would usher in a new era of human rights and dignity; if they did not, it would remain but a scrap of paper."[101] If ICERD cannot address the situation of the Dalits in India, it would remain the proverbial scrap of paper.

India has not reported to CERD since 2007. That India accepts caste discrimination occurs and warrants combating is evident from its constitution and domestic caselaw. In 2006, CERD member January-Bardill asked India why it regarded the Convention as a threat rather than an opportunity to challenge caste discrimination. She inquired whether the Government could not use the Convention as a tool to assist in the fraternity project aimed at building substantive citizenship.[102] India's position has meant the loss of the Indian voice in the global fight against racial discrimination for over twenty years. It is far more damaging than beneficial to India. The optimum means to end India's opposition is for India itself to set out in its next state report to CERD, that it withdraws its objections to CERD's interpretation of "descent" as including caste.

## Indian Judicial System

In a summary of the Supreme Court of India decision in *Safai Karamchari Andolan and Ors v India and Ors*, Surendra Kumar highlights how the Court applied ICERD in the context of the situation of manual scavengers. In doing so, "[t]he Court seemed oblivious, while unknowingly or unwittingly giving a judicial stamp to an interpretation that racial discrimination included caste."[103] The Court cited Article 2(1)(c) ICERD, that states parties condemned racial discrimination and undertook to pursue by all appropriate means and without delay a policy of eliminating racial discrimination in all its forms. It found that these provisions were binding upon India to the extent that they were not inconsistent with Indian domestic law. Kumar believes the Court "missed an opportunity to address the interrelationship between caste and race". In particular, it "seemingly applied or possibly conflated racial discrimination to

---

101   UN Doc. A/C.3/SR.1374, 15 December 1965, para. 23.

102   CERD, Summary Records – India (2007), UN Doc. CERD/C/SR.1796, paras. 48–50, quoted in: Waughray/Keane, CERD and Caste-Based Discrimination, 147.

103   Surendra Kumar, Case Review of *Safai Karamchari Andolan v Union of India* (2014) 11 SCC 224 ILDC 2829, in: *Oxford Reports on International Law in Domestic Courts*, <https://opil.o uplaw.com/view/10.1093/law-ildc/2829in14.case.1/law-ildc-2829in14?rskey=1fD1il&resul t=24&prd=OPIL> [last accessed: October 30, 2021].

caste discrimination." Kumar's point is that in *Andolan*, the Supreme Court was able to cite provisions of ICERD in support of a ruling on a caste-based practice, without recognizing that India does not understand ICERD as applying to caste-based discrimination. It is clear the Court did not "overrule" the Indian position before CERD—it simply did not refer to or recognize it. This is almost certainly an unintentional omission on the Court's part, in which it simply appears unaware of the long-running interpretive dispute between India and CERD. Hence it referred to provisions of ICERD as applicable and relevant without recognizing that India does not accept the application of ICERD to caste-based discrimination. This leaves open the possibility that the Supreme Court may in future engage with India's position at the international level.[104]

In the context of India's constitutional provisions on caste-based discrimination, the prohibition on untouchability, or statutory laws that relate to the prevention of atrocities, the Supreme Court may view provisions of ICERD or recommendations of CERD as relevant. In that light it could engage with the question as to whether caste-based discrimination comes under the scope of ICERD. It could thus challenge the Government of India's position. The extent to which the Supreme Court could "overturn" a Government position before a UN human rights treaty body is an interesting question. The Supreme Court could certainly ensure that provisions of ICERD are applicable in the implementation of domestic laws, thus implicitly overruling the current Indian position. However before CERD, it is the state, and not its judiciary, that drafts the state reports, and appears before the Committee. Ultimately a Supreme Court position could persuade the Government but could not mandate such a shift. Nevertheless it would potentially make the Indian position untenable should its highest court engage specifically with the interpretive dispute, and expressly rule that ICERD applies to legal provisions or statutes that relate to caste and caste-based discrimination. A Supreme Court citation of CERD concluding observations or its GR 29 could have such an effect.

---

104    Surendra Kumar, Case Review of *Safai Karamchari Andolan v Union of India* (2014) 11 SCC 224 ILDC 2829, in: *Oxford Reports on International Law in Domestic Courts*, <https://opil.o uplaw.com/view/10.1093/law-ildc/2829in14.case.1/law-ildc-2829in14?rskey=1fD1il&resul t=24&prd=OPIL> [last accessed: October 30, 2021].

## Other States Parties to ICERD

ICERD has a compulsory inter-state communications mechanism found in Articles 11-13, which applies to all states parties upon ratification.[105] This compulsory character is unique among the UN international human rights treaties. Article 11(1) ICERD reads: "If a State Party considers that another State Party is not giving effect to the provisions of this Convention, it may bring the matter to the attention of the Committee." There have been three inter-state communications to CERD to date – *Qatar v Kingdom of Saudi Arabia* (2018),[106] *Qatar v United Arab Emirates* (2018)[107] and *Palestine v Israel* (2018).[108] Scott Leckie has written that the inter-state communications mechanism is often perceived as a "hostile and quite drastic response by a state desiring to address human rights questions in another state."[109] However he also believes that the procedure "could be considered more seriously by more states as a useful and constructive policy tool with the potential effect of enhancing human rights throughout the world."[110] The procedure was not used at all under any of the UN human rights treaties prior to the three CERD communications in 2018. This is however partly explained by the fact that the procedure is usually optional, in that both states must have made a requisite declaration accepting the competence of the committee to receive such communications. As noted, Articles 11-13 ICERD are compulsory and as a result, any of the 182 states parties can bring an inter-state communication in relation to any other.

The progress of the current inter-state communications emphasizes the viability of the mechanism. On 29 August 2019, CERD reached its first de-

---

105    ICERD also has a dispute-resolution mechanism before the International Court of Justice under Article 22. India has entered a reservation to this provision, which reads: "The Government of India declare that for reference of any dispute to the ICJ for decision in terms of Article 22 ICERD, the consent of all parties to the dispute is necessary in each individual case." India would be highly unlikely to consent to an Article 22 dispute involving caste and the interpretation of descent in Article 1(1).

106    Qatar v Kingdom of Saudi Arabia, CERD-ISC 2018/1.

107    Qatar v United Arab Emirates, CERD-ISC 2018/2.

108    Palestine v Israel, CERD-ISC 2018/3.

109    Scott Leckie, The Inter-State Complaint Procedure in International Human Rights Law: Hopeful Prospects or Wishful Thinking?, in: *Human Rights Quarterly* 10 (2/1988), 249–303, see 253.

110    Leckie, The Inter-State Complaint Procedure in International Human Rights Law, 299.

cisions on jurisdiction and admissibility in *Qatar v Kingdom of Saudi Arabia*
and *Qatar v United Arab Emirates*.[111] The Chair of the Committee stressed that
"the decisions on the inter-state communications were the first such decisions that any human rights treaty body had ever adopted".[112] A state party
to ICERD could bring an Article 11 inter-state communication against India,
challenging its position on caste-based discrimination. There is no obligation
that the communicant state is in any way a "victim"—a state party must only
consider that another state party "is not giving effect to the provisions of this
Convention". Thus Denmark for example, home to the *International Dalit Solidarity Network*, could bring an inter-state communication against India on
the basis that it is not giving effect to the provisions of the Convention in
the context of caste-based discrimination. As Leckie underlines, this should
be considered a constructive means of resolving a dispute. The Articles 11-
13 mechanism seeks an "amicable solution" to the dispute through a process
of conciliation. It should be emphasized that CERD is not the arbiter of the
"merits" of inter-state communications. It decides under Article 11 only preliminary issues of jurisdiction and admissibility. Articles 12-13 then establish
an ad hoc Conciliation Commission, a separate body composed of five persons "who may or may not be members of the Committee"—it is constituted
independently for the resolution of each dispute, reporting its findings and
recommendations to CERD.

A further dimension is that India is not the only state party to oppose
CERD's interpretation of descent. Japan, as noted, has twice denied descent-
based discrimination on its territory. This position has not been challenged
more widely, beyond exchanges between CERD and the state party. But
Japan's position supports that of India, and has a major effect on millions

---

111   CERD, Jurisdiction of the Inter-State Communication submitted by Qatar against the
      United Arab Emirates, UN Doc. CERD/C/99/3, 30 August 2019; CERD, Admissibility of
      the Inter-State Communication submitted by Qatar against the United Arab Emirates,
      UN Doc. CERD/C/99/4, 30 August 2019; CERD, Jurisdiction of the Inter-State Communi-
      cation submitted by Qatar against the Kingdom of Saudi Arabia, UN Doc. CERD/C/99/5,
      30 August 2019; CERD, Admissibility of the Inter-State Communication submitted by
      Qatar against the Kingdom of Saudi Arabia, UN Doc. CERD/C/99/6, 30 August 2019.

112   CERD, Committee on the Elimination of Racial Discrimination closes ninety-ninth ses-
      sion, adopts decisions on inter-State communications by Qatar against Saudi Arabia
      and the United Arab Emirates, 29 August 2019, <https://www.ohchr.org/EN/NewsEv
      ents/Pages/DisplayNews.aspx?NewsID=24931&LangID=E> [last accessed: October 30,
      2021].

of Dalits who experience caste-based discrimination, in addition to its own *Buraku* population. To what extent Japan accepts the repercussions of its position in South Asia is not known. An inter-state communication under Article 11 in relation to Japan could also be considered—indeed the same state could take two inter-state communications, as Qatar has done in relation to the Kingdom of Saudi Arabia and the United Arab Emirates. Hence Denmark or another state party could consider issuing two inter-state communications in support of CERD's interpretation of "descent". This would have the added effect of emphasizing that CERD's interpretation of descent and GR 29 are not aimed at just one state.

A potential preliminary objection is that in principle, Articles 11-13 do not cover purely interpretive disputes. This point was raised before the International Court of Justice in *Ukraine v Russian Federation*, taken under Article 22 ICERD, in which Ukraine was arguing on a technical matter related to the preconditions of Article 22. Ukraine's point was that Article 22 governs disputes related to the interpretation or application of the treaty, while Article 11 relates only to the application of the treaty. Hence a communicant state would have to emphasize that this is not purely an interpretive dispute, but rather that India's refusal to accept CERD's interpretation of descent is preventing also the application of the treaty, the giving of effect to its provisions. The question underlines how the Articles 11-13 mechanism could be an excellent forum for deciding the question of caste, descent and racial discrimination, drawing out the arguments of all sides. It remains unlikely given the traditional reluctance of states parties to bring such communications. Nevertheless CERD has emphasized how "the obligations contained in the Convention [...] are subject to a collective guarantee and enforcement".[113]

## UN Bodies

Recent UN initiatives by the UN Special Rapporteur on Minorities and the Guidance Tool have been discussed above. The UN should consider appointing again a Special Rapporteur. The previous two Special Rapporteurs were on work and descent, and issued Draft Guidelines that have not been supported. There has been no such initiative since then. Rather than stopping special procedures in the realm of descent and caste-based discrimination,

---

113    CERD, Jurisdiction of the Inter-State Communication submitted by Palestine against Israel, UN Doc. CERD/C/100/5 (2019), Part III, para. 3.37.

this should emphasize their need. There should be a UN Independent Expert or Special Rapporteur on Descent-based Discrimination. This title, without a reference to "work", would reflect the clarity of terminology required. Such a Special Rapporteur could coordinate and continue the work of the UN Charter bodies since 2000. Beyond this particular initiative, the UN treaty and Charter bodies should continue to focus on caste and descent-based discrimination, in line with the recommendations and clarity of purpose evinced in the Guidance Tool.

## Conclusion

The internationalization of caste has been both successful and unsuccessful for Dalits. There have clearly been many gains. The "movement" generated from 1996 with the support of the UN bodies has assisted Dalit NGOs in India, Nepal, South Asia, and globally, to understand caste-based discrimination as a violation of international human rights law. On the other hand, India's entrenched opposition to CERD's interpretation of "descent" has limited the gains. Caste continues to be viewed primarily as a domestic issue in India. The framework of racial discrimination is not accepted. For the state of India, the results have been similarly mixed. It has succeeded in preventing caste from coming under the scope of ICERD. However it has done this by limiting its engagement with the treaty body. To maintain its position on caste, India has had to sacrifice its role as a leading international voice against racial discrimination.

India's opposition to caste as a form of descent-based discrimination, and within the scope of Article 1(1) ICERD, appears increasingly difficult to sustain. The argument that "caste" is not "race" is a misreading of the terms of the debate. Caste can be different from race and still be a form of racial discrimination, the umbrella term of Article 1(1). The Dalits as a group clearly belong within the scope of ICERD. The elimination of caste-based discrimination fits with the object and purpose of the treaty, as applied in an Indian context. It appears impossible to give the treaty meaning in India without addressing caste-based discrimination. India's position should eventually change but the sooner it does the better; there has been much lost in the 25 years that India has been effectively absent from ICERD. The solutions proposed in this chapter begin with the recommendation that India itself should reconsider. Without this, its judicial system, other states parties to the treaty, and the UN bodies, should each or in combination challenge India to justify its position, and by doing so, possibly change it. The urgency grows as discrimination and atrocities against Dalits continue.

## References

Anderson, Carol, From Hope to Disillusion: African Americans, the United Nations, and the Struggle for Human Rights, 1944–1947, in: *Diplomatic History* 20 (4/1996), 531–563.

Banton, Michael, *International Action against Racial Discrimination*, Oxford 1996.

Bhimraj, M., The 'Caste' as 'Discrimination Based on Work and Descent' in International Law: Convincing or Compromising?, in: *International Journal on Minority and Groups Rights* 27 (4/2020), 796–825.

Bob, Clifford, "Dalit Rights are Human Rights": Caste Discrimination, International Activism and the Construction of a New Human Rights Issue, in: *Human Rights Quarterly* 29 (1/2007), 167–193.

Davis, Alexander E./Thakur, Vineet, 'An Act of Faith' or a 'New Brown Empire'? The Dismissal of India's International Anti-Racism, 1945–1961', in: *Commonwealth & Comparative Politics* 56 (1/2018), 22–39.

Du Bois, W.E.B. (ed.), *An Appeal to the World: A Statement on the Denial of Human Rights to Minorities in the Case of Citizens of Negro Descent in the United States of America and an Appeal to the United Nations for Redress*, New York 1947.

Keane, David, Caste-based Discrimination in International Human Rights Law, New York 2007.

Keane, David, Mapping the International Convention on the Elimination of Racial Discrimination as a Living Instrument, in: *Human Rights Law Review* 20 (2/2020), 236–268.

Khan, M. Muslim, India-South Africa Unique Relations, in: *The Indian Journal of Political Science* LXII (2/2019), 613–634.

Leckie, Scott, The Inter-State Complaint Procedure in International Human Rights Law: Hopeful Prospects or Wishful Thinking?, in: *Human Rights Quarterly* 10 (2/1988), 249–303.

Lloyd, Lorna, 'A Most Auspicious Beginning': The 1946 United Nations General Assembly and the Question of the Treatment of Indians in South Africa, in: *Review of International Studies* 16 (2/1990), 131–153.

McVeigh, Robbie, 'Ethnicity Denial' and Racism: The Case of the Government of Ireland against Irish Travellers, in: *Translocations* 2 (1/2007), 90–133.

O'Malley, Alanna, India, Apartheid and the New World Order at the UN, 1946–1962, in: *Journal of World History* 31 (1/2020), 195–223.

Rao, G. Kalyan, *Antarani Vasantam* [*The Untouchable Spring*], New Delhi 2000.

Schwelb, Egon, The International Convention on the Elimination of All Forms of Racial Discrimination, in: *International and Comparative Law Quarterly* 15 (4/1966), 996–1068.

Thakur, Vineet, The "Hardy Annual": A History of India's First UN Resolution, in: *India Review* 16 (4/2017), 401–429.

Thornberry, Patrick, Confronting Racial Discrimination: A CERD Perspective, in: *Human Rights Law Review* 5 (2/2005), 239–269.

Thornberry, Patrick, The Convention on the Elimination of Racial Discrimination, Indigenous Peoples, and Caste/Descent-Based Discrimination, in: Castellino, Joshua/Walsh, Niamh (eds.), *International Law and Indigenous Peoples*, Leiden 2005, 17–53.

Thornberry, Patrick, *The International Convention on the Elimination of All Forms of Racial Discrimination: A Commentary*, Oxford 2016.

Waughray, Annapurna/Keane, David, CERD and Caste-Based Discrimination, in: Keane, David/Waughray, Annapurna (eds.), *50 Years of the ICERD: A Living Instrument*, Manchester 2017, 121–149.

# Equality under the Indian Constitution

*Gautam Bhatia*

**Abstract**

*This chapter explores the concept of equality under the Indian Constitution, through the lens of affirmative action ["reservations"]. Because of historical reasons, the idea of equality in Indian political and constitutional thought has always been linked with the mitigation of social disadvantage, and the redressal of social and historical injustices. During the framing of the Constitution, the framers drew upon prior institutional experience, and envisioned affirmative action in the form of quotas—also known as reservations—to be the vehicle through which substantive equality could be achieved in society. The constitutional provisions, however, were framed in abstract terms. Consequently, it was left to the judiciary to resolve—over seven decades—disputes over who were to be the beneficiaries of reservations, how they were to be identified, and how much reservation was permissible. This chapter discusses the past, present, and possible future(s) of that jurisprudence.*

## Introduction

In this chapter, I explore the history of equality under the Indian Constitution, with a specific focus on how the Constitution and the Courts have understood structural and institutional *inequality*, and the role of law in mitigating that inequality. The most common tool for mitigating structural inequality has been "reservations," a set of quota-based affirmative policies that are implemented in public employment and in access to institutions of higher education. This chapter considers the intersection between the history of equality in India, and the history and evolution of reservations, from the following perspectives: what was, and is, the *philosophy* of equality that underlies reservations, and how did it evolve? How ought the State *identify* beneficiaries of reservations, and on what bases? And how are reservations to be implemented?[1]

Reservations received constitutional sanction during the framing of the Indian Constitution. The framers were aware that they were inheriting a highly stratified society, riven along multiple axes. Some of these stratifications pre-dated colonial rule, while others had been deepened and intensified because of colonialism. There also existed an awareness—at least five decades old—that affirmative State measures were required to overcome this social stratification, and achieve substantive—as opposed to merely formal—equality. The post-Constitutional history of Indian equality jurisprudence, thus, has been shaped by debates around the *nature* of inequality, the *measures* that the Constitution mandates or allows to overcome it, and the *subjects* of the government's affirmative measures (beneficiaries).

I will begin by tracing the history of affirmative action in colonial India, leading up to the debates in the Constituent Assembly and the framing of the Indian Constitution's "equality code," set out under Articles 14, 15, and 16 of the Constitution. I will then trace the development of the Supreme Court's equality jurisprudence over the last seven decades, noting a shift from "formal" to "substantive" equality, and more recent attempts to strike a balance between the two. This jurisprudence evolved in the context of Indian society's stratification along the lines of caste, with caste—as a heuristic for social disadvantage—being the primary factor in *identifying* beneficiaries of affirmative action programs. Finally—and in view of this tension between formal and substantive equality—I will examine the future prospects for groups of beneficiaries that are not explicitly mentioned under the Constitution (such as, for

---

1    Some important work on the subject includes Marc Galanter, *Competing Equalities: Law and the Backward Classes in India*, Berkeley, Los Angeles, London 1984; Vinay Sitapati, Reservations, in: Sujit Chaudhary/Madhav Khosla/Pratap Bhanu Mehta (eds.), *The Oxford Handbook for the Indian Constitution*, Oxford 2015, 720–742; Kalpana Kannabiran, *Tools of Justice: Non-Discrimination and the Indian Constitution*, Milton Park, Abingdon 2012; Rochana Bajpai, *Debating Difference: Group Rights and Liberal Democracy in India*, Oxford 2011; H.M. Seervai, *Constitutional Law of India*, Vol. 1, 4th ed., Allahabad 2015; Karuna Ahmad, Towards Equality: The Consequences of Protective Discrimination, in: *Economic and Political Weekly* 13 (2/1978), 69–72; Marc Galanter, Who are the Other Backward Classes? An Introduction to a Constitutional Puzzle, in: *Economic and Political Weekly* 13 (43/44 1978), 1812–1828; N. Radhakrishnan, Units of Social, Economic, and Educational Backwardness: Caste and Individual, in: *Journal of the Indian Law Institute* 7 (3/1965), 262–272.

example, the transgender community), but nonetheless share characteristics of structural and institutional disadvantage.

## The Colonial Era and the Framing of the Indian Constitution

Dr. B.R. Ambedkar—who would go on to become the chairperson of the drafting committee of the Indian Constitution, and who himself was a *dalit*—once described the caste system as a system of "graded inequality."[2] Through a complex structure of religious and social injunctions, involving economic boycotts, physical segregation, and violence, caste was the axis around which individuals were excluded from accessing basic social goods essential for a life with dignity.[3] Many centuries of the operation of the caste system had, thus, resulted in the erection of structural and institutional barriers to equal participation and representation, for many caste groups in India.[4] The caste system, thus, was an example of "structural inequality," i.e., a situation in which "the rules of a society's major institutions reliably produce disproportionately disadvantageous outcomes for the members of certain salient social groups and the production of such outcomes is unjust."[5]

In its social operation, thus, the caste system could—in some respects—be compared with racial discrimination: both caste and race worked through social (and sometimes legal) norms and rules, to "lock in" people into disadvantaged positions, based upon their affiliation with certain groups. In its particular form of graded hierarchies and occupation-based discrimination, however, the structural inequality of the caste system remained, in other respects, *sui generis*.

---

2    See generally, B.R. Ambedkar, Castes in India: Their Mechanism, Genesis and Development. Paper presented at the Anthropology Seminar, Columbia University, New York, May 9, 1916, in: Vasant Moon (ed.), *Dr. Babasaheb Ambedkar: Writing and Speeches*, Vol. I, New Delhi 1979, 3–22.

3    See e.g., J.H. Hutton, *Census of India, 1931: Vol. I – India, Part I Report*, Delhi 1933, <https://ia802506.us.archive.org/14/items/CensusOfIndia1931/Census%20of%20India%201931.pdf> [last accessed: October 30, 2021].

4    Galanter, *Competing Equalities*, 7–17.

5    A. Altman, Discrimination, in: *The Stanford Encyclopedia of Philosophy*, <https://plato.stanford.edu/entries/discrimination/#OrgInsStrDis> [last accessed: October 30, 2021].

While the hegemony of the caste system had been challenged throughout Indian history,[6] in the colonial period, it began to attract the attention of thinkers and social reformers towards the end of the 19th century. Radical writers and activists such as Jotiba Phule launched a frontal attack upon these structures and institutions of segregation and oppression.[7] At the beginning of the twentieth century, these ideas began to percolate into governmental policies. At the time, India was divided into territory ruled directly by the British crown, and numerous "princely states," which were under a system of effective vassalage to the British, but retained a degree of freedom to set internal policy.

In 1905, India saw the first recorded instance of affirmative action: In the princely state of Kolhapur, the ruler—Shahuji Maharaj—issued an order reserving 50% of posts in the administration for "backward castes."[8] As part of his reasons for doing so, Shahuji cited an absence of equitably distributed educational opportunities through his state. As I have argued elsewhere, this was an early articulation of the concept of structural disadvantage and discrimination, and the identification of beneficiaries was done by asking *who* it was that had been unable to access opportunities on an equitable basis. The *method* of doing so was to look at representation that presently existed within state institutions, and to correct for imbalances by providing a set quota for the disadvantaged class of people.[9] The *unit* of identifying disadvantage (termed "backwardness," which was used throughout the colonial period) was that of caste. While there was no *one* set of criteria to determine what constituted "backwardness," key indicators—as highlighted in census reports—included social discrimination (such as social boycotts, "untouchability" etc.), spatial segregation and denial of the use of public commons (such as roads and wells), and poverty.

Meanwhile, Kolhapur's example was followed by multiple princely states across the country, as well as in provincial legislative councils in British Indian territory. By the mid-1920s, the use of quotas for specific, identified castes

6    Gail Omvedt, *Seeking Begumpura: The Social Vision of Anticaste Intellectuals*, New Delhi 2009.

7    Jotirao Phule, *Slavery: Collected Works of Mahatma Jotiba Phule (P.G. Patil trans.)*, Bombay 1991.

8    Dr. Jayasingrao Pawar, *Rajarshi Shahu Chatrapatinche Jahirname va Hukumname*, Bombay 2018.

9    Gautam Bhatia, *The Transformative Constitution: A Radical Biography in Nine Acts*, New Delhi 2019, 74–114.

was no longer exceptional. This was accompanied by the rise of a strong anti-caste movement, led by Ambedkar and others, that put issues of caste discrimination and structural inequality at the center stage of Indian nationalist politics.[10]

It was in this context that the Constituent Assembly met—between 1947 and 1949—to draft the Indian Constitution. The members of the Constituent Assembly were clear about the fact that it was the State's task to identify—and address—the social stratification that characterized Indian society, and that it would be the Constitution's task to facilitate this enterprise. For this reason, the Indian Constitution—in its bill of rights—contained both the formal equality clause that is familiar to constitutional scholars all over the world, but *also*—drawing upon the five-decade-old history of quotas that had been prevalent in different parts of the country—contained specific enabling provisions allowing the government to bring in affirmative action measures in certain cases. The debates around the equality clauses demonstrate how the framers borrowed from other constitutions, and used those borrowings as a base to articulate a richer, and most sophisticated set of constitutional ideas that were relevant to the soil in which Indian Constitutionalism was meant to take root.

These provisions constituted what the Supreme Court would later go on to call the "Equality Code:" Articles 14 through 16 of the Indian Constitution. Article 14 stipulated that the State would not deny to any person equality before law, or the equal protection of laws, within India.[11] Article 15 prohibited discrimination on grounds of race, caste, sex, religion, and place of birth, while allowing for "special provisions" to be made for women and children.[12] Article 16(1) guaranteed equality of opportunity.[13] The provision for affirmative action was set out in Article 16(4), which stated:

"Nothing in this article shall prevent the State from making any provision for the reservation of appointments or posts in favor of any backward class of citizens which, in the opinion of the State, is not adequately represented in the services under the State."[14]

---

10    Anand Teltumbde, *Mahad: The Making of the First Dalit Revolt*, New Delhi 2016.
11    Article 14, Constitution of India, 1949.
12    Article 15, Constitution of India, 1949.
13    Article 16(1), Constitution of India, 1949.
14    Article 16(4), Constitution of India, 1949.

As is obvious, Article 16(4) was drafted as an enabling cause, allowing the State to make "any provision for reservation" (the *what*) for appointments or posts in public services (the *where*), for "any backward class" not adequately represented (the *whom*).

The wording of Article 16(4) was subject to significant debate in the Constituent Assembly. While there was consensus about the fact that India *did* need affirmative action measures to ensure the upliftment of disadvantaged sections of society, members of the Constituent Assembly disagreed over how to *identify* the beneficiaries of the State's affirmative action policies. Initially, the draft Article only made a lack of adequate representation as the basis of affirmative action policies. However, it was pointed out that there might be a whole host of reasons why a particular group of people might not be adequately represented in public employment, which had nothing to do with disadvantage, or with any underlying *rationale* for affirmative action in the first place. Fears were also expressed that this would serve as a license to the government to parcel up all of public employment into slivers of quotas for different interest groups, and render any kind of open competition redundant.[15]

To allay both sets of fears, B.R. Ambedkar proposed adding the phrase "backward classes" to the Draft Article. He noted that while the equality of opportunity was a generic principle in the Constitution:

> "At the same time, as I said, we had to reconcile this formula with the demand made by certain communities that the administration which has now—for historical reasons—been controlled by one community or a few communities, that situation should disappear and that the others also must have an opportunity of getting into the public services."[16]

The term "backward classes" was supposed to serve both as a means of *identifying* beneficiaries of government affirmative action policy, as well as *limiting* the application of affirmative action policies. The term "backward classes" had been used before, in different forms (for example "depressed classes"), especially in colonial survey documents. Although there did not exist a *legal* defi-

---

15    Parliament of India, *Constituent Assembly Debates*, Vol. VII, 30 November 1948, <https ://www.constitutionofindia.net/constitution_assembly_debates/volume/7/1948-11-30> [last accessed: October 30, 2021].

16    Parliament of India, *Constituent Assembly Debates*, Vol. VII, 30 November 1948 (speech of B.R. Ambedkar).

nition of the term, it was broadly understood to refer primarily to the group of people known as "untouchables" (later, *dalits*), who occupied the bottom of the caste hierarchy. There was, thus, an understanding in the Constituent Assembly that the purpose of affirmative action was to identify groups that had been subjected to structural discrimination, and were therefore placed in positions of enduring disadvantage. This did not mean, however, that the Constitution was committed to a vision of society that took the group as its constituent unit. As Ambedkar clarified, the basic unit of the Constitution remained the individual.[17] According to the vision of the Constitution, individuals had been historically subjected to discrimination *because* they belonged to certain groups, and thus, to bring about substantive equality, the Constitution would have to *go through* groups in order to reach individuals. This was buttressed by the fact that the Constitutional framers—optimistically—believed that affirmative action would need to last no longer than ten years, before genuine equality was achieved.

The vision of equality under the Indian Constitution, as it finally took shape, had a few other elements. The first was that the Constitution seemed to envisage the *State* (i.e., the government) to be the primary arm for implementing affirmative action policies, as opposed to judicial action. This is indicated from the fact that Article 16(4) was drafted in enabling language: it did not *obligate* the State to undertake affirmative action, but *permitted* it to do so. Added to this was the fact that the Indian Constitution appeared to hold two different concepts of equality in tension with each other. Article 16(1) guaranteed the equality of opportunity. Article 16(4) then began with the phrase: "*Nothing in this Article shall prevent the State [...]*." This notwithstanding clause appeared to suggest that *had it not been* for the existence of Article 16(4), affirmative action measures would have been illegal under the Indian Constitution (or, permitted in very narrow circumstances, as in American jurisprudence). In other words, therefore, Article 16(4)—which was committed to a substantive, material understanding of equality, was an *exception* to the formal vision of equality contained in the rest of the Equality Code: and that, therefore, any deviations from the rule of formal equality were justified only insofar as permitted by the Constitution (for example, through Article 16(4)), or not at all.

---

17    Parliament of India, *Constituent Assembly Debates*, Vol. VII, 4 November 1948 (speech of B.R. Ambedkar).

We can therefore see that the debates in the Indian Constituent Assembly, and the final form of the Equality Code, set out a constitutional program in specific terms, but also left a significant number of questions unanswered and unresolved. *First*, on the question of beneficiaries, or *who* would be entitled to claim the benefits of affirmative action. The Constitution used the term "backward class," which bore a certain legal history, but was also underdetermined. It was evident that structural disadvantage was the animating feature of affirmative action policy, but what—precisely—constituted a "backward class" was not spelt out in the Constitution. *Secondly*, the unit of affirmative action was the group ("backward class"), but at the same time, both the Constituent Assembly Debates, and the overall framing of the Equality Code indicated that that the normative unit of the *Constitution* was the individual, and that the use of groups in Article 16(4) was instrumental. And *thirdly*, the Constitution appeared to subscribe to both formal and substantive equality, framing them as rule/exception, but without further clarity as to how these opposing impulses were to be reconciled.

Inevitably, therefore, these questions—which went to the heart of the philosophical vision of equality—would have to be resolved by courts, and it is there that we turn in the next section of this chapter.

## The Jurisprudential Evolution of Equality

As we have seen in the previous section, colonial India had, over five decades, grown familiar with quota systems, as forms of affirmative action, to mitigate structural disadvantage and ensure equitable representation. But in the new Constitution, while quotas were allowed for backward "classes," discrimination on account of caste and religion—including in the field of public employment—was categorically forbidden.[18] This—as we have seen—set up a conceptual tension within the Indian Constitution's Equality Code.

The compatibility of quotas with the new constitutional order was called into question immediately after the framing of the Constitution. There existed, in the state of Madras, a Government Order that set out a quota, based on caste and religion, for admission to certain higher educational institutions. An unsuccessful upper-caste candidate challenged this government order on

---

18    See Article 16(2), Constitution of India, 1949.

the basis that it violated her rights to equal protection and equality of opportunity under the Indian Constitution.[19] The State defended it on the basis that uplifting disadvantaged sections of society was integral to the constitutional vision, as set out in the (unenforceable) Directive Principles of State Policy: it was the State's obligation to "promote [...] with special care the educational and economic interests of the weaker sections of the people."[20]

Both the Madras High Court and the Indian Supreme Court agreed with the candidate, and struck down the Government Order (*State of Madras v. Champakam Dorairajan*). At the heart of the Supreme Court's judgment was the assumption that the affirmative action provision (Article 16(4) of the Constitution) was an *exception* to the *general rule* of formal equality.[21] It followed from this that affirmative action—or reservations—was allowed only where, and to the extent that, the Constitution specifically permitted it (or, in other words, reservations were presumptively unconstitutional unless explicitly saved by a constitutional clause). Article 16(4) of the Indian Constitution only spoke of reservations in public employment. There was no constitutional clause that allowed reservations in admissions to educational institutions. For this reason—the Supreme Court held—the Government Order unlawfully discriminated against the candidate on the basis of her caste and religion, and was unconstitutional.

As India's first Prime Minister, Jawaharlal Nehru, recognized at the time, in the working of the Constitution, the government was finding out that to achieve a certain kind of (substantive, material) equality, it would need to violate another kind of (formal) equality. The Indian Parliament responded to the *Champakam Dorairajan* by amending Article 15 of the Constitution, and introducing a new Article 15(4) (this was the first amendment to the Indian Constitution). Article 15(4) stated:

> "Nothing in this article or in clause (2) of Article 29 shall prevent the State from making any special provision for the advancement of any socially and educationally backward classes of citizens or for the Scheduled Castes and the Scheduled Tribes."[22]

---

19   *State of Madras v. Champakam Dorairajan*, 1951 Supreme Court Reports (SCR) 525 (Supreme Court of India).

20   Article 46, Constitution of India, 1949.

21   *State of Madras v. Champakam Dorairajan*, para. 14.

22   Article 15(4), Constitution of India, 1949.

It will be seen that, with a few differences, Article 15(4) mirrored the language of Article 16(4), down to the notwithstanding clause. In other words, Parliament's response to the judicial finding that reservations were "exceptions" to the general rule of equality was to widen the scope of the exception. This did mean, however, that throughout the 1950s and 1960s—as long as the "exception" theory continued to hold, any attempts to introduce affirmative action policies that went beyond Articles 15(4) and 16(4)—or covered beneficiary groups not strictly within the contours of these two Articles (such as, for example, veteran freedom fighters), were struck down by the Courts as unconstitutional.[23]

The "exception theory" underlying the Equality Code also had a corollary impact on the question of *who* the beneficiaries were under affirmative action/reservation programs. The Constitutional term under Article 16(4) was "backward classes," whose provenance we discussed briefly in the previous section. In *Balaji's Case*, the question before the Supreme Court was: what, precisely, did a "class" mean? The question was triggered by the fact that—as we have seen above—quotas were shaped primarily around the axis of caste. In *Balaji's Case*, it was argued that this was impermissible, as caste-based discrimination was expressly outlawed by the Constitution.[24]

The Court responded by holding that, in many respects, castes and classes overlapped. After all, a caste—like class—possessed certain internal unity and coherence, and could only be understood in relation to *other* castes. Consequently, caste was "relevant factor" in determining class.[25] That said, because of the fact that the Constitution *specifically* used the term "class," and *also* prohibited discrimination on grounds of caste, the Court was keenly aware that it could not equate the two. Its answer was to hold that caste could be the *starting point* of locating and identifying disadvantaged classes, but it could not be *end point*. In other words, caste could serve as a heuristic, but after that, other factors—such as social, cultural, or economic disadvantage—would have to be identified to bring *a* particular class group within the protective provisions of the Constitution (or, class was "caste-plus").

Based upon these judgments—and on the basis of multiple Commission reports spanning forty years from the time India became independent—the

---

23   *Sukhnandan Thakur v. State of Bihar*, All India Reporter (AIR) 1957 Pat 617 (High Court of Patna).

24   *M.R. Balaji v. State of Mysore*, 1963 Supp. (1) SCR 439 (Supreme Court of India).

25   *M.R. Balaji v. State of Mysore*, para. 25.

government would eventually settle upon an immensely complex 21-point criteria, including social, cultural, and economic components, to identify the disadvantage ("backwardness") that justified bringing a particular group of beneficiaries within the scope of Articles 15 or 16.[26]

In *Balaji's Case*, the "exception theory" had another consequence. In the State of Mysore—whose reservation policies had been challenged in the case—68% of available places in public educational institutions had been reserved. The Court held that *this*, in itself, was unconstitutional: if, indeed, reservations/affirmative action was an *exception* to the *rule* of equality, then any quota policy that exceeded 50%, without special justification, was presumptively unconstitutional, as that would amount to the "exception" swallowing up "the rule." In effect, therefore, *Balaji* imposed a judicial cap of 50% upon reservations, based upon the judicial theory that reservations were exceptions to—and incompatible with—equality as understood by the Indian Constitution.

The "exception theory" held sway at the Indian Courts for the first two and a half decades after Independence, although it was challenged in powerful dissenting opinions, both at the High Courts, and at the Indian Supreme Court. Dissenting judges pointed out that the "exception theory" misunderstood the constitutional vision of equality by ignoring the social and material *inequalities* that existed in the Indian polity, and by treating individuals and groups before it as being formally equal. In *T. Devadasan's* case, for example, where once again the question of quota caps (50%) was at issue in situations where vacancies "carried forward" between years, Subba Rao J. noted:

> "If [Article 16(1)] stood alone all the backward communities would go to the wall in a society of uneven basic social structure; the said rule of equality would remain only an [sic] utopian conception unless a practical content was given to it."[27.]

Justice Subba Rao went on to note that:

---

26  National Commission for the Backward Classes, *Report of the Backward Classes Commission* ["the Mandal Commission Report"], 1980, <http://www.ncbc.nic.in/Writereaddata/ Mandal%20Commission%20Report%20of%20the%201st%20Part%20English635228 715105764974.pdf> [last accessed: October 30, 2021].

27  *T. Devadasan v. Union of India*, 1964 (4) SCR 680, ¶26 (Supreme Court of India) (dissenting opinion of Subba Rao J.).

"Centuries of calculate [sic] oppression and habitual submission reduced a considerable section of our community to a life of serfdom [...] That is why the makers of the Constitution introduced clause (4) in Art. 16. The expression 'nothing in this article' is a legislative device to express its intention in a most emphatic way that the power conferred thereunder is not limited in any way by the main provision but falls outside it".[28]

Consequently, it was Justice Subba Rao's view that the entire structure of Article 16—including both Articles 16(1) and 16(4)—*reflected* the social reality of the country, and that the articulation of equality *incorporated* this reality: in other words, the constitutional vision of equality had to take into account existing, material inequalities, and reservations/affirmative actions were, therefore, in *service* of that vision of equality. The dispute turned upon the meaning of the notwithstanding clause: did the phrase "nothing in this Constitution shall" mean that Article 16(4) was carving out an exception where general constitutional rules did not apply, or was it simply *restating* what those rules were?

Finally, in 1975, the Supreme Court itself turned tack and accepted the latter argument.

This happened in the case of *State of Kerala v N.M. Thomas*.[29] While the facts of the case were fairly prosaic—involving a dispute over extended timelines for certain candidates for employment to fulfill certain eligibility criteria—the case is important because of the stark judicial shift initiated by the Supreme Court. A majority of the seven-judge bench of the Supreme Court held that Article 16(4) was not an exception to Article 16(1), but an "emphatic restatement" of it. So, Chief Justice Ray noted:

"[...] equality within Articles 14 and 16(1) will not be violated by a rule which will ensure equality of representation in the services for unrepresented classes after satisfying the basic needs of efficiency of administration."[30]

In other words, affirmative action/reservations were not in conflict with—or in tension with—the equality of opportunity, but were themselves a *part*—and implementation of—the equality of opportunity. "Equality of representation"

28    *T. Devadasan v. Union of India*, ¶26 (dissenting opinion of Subba Rao J.).
29    *State of Kerala v. N.M. Thomas*, (1976) 2 Supreme Court Cases (SCC) 330 (Supreme Court of India).
30    *State of Kerala v. N.M. Thomas*, ¶37 (Supreme Court of India) (majority opinion of Ray CJI).

for classes that were under-represented *was* what equality under the Indian Constitution meant and required.

In a concurring opinion, Justice Mathew spelled out the theory of equality underlying this articulation:

> "The notion of equality of opportunity is a notion that a limited good shall in fact be allocated on the grounds which do not, a priori, exclude any section of those that desire it. All sections of people desire and claim representation in the public service of the country, but the available number of posts are limited and therefore, even though all sections of people might desire to get posts, it is practically impossible to satisfy the desire. The question therefore is: on what basis can any citizen or class of citizens be excluded from his or their fair share of representation?
>
> [...] what, then, is *a priori* exclusion? It means exclusion on grounds other than those appropriate or rational for the good (posts) in question. The notion requires not merely that there should be no exclusion from access on grounds other than those appropriate or rational for the good in question, but the grounds considered appropriate for the good should themselves be such that people from all sections of society have an equal chance of satisfying them.
>
> [...] what one is doing there is to apply the same criteria to X as affected by favourable conditions and to Y as affected by unfavourable but curable conditions. Here there is a necessary pressure to equal up the conditions. To give X and Y equality of opportunity involves regarding their conditions, where curable, as themselves part of what is done to X and Y and not part of X and Y themselves. Their identity for this purpose does not include their curable environment, which is itself unequal and a contributor of inequality."[31]

According to Justice Mathew, therefore, the background socio-economic conditions within which people lived their lives and "competed" for scarce resources (such as public employment, or seats in higher educational institutions) could not be treated as normatively irrelevant. These conditions were not "natural," just a part of the background environment, but were the result of the historically unequal evolution of society, and how disadvantaged groups had been treated over time. Under the Indian Constitution, thus, these

---

31    *State of Kerala v. N.M. Thomas*, ¶¶58, 59, 62 (Supreme Court of India) (concurring opinion of Mathew J.).

socio-economic conditions had to be treated as an integral aspect of existing *inequalities*, which had to be leveled to *equality*, through affirmative State action.

As we can see, it is evident that such a finding would require the Court to fundamentally alter its view not just on Article 16(4) and the relationship between Articles 16(1) and 16(4), but at a more foundational level, about the constitutional vision of equality. Reading Article 16(4) into 16(1) called for a new understanding of the meaning of "equality of opportunity"—and, by extension, of equality itself. The Court therefore noted that equality under the Indian Constitution was not *formal* equality, but *substantive*: the socio-economic conditions of individuals and groups was not something that was to be taken into account in exceptional cases, but in *every* case, and equality *itself* required a mitigation of those unequal background conditions.

The Court marshaled a range of argumentative resources to justify this conclusion, from the political theory of Bernard Williams (in Justice Mathew's concurring opinion, cited above), to foreign precedent. Most specifically, it relied on the Directive Principles of State Policy, which enjoined the State to take specific efforts to ameliorate the situation of disadvantaged groups in India. In a concurring opinion Krishna Iyer J. observed that:

> "[...] 'equal opportunity' for members of a hierarchical society makes sense only [through] a strategy by which the underprivileged have environmental facilities for developing their full human potential [...] the distinction would seem to be between handicaps imposed accidentally by nature and those resulting from societal arrangements such as caste structures and group suppression. Society being, in a broad sense, responsible for these latter conditions, it also has the duty to regard them as relevant differences among men and to compensate for them whenever they operate to prevent equal access to basic, minimal advantages enjoyed by other citizens."[32]

This was also affirmed by Justice Mathew:

> "[...] if we want to give equality of opportunity for employment to the members of the Scheduled Castes and Scheduled Tribes, we will have to take note of their social, educational, and economic environment. Not only is the directive principle embodied in Article 46 binding on the law-maker as ordinarily

---

32    *State of Kerala v. N.M. Thomas*, ¶141 (Supreme Court of India) (concurring opinion of Krishna Iyer J.).

understood but it should equally inform and illuminate the approach of the Court."[33]

The Constitution's fundamental rights chapter, the Supreme Court argued, had to be *informed* by the Directive Principles, even though they were unenforceable. Consequently, if the Constitutional text itself was ambiguous—or ambivalent—about which concrete vision of equality it espoused, the Directive Principles would assist the Court in making that decision.[34]

Taken to its logical conclusion, the judgment in *N.M. Thomas*—which, for the purposes of convenience, we can categorize as "Stage 2" in the jurisprudential evolution of equality under the Indian Constitution—would lead to a number of far-reaching changes. Most importantly, if Article 16(4) was indeed a "facet" of Article 16(1), then it would follow that reservations/affirmative action were *themselves* a part of 16(1). From this, two corollaries would flow: *first*, individuals or groups other than those mentioned in Article 16(4) ("backward classes") would be entitled to claim the benefits of affirmative action, if they could show that they were substantively disadvantaged; *secondly*, while Article 16(4) was framed in permissive terms (*allowing* the government to take affirmative action measures), Article 16(1) was framed as a *right*—the right to equality of opportunity. Thus, arguably, after *N.M. Thomas*, there was now an enforceable *right* to affirmative action against the government, in case it failed in its obligations to identify—and mitigate—substantive disadvantage.

Finally, it also followed from the logic of *N.M. Thomas* that the "50% rule" articulated in *Balaji* was no longer applicable. The underlying rationale of the "50% rule" was that the "exception" could not "swallow up the rule." However, according to *N.M. Thomas*, the Equality Code of the Constitution did not have rules and exceptions: there was one unified vision of substantive equality, where affirmative action/reservations were best understood as *advancing* the goals of equality, and not being in conflict or tension with it. This being the case, there was no longer any warrant for a 50% cap: the extent and degree of reservations would, rather, have to be *proportionate* to the extent and degree of disadvantage in a particular place.

---

33    *State of Kerala v. N.M. Thomas*, ¶75 (Supreme Court of India) (concurring opinion of Mathew J.).

34    See e.g. Gautam Bhatia, Directive Principles of State Policy, in: Sujit Chaudhary/ Madhav Khosla/Pratap Bhanu Mehta (eds.), *The Oxford Handbook for the Indian Constitution*, Oxford 2015, 644–662.

Apart from an odd High Court decision,[35] however, the path laid out by *N.M. Thomas* was not followed by too many subsequent judgments. In *Jagdish Rai v State of Punjab*, the Punjab & Haryana High Court did uphold reservations for ex-armed forces personnel, noting that:

> "[...] while the best and the most meritorious of those seeking appointment under the State should be selected, it is also equally fair and equitable that a just proportion of the posts should be given to those who, because of a peculiar handicap, may not stand a chance against those not so handicapped. It would be an extension of the principle of Article 16(4) to those that do not fall under Article 16(4). Defence Personnel who on account of their service with the Army, the Navy, and the Air Force over the years have lost opportunities for entering Government service and have also lost contact with ordinary civilian life may find it extremely difficult, on demobilization, to compete with civilians for civilian jobs despite the qualities of discipline, sacrifice, sense of public duty, initiative, loyalty, and leadership which they would have undoubtedly acquired as members of the Defence Forces."[36]

Thus, therefore, beneficiary groups could now be expanded to whomever could successfully demonstrate suffering from structural or institutional disadvantage. This, as we have seen, was a key feature of the *N.M. Thomas* case.

There were, however, no further developments, and in 1992, a nine-judge bench of the Supreme Court decided the case of *Indra Sawhney v Union of India*[37], which—because of the size of the bench—is widely regarded as authoritatively laying down the law on reservations and equality under the Indian Constitution. *Indra Sawhney* involved a challenge to the overhaul of India's reservation structure, following a report from the Mandal Commission. Using a twenty-one point criteria (as indicated above), the Mandal Commission had recommended reservations for a set of caste groups broadly termed "Other Backward Classes" (OBCs), in addition to reservations for Scheduled Castes and Scheduled Tribes.

While the Supreme Court upheld the government's new reservation policy based on the Mandal Commission Report, it also signaled a retreat from the vision of equality articulated in *N.M. Thomas* (while, at the same time,

---

35   *Jagdish Rai v. State of Punjab*, AIR 1977 P&H 56 (High Court of Punjab & Haryana).

36   *Jagdish Rai v. State of Punjab*, ¶10 (High Court of Punjab & Haryana).

37   *Indra Sawhney v. Union of India*, (1992) Supp. 3 (SCC) 217 (Supreme Court of India).

formally endorsing it). For example, *Indra Sawhney* upheld once again *Balaji's* 50% cap on reservations (barring "exceptional cases"), which, as we have seen, was logically inconsistent with the reasoning of *N.M. Thomas*.[38] *Indra Sawhney*—and subsequent cases‾also made an important rhetorical shift from *N.M. Thomas*, by articulating the relationship between Articles 16(1) and 16(4) as needing a "balance," which would be drawn by the Court. The idea of "balance," thus, came to occupy an uncertain middle ground between the "exception theory" that had dominated the first twenty-five years of constitutional jurisprudence, and the "facet theory" that had been advanced in *N.M. Thomas*.[39] Reservations were now *neither* exceptions to the rule of equality, *nor* integral to equality, but had to be "balanced" with formal equality claims (such as claims to "merit," as measured by competitive examinations, or the claim of "efficiency in government services," as required by Article 335 of the Constitution).[40] This concept of "balance" has been repeated in judgments after *Indra Sawhney*.[41] Unfortunately, however, the Court did not—and still has not—provided either a theoretical justification for this "midway point," nor precisely articulated *what* this balance entails (other than a consistent reiteration of the 50% rule).

The *Indra Sawhney* judgment also opened another front in the dispute over the identification of beneficiaries. The judgment introduced the concept of the "creamy layer," i.e., members of beneficiary groups that had attained social, cultural, or economic privileges to the extent that they—*qua* individuals—no longer suffered from the kind of structural disadvantage that constituted the basis for reservations in the first place (and were therefore no longer "deserving" of reservations).[42]

---

38   *Indra Sawhney v. Union of India* (Supreme Court of India), para 95 (plurality opinion of B.P. Jeevan Reddy J.).

39   Sitapati, Reservations, 738–740.

40   Article 335, Constitution of India, 1949. The implicit assumption here is that selection through reservations will affect "efficiency." This assumption was challenged in the Supreme Court's decision in *B.K. Pavitra v. Union of India*, (2019) 16 SCC 129 (Supreme Court of India), which contains a subtle and powerful discussion of the concept of "merit." There has been no further judicial development in that regard, however.

41   See e.g. *M. Nagaraj v. Union of India*, (2006) 8 SCC 212; *Ajit Singh (II) v. State of Punjab*, (1997) 7 SCC 209.

42   *Indra Sawhney v. Union of India*, ¶843 (Supreme Court of India) (Plurality Opinion of B.P. Jeevan Reddy J.).

The concept of the "creamy layer" has been controversial in the three decades since its articulation in *Indra Sawhney*; there has been confusion, for example, over whether it applies only to the "Other Backward Classes," or whether it applies to "Scheduled Castes" and "Scheduled Tribes" as well –the most recent judgments of the Supreme Court clarify that it does not.[43] The theoretical underpinning of the "creamy layer" doctrine, however, takes us back to the original disputes at the time of the framing of the Indian Constitution: is equality under the Indian Constitution equality between individuals, or between groups? The "creamy layer" doctrine suggests—consistent with B.R. Ambedkar's observations in the Constituent Assembly—that the Constitution's fundamental unit is the individual, with groups playing nothing more than a purely *instrumental* role, in serving as a heuristic for, and allowing the State to identify, disadvantaged individuals (with a certain degree of inevitable bluntness). The non-application of the "creamy layer" doctrine to Scheduled Castes and Scheduled Tribes suggests, however, that for *those* groups of beneficiaries, different considerations are at play: in the case of Scheduled Tribes, there is a constitutional interest in protecting their ways of life *as groups*;[44] while in the case of Scheduled Castes, who occupied the lowest rung of the caste hierarchy, there is an understanding that however privileged individuals might be within the caste, the social stigma and barriers that attach to them *because* of their caste location, are insuperable.

The "creamy layer" doctrine does reveal, however, the essential *fungibility* of groups as the units on which affirmative action policies are based. It is also related to another important, ongoing controversy with respect to the identification of beneficiaries: that of sub-classification. B.R. Ambedkar's acute observation about the caste system being a "graded hierarchy" speaks to the fact that while, for the purposes of the Constitution, "Scheduled Castes" are referred to as a unity (and, for the purposes of State policy, "OBCs" are also referred to as a unity), in actual fact, discrimination in Indian society is far more fine-grained. In *E.V. Chinnaiah*, this precise issue was before the Court: was further *sub-classification* within beneficiaries—on the basis of relative *intra-*

---

43   *Jarnail Singh v. Lacchmi Narain Gupta*, (2018) 10 SCC 396 (Supreme Court of India).

44   For an articulation of this constitutional principle, see *Samata v. State of UP*, AIR (All India Reports) 1997 SC 3297 (Supreme Court of India). See also the V[th] and VI[th] Schedules of the Indian Constitution, which provide specific safeguards and provisions for indigenous peoples.

*group* disadvantage—permissible?[45] Without providing substantive reasons, the Supreme Court held that it was not. While *E.V. Chinnaiah* held the field for around two decades, its lack of reasoning meant that its hold was tenuous at best; and in 2020, its correctness was "referred" to a larger bench for resolution (which is still awaited).

The controversy over both the "creamy layer" doctrine and sub-classification reveals, as well, the limits of the law in enforcing substantive equality: how fine-grained can classifications be, to capture the reality of inequality and discrimination, and ensure that—both in absolute and relative terms—beneficiaries are genuinely *entitled* to the benefits of affirmative action? The absence of clear answers, even after three decades of jurisprudence, suggests that the disputes might be intractable.

## Other Beneficiaries

As indicated in the previous Section, while in practice the Supreme Court has walked back on the findings in the *N.M. Thomas* judgment, formally and *doctrinally*, *N.M. Thomas* has not been overruled, and indeed, continues to hold the field. And in one respect, the logic of *N.M. Thomas* has been carried forward. In *NALSA v Union of India*[46], the Supreme Court affirmed that transgender individuals' gender identity—and its expression—was constitutionally protected under Articles 14 and 15, and under Article 19(1)(a) (the right to freedom of speech and expression).[47] However, the Supreme Court went further: it *also* held that the transgender community was entitled to affirmative action under Article 16, and directed the government to make provisions for the same (seven years after the judgment, this has not yet happened).

The Supreme Court's judgment in *NALSA* is important in two respects, as far as the question of affirmative actions and beneficiary groups goes. *First*—and following *N.M. Thomas'* logic—the Court does not limit the question of affirmative action and reservations to Article 16(4). Arguably, the transgender community does not fall within the technical definition of "backward

---

45    *E.V. Chinnaiah v. State of Andhra Pradesh*, (2005) 1 SCC 394 (Supreme Court of India). For a critique, see K. Balagopal, Justice for Dalits among Dalits: All the Ghosts Resurface, in: *Economic and Political Weekly* 40 (29/2005), 3128–3133.

46    *NALSA v. Union of India*, AIR 2014 SC 1863 (Supreme Court of India).

47    *NALSA v. Union of India* (Supreme Court of India), para. 65.

classes" (see above). This—as has been argued—follows inevitably from the understanding that Article 16(4) is a facet of Article 16(1), and is designed to give full *effect* to substantive equality, rather than provide a shield from the operation of equality in certain exceptional cases. Thus, Article 16(4) does not *exhaust* the scope of affirmative action; rather, affirmative action is part of the constitutional guarantee of the equality of opportunity.

*Secondly*, it follows from this that once it has been found that a particular individual and group suffers from substantive disadvantage, it *follows* that that individual or group has a *claim* to affirmative action (as Article 16(1) is framed in the language of right). Thus, in *NALSA*, after finding that the transgender community had been subjected to structural and institutional discrimination, the Court took this through to its natural, *N.M. Thomas*-grounded conclusion, and found that there existed a judicial right to affirmative action.

This finding, however, needs some clarification. The Indian Supreme Court has often stated that there is no "right to reservation" under the Indian Constitution. While this is trivially true, it is also a limited statement: there is no "right to reservation" in that an individual cannot claim a specific *quota* for themselves or their own group. That continues to be covered by Article 16(4), and remains at the discretion of the State. *However*, quotas do not exhaust the scope of affirmative action. Thus, the fact that there is no enforceable right to a specific *quota* does not mean that the State is exempted from its obligation—under the substantive vision of equality—to identify sites and axes of structural and institutional inequality, and frame laws and policies to ameliorate them (whether or not they take the form of quotas).

As Karan Lahiri has persuasively argued, for example, under the *N.M. Thomas* logic, there is a "power plus duty" upon the State: the State has the power to make reservation and quota policies, but it also has a constitutional *duty* to identify sites of discrimination and inequality—and its failure to do so—or its failure to act upon its findings—will attract judicial scrutiny and review in the normal course.[48] This doctrine, however, has not yet been accepted by the Court, and it remains to be seen if it will become part of Indian equality and affirmative action jurisprudence in the future. If it does—as it

---

48    Karan Lahiri, Does Article 16 Impose a "Power Coupled with a Duty" upon the State?, in: *The Indian Constitutional Law and Philosophy Blog*, 13 November 2015, <https://indconlawphil.wordpress.com/2015/11/13/guest-post-does-article-16-impose-a-power-coupled-with-a-duty-upon-the-state-i/> [last accessed: October 30, 2021].

should—the door will be open for potential beneficiaries (such as, for example, the disabled, or the old), who are not presently covered by Article 16(4), to make direct claims upon the State. The Supreme Court's *NALSA* judgment demonstrates how that might be possible in practice.

## Conclusion

During the framing of the Indian Constitution, during the time of Independence, it became clear that the Constitution would not limit itself to the straightforward—and familiar—"equal protection clause," as was the default in many other Constitutions. The Indian struggle for Independence had not only been a *political* struggle against colonial rule, but also, a *social* struggle against inequalities and stratifications within the community and the society, along the lines of caste, gender, and so on. For this reason, the framers of the Constitution ensured that this insight was reflected in the wording of the Constitution: whether in the language of "special provisions" for women (that this chapter has not discussed),[49] or in the language of enabling, affirmative action provisions for "backward classes."

The language of the constitutional clauses, however, left several questions unanswered. Some of these questions were reflected in the Constituent Assembly Debates, but found no resolution; others remained unarticulated, both in the Debates and in the constitutional text, but were very real nonetheless.

*First*, what was the Constitutional vision of equality? Was it *formal equality*, and were the affirmative action provisions a narrow exception to that rule, specifically carved out in the constitutional text, beyond which no such provisions could be made?

*Secondly*, what was the role of groups in the question of affirmative action? Were groups the basic normative units of the Constitution? Or was their purpose instrumental, in order to help identify disadvantage—as disadvantage had historically existed along group axes—while the basic normative unit of the Constitution remained the individual?

*Thirdly*, how were beneficiaries of affirmative action to be identified? What was the meaning of the term "backward classes," and how did it relate to caste? What about beneficiaries who faced disadvantage, but did not fall within the meaning of "backward classes"?

---

49    See Gautam Bhatia, *The Transformative Constitution*, 74–114.

As the Constitution left these questions unresolved, it was up to the courts to answer them. Over the seventy years of its existence, the Supreme Court—and, often, the numerous Indian High Courts—have developed a complex, and often contradictory, approach to these questions. Broadly, the history of the jurisprudence can be divided into three periods. The first period—between 1950 to 1975—was when the Supreme Court considered reservations to be narrow, explicit exceptions to the general rule of equality, and when—therefore—reservations were explicitly capped at 50%, and no individual or group outside the ones strictly defined by Article 16(4) were eligible.

The second period began with the *N.M. Thomas Case*. The Supreme Court reversed its position and held that Article 16(4) was a facet—or an emphatic restatement of—Article 16(1). In other words, reservations were not in conflict with, or in tension with, the Constitutional vision of equality, but in harmony: it was through reservations that substantive equality would become truly real.

However, the Supreme Court did not take forward the findings in *N.M. Thomas*, and its judgment in *Indra Sawhney* (1992) inaugurated the third period, which—arguably—continues to today. In *Indra Sawhney*, the Court embarked on an untheorized "middle path" between exception and facet, that of balance: claims under Article 16(4) had to be "balanced" with right to equality of opportunity under Article 16(1), with neither to be given primacy over the other. This threw up a host of other questions and issues, which remain the subject of litigation to this day. These include, for example, the scope of the "creamy layer" doctrine, which speaks directly to the controversy around what, precisely, is the basic normative unit of the Indian Constitution, the individual or the group. They also include the issue of sub-classification, which presently awaits a hearing by a seven-judge bench of the Supreme Court. But while these disputes remain locked in place, an opening—of sorts—was created by the Supreme Court in its 2014 *NALSA* decision. By holding that the transgender community was entitled to claim affirmative action under the Indian Constitution, the Supreme Court signaled that the logic of *N.M. Thomas*—according to which the constitutional vision of substantive equality required the government to take positive steps to identify and ameliorate structural and institutional disadvantage—could be taken forward in one important respect, that is, with respect to beneficiary groups that did not fall within the strict contours of Article 16(4). It remains to be seen whether, in the coming years, the Supreme Court takes up this invitation.

# References

Ahmad, Karuna, Towards Equality: The Consequences of Protective Discrimination, in: *Economic and Political Weekly* 13 (2/1978), 69–72.

Altman, Andrew, Discrimination, in: *The Stanford Encyclopaedia of Philosophy*, <https://plato.stanford.edu/entries/discrimination/#OrgInsStrDis> [last accessed: October 30, 2021].

Ambedkar, B.R., Castes in India: Their Mechanism, Genesis and Development. Paper presented at the Anthropology Seminar, Columbia University, New York, May 9, 1916, in: Moon, Vasant (ed.), *Dr. Babasaheb Ambedkar: Writing and Speeches*, Vol. I, New Delhi 1979, 3–22.

Bajpai, Rochana, *Debating Difference: Group Rights and Liberal Democracy in India*, Oxford 2011.

Balagopal, K., Justice for Dalits among Dalits: All the Ghosts Resurface, in: *Economic and Political Weekly* 40 (29/2005), 3128–3133.

Bhatia, Gautam, Directive Principles of State Policy, in: Chaudhary, Sujit/ Khosla, Madhav/Mehta, Pratap Bhanu (eds.), *The Oxford Handbook for the Indian Constitution*, Oxford 2015, 644–662.

Bhatia, Gautam, *The Transformative Constitution: A Radical Biography in Nine Acts*, New Delhi 2019.

Galanter, Marc, Who are the Other Backward Classes? An Introduction to a Constitutional Puzzle, in: *Economic and Political Weekly* 13 (43/44 1978), 1812–1828.

Galanter, Marc, *Competing Equalities: Law and the Backward Classes in India*, Berkeley, Los Angeles, London 1984.

Hutton, J.H., *Census of India, 1931: Vol. I – India, Part I Report*, Delhi 1933, <https://ia802506.us.archive.org/14/items/CensusOfIndia1931/Census%20of%20India%201931.pdf> [last accessed: October 30, 2021].

Kannabiran, Kalpana, *Tools of Justice: Non-Discrimination and the Indian Constitution*, Milton Park, Abingdon 2012.

Lahiri, Karan, Does Article 16 Impose a "Power Coupled with a Duty" upon the State?, in: *The Indian Constitutional Law and Philosophy Blog*, 13 November 2015, <https://indconlawphil.wordpress.com/2015/11/13/guest-post-does-article-16-impose-a-power-coupled-with-a-duty-upon-the-state-i/> [last accessed: October 30, 2021].

Omvedt, Gail, *Seeking Begumpura: The Social Vision of Anticaste Intellectuals*, New Delhi 2009.

Pawar, Dr. Jayasingrao, *Rajarshi Shahu Chatrapatinche Jahirname va Hukum-name*, Bombay 2018.

Phule, Jotirao, *Slavery: Collected Works of Mahatma Jotiba Phule* (P.G. Patil trans.), Bombay 1991.

Radhakrishnan, N., Units of Social, Economic, and Educational Backward-ness: Caste and Individual, in: *Journal of the Indian Law Institute* 7 (3/1965), 262–272.

Seervai, H.M., *Constitutional Law of India*, Vol. 1, 4th ed., Allahabad 2015.

Sitapati, Vinay, Reservations, in: Chaudhary, Sujit/Khosla, Madhav/Mehta, Pratap Bhanu (eds.), *The Oxford Handbook for the Indian Constitution*, Oxford 2015, 720–742.

Teltumbde, Anand, *Mahad: The Making of the First Dalit Revolt*, New Delhi 2016.

# Authors and Editors

**Gautam Bhatia** is a lawyer and a D.Phil. (graduate) from the University of Oxford.

**Ulrike Davy** is Professor of Constitutional and Administrative Law, German and International Social Security Law and Comparative Law at the Faculty of Law, Bielefeld University, and Visiting Professor at the Faculty of Law, University of Johannesburg, South Africa. She is a Principal Investigator of the Collaborative Research Center SFB 1288 "Practices of Comparing."

**Antje Flüchter** is Professor of Early Modern History at the Faculty of History, Philosophy and Theology, Bielefeld University. She is the Speaker and a Principal Investigator of the Collaborative Research Center SFB 1288 "Practices of Comparing."

**Lynn Hunt** is Eugen Weber Professor of Modern European History (emerita) and Distinguished Research Professor at the Department of History, University of California, Los Angeles.

**David Keane** is Professor in Law at the School of Law and Government, Dublin City University.

**Malika Mansouri** is a Doctoral Researcher in Law at the Faculty of Law, Bielefeld University, and in the Collaborative Research Center SFB 1288 "Practices of Comparing".

**Helmut Walser Smith** holds the Martha Rivers Ingram Chair of History and is Professor of History at the History Department of Vanderbilt University, Nashville.

# Bielefeld University Press

Silke Schwandt (ed.)
**Digital Methods in the Humanities**
Challenges, Ideas, Perspectives

2020, 312 p., pb., col. ill.
38,00 € (DE), 978-3-8376-5419-6
E-Book: available as free open access publication
PDF: ISBN 978-3-8394-5419-0

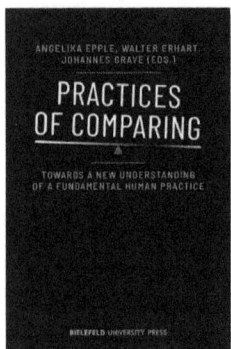

Angelika Epple, Walter Erhart, Johannes Grave (eds.)
**Practices of Comparing**
Towards a New Understanding
of a Fundamental Human Practice

2020, 406 p., pb., col. ill.
39,00 € (DE), 978-3-8376-5166-9
E-Book: available as free open access publication
PDF: ISBN 978-3-8394-5166-3

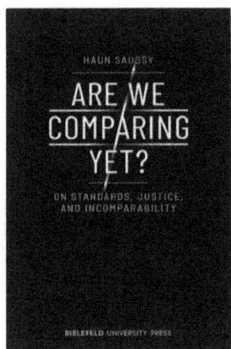

Haun Saussy
**Are We Comparing Yet?**
On Standards, Justice, and Incomparability

2019, 112 p., pb.
19,99 € (DE), 978-3-8376-4977-2
E-Book: available as free open access publication
PDF: ISBN 978-3-8394-4977-6

**All print, e-book and open access versions of the titles in our list
are available in the online shop www.bielefeld-university-press.de**

# Bielefeld University Press

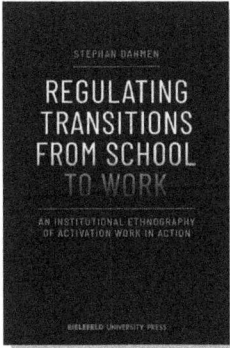

Stephan Dahmen
**Regulating Transitions from School to Work**
An Institutional Ethnography of Activation Work in Action

June 2021, 312 p., pb., ill.
36,00 € (DE), 978-3-8376-5706-7
E-Book: available as free open access publication
PDF: ISBN 978-3-8394-5706-1

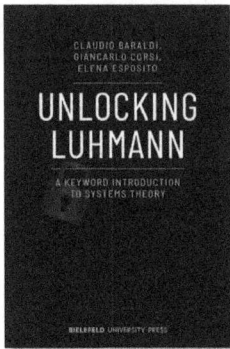

Claudio Baraldi, Giancarlo Corsi, Elena Esposito
**Unlocking Luhmann**
A Keyword Introduction to Systems Theory

April 2021, 276 p., pb.
40,00 € (DE), 978-3-8376-5674-9
E-Book: available as free open access publication
PDF: ISBN 978-3-8394-5674-3

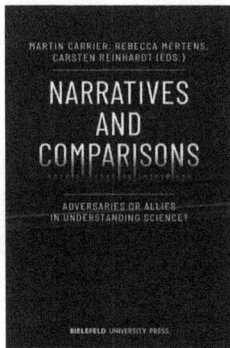

Martin Carrier, Rebecca Mertens, Carsten Reinhardt (eds.)
**Narratives and Comparisons**
Adversaries or Allies in Understanding Science?

January 2021, 206 p., pb., col. ill.
35,00 € (DE), 978-3-8376-5415-8
E-Book: available as free open access publication
PDF: ISBN 978-3-8394-5415-2

**All print, e-book and open access versions of the titles in our list
are available in the online shop www.bielefeld-university-press.de**

GPSR Authorized Representative: Easy Access System Europe, Mustamäe tee
50, 10621 Tallinn, Estonia, gpsr.requests@easproject.com